Elbert Hubbard's

The Philistine

A Periodical of Protest

1895 - 1915

A Major American "Little Magazine"

Bruce A. White

STAND ALONE x UNDERWORLD AMUSEMENTS

Elbert Hubbard's The Philistine, a Periodical of Protest (1895-1915)

Design and new typestting by Kevin I. Slaughter

isbn: 978-1-943687-13-8

First edition 1989 by University Press of America, Inc.

This updated and expanded second edition
published by Underworld Amusements.
www.UnderworldAmusements.com

SA1075 | This edition is part of the *Stand Alone* series produced by the Union of Egoists. The sale of this book furthers the archival, historical, biographical and bibliographical work at www.UnionOfEgoists.com.

Dedicated to the American taxpayers, who have subsidized my education and my livelihood.

Acknowledgments

I wish to thank Gallaudet University for funding some of my travel expenses and for providing me with a semester's sabbatical leave to complete this book; special thanks go to Dr. Michael A. Karchmer and Susan J. King of the Graduate Studies and Research office for their assistance in preparing this book for publication.

To Mr. William H. Loos, Curator of the Rare Book Room of the Buffalo and Erie County Public Library, to Ms. Cathy Henderson, Research Librarian at the Harry Ransom Humanities Research Center, The University of Texas at Austin, and to the Governing Board of the Elbert Hubbard Museum, East Aurora, New York, I extend my gratitude for their gracious assistance. I am especially indebted to Mr. Charles F. Hamilton, author and Hubbard scholar, for continued encouragement and counsel and a magnanimous gift of *Philistine* magazines to facilitate my research.

My former mentor at the University of Maryland at College Park, Dr. Peter Van Egmond, already knows how grateful I am for his guidance. To everyone else who has helped me along the way, thank you.

Author's Note to the Paperback Edition

Fifty years ago a bookstore owner on Cape Cod brought me to a nearby residence to see a trunkful of *Philistine* magazines, which became the nucleus of my collection of works by Elbert and Alice Hubbard. While agonizing over a dissertation topic years later, I looked at my shelves of *Philistines* and decided the Hubbards and their little magazine merited serious study. The Hubbards were famous for what they made, including Roycroft furniture, but I was more interested in what they wrote. The revised dissertation was published by an academic press in 1989 and I made a study of the Hubbards' other writings and journalism available online in 2009. That, I thought, was the end of my efforts to bring attention to their written work. But at the end of 2017 Kevin Slaughter reached out to me about my *Philistine* book and this paperback reprint is the result. I am grateful for his enthusiastic support, and hope that the Hubbards' writings will long continue to be enjoyed and studied.

Benjamin DeCasseres admiring a portrait of his relative Baruch Spinoza, at an event on Nov. 29, 1932 celebrating the philosopher's 300th birthday. It was that year his book *Spinoza: Liberator of God and Man* was published (New York: E. Wickham Sweetland, 1932).

Courtesy of the Union of Egoists

Publisher's Preface

I wanted to tell you, from my own perspective, how I came to reprint Mr. White's excellent history of *The Philistine*. In my self-guided study of forgotten or neglected freethinkers, it is all too common to find groups on similar paths that never overlap to compare notes, or at least share stories over a drink, so I'm most interested when I do find those moments of overlap and connectivity.

I set up the website BenjaminDeCasseres.com in 2012 to make my ongoing research and related publishing available. My studies of DeCasseres became interwoven with a handfull of fascinating writers: Dora Marsden, Malfew Seklew, Ragnar Redbeard, Max Stirner. They formed the nucleus of a much larger research and publishing project at UnionOfEgoists.com, launched in early 2016 with my co-editor Trevor Blake. The project spread to folks connected with the core group, such as Benjamin R. Tucker, Stephen Byintgon, James L. Waker, Renzo Novatore, Sidney E. Parker, John Henry Mackay and others. These were all people who had identified with a worldview first articulated by Max Stirner in his 1845 work *Der Einzige und sein Eigentum*. While today the term "egoism" is associated with Objectivist philosopher Ayn Rand, it has been adopted and extrapolated by individuals across the political and social spectrum for close to two centuries. Egoists came in forms from French anarchist criminal gangs to folksy "back to nature" advocates to diabolical showmen. UnionOfEgoists.com has a focus on the various journals they published, edited or wrote for.

Hubbard was always *just on the periphery* of my studies. I would encounter his name time and again, but almost always in a tertiary manner, never demanding I follow him down a rabbit hole away from the one I was already in. There was exactly one point where all of this came crashing together in one place: Benjamin DeCasseres' ghost writing a biographical sketch of Max Stirner for Elbert Hubbard's other journal, *The Fra* (see Appendix E).

A couple years ago I obtained a sizable collection of *The Philistine* and I was sure more of DeCasseres' work *should* be in those issues. The copies were too brittle for casual, repeated handling. Finding anything was a matter of serendipity (flipping through at random), brute force (page by page by page by page) or finding a reference work (a table of contents or an index). The last option is clearly the most desirable. I found *one* sale listing for *one* copy of Mr. White's 1986 book online, and at a price reflecting such a scarce work published for an academic market. I decided that I would instead try to find the author himself. At a minimum, I would see if he still had any extra copies around that I could buy directly from him, but I also had another idea.

To my delight I got a response to one of the many emails I sent out to find him. I proposed reprinting his book as part of a quasi-journal project meant to make available obscure "lost" works relating to the UnionOfEgoists.com project. Sight unseen I was taking a risk. Mr. White has been kind enough to agree.

It was during the design and typesetting of this new edition that I obtained scans of another rare journal, *The Free Comrade*, edited by Egoist socialist poet J. Wm. Lloyd, and published by Egoist Anarchist Clarence L. Swartz. It was in that journal the following quote was found:

> "Comrade Elbert Hubbard, *our* Elbert Hubbard, uttering through *The Philistine*, is the Cutest Tongue in the Mouth of Freedom. A Gentle Genius and Laughing Liberator. This is a free Praisement and he knows nothing of it. And before he finds out send him your dollar and get yourself a niche in the American Academy of Immortals."
>
> –J. Wm. Lloyd, *The Free Comrade*, May 1899

In is most famous work, *A Message to Garcia*, he very explicitly states:

> I am an Anarchist. All good men are Anarchists...
> Being an Anarchist I am also a Socialist. Socialism is the antithesis of Anarchy. One is the North Pole of Truth, the other

> the South. The Socialist believes in working for the good of all, while Anarchy is pure Individualism. I believe in every man working for the good of self; and in working for the good of self, he works for the good of all.

While it is easy to criticise his definitions of "anarchism" and "socialism", seeing him apply the terms to himself placed him closer to *my studies* than I expected. That this text explicitly used those terms and was printed as promotional material by the Boy Scouts of America and the US Marine Corps tells me maybe times have changed in ways even I could find surprising. Mr. White tells a more complete story in Chapter V.

What dawned on me is that Hubbard was "comrade" with these other figures not as much because of anarchism or socialism (which he later largely abandoned for "free enterprise"), but because nearly all of them were of the mettle to create their own platforms to articulate their understanding of the world as it is, or as it should be. They were freethinkers and challenged the status quo, and most central to that view was the primacy of the individual. From Benjamin R. Tucker's *Liberty* (1881) here in the US, to Dora Marsden's feminist-individualist journal *The Freewoman* (1911, later *The New Freewoman*, later *The Egoist*) in the UK, they were all part of the movement of "Modern Journals" that shaped the sense and sensibilities of the modern world. They were inheritors of a sensibility established by Ralph Waldo Emerson's *The Dial* (1840) from Boston, and *The Savoy* (1896), edited by Arthur Symons, in London. Regardless of professed beliefs, they all sang a song of the self, and we can still hear the echos to this day.

Hubbard was his own man, and an American artist and craftsman who should not be forgotten. If this small work in some way keeps his name alive, I am proud to make it available once more. If this is a key for another scholar (academic or autodidact) to tap into this vein of fascinating material for their own ends, then *doubly-so*.

Kevin I. Slaughter
May, 2018

A Periodical of Protest

NEUTRALITY: The attempt of a prejudiced mind to convince itself that it is not prejudiced.

Printed Every Little While for the Society of the Philistines and Published by Them Monthly. Subscription, One Dollar Yearly
Single Copies, Ten Cents
JULY, 1915

VALEDICTORY

The last issue of *The Philistine*, Vol. 41 No. 2, July 1915.
Depicted actual size.

Courtesy of the
Union of Egoists

Contents

Elbert Hubbard
For Claire MacDonald
Aug 17th
1901

Chapter I

Introduction

"A Business Man with a Literary Attachment"

Elbert Hubbard (1856-1915) co-founded *The Philistine: A Periodical of Protest* in 1895, and was its editor and principal contributor until his death aboard the *Lusitania*, when publication of the *Philistine* ceased. This 32-page monthly, printed at his community of Roycrofters in East Aurora, N.Y., was the longest-lived of the "little magazines" which flourished during the 1890s. Financially self-sustaining from the beginning, the *Philistine* brought fame to Hubbard, especially after the 1899 appearance of his "A Message to Garcia," which doubled the magazine's circulation to 100,000. Though he is not well known today, interest in Hubbard and his work has been increasing recently. *Books in Print* for 1986-1987 lists a 1983 paperback reprint of Freeman Champney's 1968 biography and more than a dozen reprints of Hubbard's work, including a ten-volume set of the *Philistine* for $1,000.

One of the earliest critics to assess Hubbard's contribution to American journalism was Algernon Tassin, in his *The Magazine in America* (1916). More than Edward W. Bok (*Ladies' Home Journal*), S. S. ("So So") McClure (*McClure's Magazine*), or Frank Andrew Munsey (*Munsey's Magazine*), Hubbard, in Tassin's estimation, the only one of these editors "who had any literary gift," was able to

> deal the editorial tradition of reticence a body blow; to develop that arrestingly and grippingly personal tone which was becoming characteristic of the American sanctum, and to demolish the last vestige of the pose which Boston culture had bequeathed American letters. (357)

Today an increasing number of scholars are beginning to find merit in the suggestion Joseph Wood Krutch made in *The Nation* in 1926: "The career of Elbert Hubbard would furnish a not unsuitable subject for scholarly investigation and no *Kulturgeschichte* of modern America can be complete without him" (4 Aug. 1926, p. 107). Seventy years after Hubbard's death, his fervent hope for lasting renown finally seems realizable, primarily because of the contributions of the *Philistine* to American literature and journalism.

Elbert Hubbard turned to a pursuit of literary fame after gaining wealth as a merchandiser: he described himself astutely as "a business man with a literary attachment" (Balch, 103). The course of his rags-to-riches journey is reminiscent of a novel by Horatio Alger, Jr. He was not content with wealth, however; and though he would defend responsible capitalists as American heroes, much to the detriment of his contemporary and posthumous reputation among genteel critics, Hubbard longed for a more elusive attainment. In 1892, at the age of thirty-six, he sold his interest in a Buffalo soap company to pursue his cultural and literary goals, emulating the career of one of his idols, Benjamin Franklin. As an Illinoisan with literary pretensions, he was keenly aware of the contempt the eastern establishment had for the nouveau riche, and he was determined to transcend his status and join the culturally elite of Boston and New York; when he failed to get his literary manuscripts accepted, he adopted the name and combativeness of the ancient Philistines and turned to attacking the literary authorities, protesting the power and orthodoxy of these "Chosen People."

Hubbard's literary career was as successful as his business career had been. He wrote six novels, hundreds of *Little Journeys* (biographical essays), and most of the contents of the *Philistine*. Life members of his Society of Philistines included (in 1904) two Supreme Court justices, eight senators, forty-six congressmen, "lawyers to incinerate," and "the chief artists, actors and literary workers of England and America" (*Philistine*, 18.4:112). Between 1909 and 1915 (daily in 1915) he contributed more than six hundred editorial columns to the Hearst syndicate's *New York American*, earning $30,000 annually (Balch, 268), and in 1914 he was the highest-paid lecturer in the United States (Balch, 248). His famous pastoral community of Roycrofters at East Aurora, New York, superbly managed by his second wife, Alice (Moore) Hubbard, was a vibrant conglomerate of gifted writers, printers, bookbinders, artists, and craftsmen, all enjoying extraordinary freedom to learn their crafts and refine their skills.[1]

Hubbard has been called "an American William Morris," and recent evaluations of his influence have included his contributions to American printing and bookmaking. Champney remarks that it is easy, in view of the negative criticism regarding the quality of the Roycroft Press publications, to overlook the point that Hubbard "brought the book as an art object into the American consciousness" (59). Susan Otis Thompson devotes the longest chapter of her *American Book Design and William Morris* to Hubbard (168-189), and describes him as one of the "most ardent American followers of the Kelmscott style, certainly its most prolific propagator, and perhaps the most widely influential" (168). In noting the critical ambivalence that still exists regarding his bookmaking accomplishments, some of the objections prompted not so much because of the books but because of the man who advertised them and the way that he advertised them, Thompson suggests that a reappraisal of Hubbard's place in American printing may be overdue (188, 219).

Thompson quotes, for example, from a *Modern Art* review by Joseph M. Bowles (Apr. 1, 1896) of Hubbard's first publication venture, *The Song of Songs* (1896), which shows how Hubbard's "salesmanship put the wrong taste in some people's mouths" (186). Bowles conceded that, had Hubbard been more humble, calling his book "an effort toward an ideal, as all our work in this country must be for a long time yet, no one could have criticized it" (186). Hubbard's second book, *The Journal of Koheleth: Being a Reprint of the Book of Ecclesiastes* (also 1896), was also negatively reviewed, in the *New York Times Book Review* (10 Oct. 1896), with the reviewer alluding to Hubbard's advertising before criticizing his workmanship (186).

Elsewhere in her book Thompson acknowledges the influence of Hubbard on Will Ransom, student of the typographer Frederic W. Goudy. Ransom was founder of the Village Press (Park Ridge, Illinois) and the Handcraft Shop (Snohomish, Washington), and "dean of writers about private presses." He sent a copy of his first work, *The Lady of Shalott* (1901), to Hubbard in exchange for a signed portrait on Japanese vellum. Both this book and his second, Wilde's *Ave Imperatrix!* (1902), according to Thompson, "clearly" show the Roycroft influence (135).[2]

The Hubbard-Morris relationship needs reappraisal as well. It so happens that "one of the most pleasing and restrained productions done by the Roycrofters" is a 1907 edition of a "little journey" to the home of William Morris (Walsdorf, 225). This 67-page book includes some letters from Morris to Robert Thomson, a description of Kelmscott House, and Hubbard's version of his meeting with Morris.[3] (A much shorter version of this "journey" appears in the September 1899 [9.4:97-106] issue of the *Philistine*, in which Hubbard makes no mention of having visited Morris and his Kelmscott House.) Here is Hubbard's account of his fateful meeting with Morris, as taken from the 1900 edition of *Little Journeys to the Homes of English Authors* (pp. 9-35), which was the first of the "journeys" to be printed by the Roycrofters (instead of by G. P. Putnam's Sons), and which has a Kelmscott appearance in its title-page border and initials in the text (Thompson, 172):

> [I] . . . passed a great pile of paper in crates that cluttered the hallway, and entered the library. There, leaning over the long, oaken table, in shirtsleeves, was the master . . . .
>
> He greeted me as if we had always known each other, and [F. S.] Ellis and piles of Chaucer proof led straight to old Professor Child of Harvard, whose work Ellis criticized and Morris upheld. They fell into a hot argument, which was even continued as we walked across the street to the Doves Bindery . . . .
>
> When we were once inside the Bindery, the Chaucerian argument between Mr. Ellis and Th' Ole Man shifted off into a wrangle with [manager T. J.] Cobden-Sanderson . . . . [The Kelmscott *Chaucer* was the last work Morris produced.] Once back in the library of Kelmscott House, Mr. Ellis and Th' Ole Man leaned over the great oaken

> table and renewed, in a gentler key, the question as to whether Professor Child was justified in his construction of the Third Canto of the "Canterbury Tales. . . ." This was my first interview with William Morris. By chance I met him again, some days after, at the shop of Emery Walker [who inspired Morris to produce books] in Clifford Court, Strand. . . . [H]e told me he had read "Huckleberry Finn," and doted on "Uncle Remus." He also told me that he had read every printed word that Emerson had written. And further he congratulated me on the success of my book, "Songs From Vagabondia." (29-32)

There is no contesting that Hubbard was inspired by his trip to see Morris, but it would seem that, at the most, they exchanged words for only a minute or two. Why Hubbard lets this misdirected praise which he attributes to Morris pass without comment, however, is troubling, and affords a good example of Hubbard's frequently lackadaisical attitude toward factual accuracy which so offended many of his contemporaries. *Songs from Vagabondia* (1894) is Bliss Carman and Richard Hovey's book, and was printed by the Kelmscott-inspired Boston publishing firm of Copeland & Day a year before the establishment of the Roycrofters (Thompson, 50-51). Hubbard knew this, of course, and in fact mentions Carman and his "Songs" in the November 1900 (11.6:188) issue of the *Philistine.* Nevertheless, subsequent editions of his essay on Morris retain this misinformation. To be charitable to Hubbard, perhaps this is his way of depreciating his significance to Morris, or a private joke on his "old friend" Carman. In any event, regardless of the nature of Hubbard's relationship with Morris, it is not possible to discuss the history of Morris's influence in the United States without mentioning Hubbard and his Roycroft Press.

Additional corroboration of the importance of Hubbard's role in American printing is provided by Richard J. Wolfe and Paul McKenna in their *Louis Herman Kinder and Fine Bookbinding in America: A Chapter in the History of the Roycroft Shop* (1985). They acknowledge the "tendency today to deflate, deprecate and depreciate the work of Hubbard and his Roycroft enterprise," but note that "this unique experiment in American bookmaking provided an equally unique opportunity for a number of highly advanced and imaginative craftsmen, of whom Kinder and Dard Hunter are but two outstanding examples, to 'do their thing'" (94). Kinder, for example, admitted that "words cannot express the feeling of gratitude I owe Mr. Elbert Hubbard, for his encouragement and cooperation which rendered [my] work not only possible, but very delightful and pleasant to me" (74). Wolfe and McKenna add that Hubbard compensated Kinder equitably, even providing him a new house in 1903 in an effort to retain his services.[4]

Hubbard's encouragement of another fine artist, Dard Hunter, is recounted by Hunter's son in *The Life Work of Dard Hunter*, Vol. 1 (1981). According to Dard Hunter II, his father, as Director of Art under Hubbard, designed and produced more than 100 books and pamphlets, including many back covers of the *Philistine*; these designs have a "unique place in the history of book illustration today and are highly esteemed and admired by competent book lovers and connoisseurs" (1). Hunter had toured the Chautauqua circuit as a "lightning crayon artist," and had met Hubbard several times.[5] At East Aurora he was "given the freedom of discovery--to work with almost anything he yearned to do, usually with the full support of both Alice and Elbert Hubbard who were most affable to him from the beginning" (11). Dard Hunter alludes to his seven-year stay (1903-1910) in East Aurora in his article on Hubbard and his "A Message to Garcia" (30), and praises the Hubbards as "remarkable individuals--sincere, kindly, generous, understanding. I shall always remember them with the deepest affection" (35).

The extent of indebtedness to Hubbard by Hunter, as well as by William W. Denslow and other artists and craftsmen, is reinforced by Robert Koch in his "Roycrofters as Artist-Craftsmen." According to Koch, Hunter was responsible in 1906 for the book which "remains as the finest design of all Roycroft publications," Elbert and Alice Hubbard's play, *Justinian and Theodora* (80). It was during his stay in East Aurora that Hunter freed himself of the influence of sixteenth-century Venetian layout and typography, an influence seen in "both Kelmscott and Roycroft books prior to 1900" (81), and turned away from the "curving organic line" of the Art Nouveau to modern angularity. Although Hunter left East Aurora in 1910 to study in Vienna, his style surfaced repeatedly in subsequent works published by Hubbard, who, according to Hunter, "probably had more influence in the development of book-collecting than any other person of his generation" (79).

Testimonials from "well known book lovers" were frequently advertised in the first years of the *Philistine.* Among them, as given in the front pages of the November 1898 (7.6) issue, are John Hay, American statesman and bibliophile, Queen Victoria (through her librarian Helen Barstow), actress Dame Ellen Terry, E. C. Stedman, American poet and critic, and Wall Street broker, W. E. Gladstone, actress Helena Modjeska (Countess Bozenta), Frances E. Willard, American temperance leader and reformer, Harold Frederic, author of *The Damnation of Theron Ware*, and Israel Zangwill, English author and Zionist.

John Hay, then Secretary of State, asked to be enrolled as a Life Member of the Society of Philistines, though he was not sure he would live 99 years. (In a letter to Hubbard dated 1 June 1899 he praises the bound "A Message to Garcia" as being a "little masterpiece of writing, printing and binding" [HRHRC, Box Recip. Uniden.-J, Folder H-J].) The Queen's copy of *Sonnets from the Portuguese* (1898), according to her librarian, has a place among her "intimate book treasures" because the "combination of paper, typography, illuminations and binding is so harmonious." Ellen Terry placed a standing order for two copies of everything published by the Roycrofters. When Terry heard that Hubbard was in Edinburgh, she sent him a message to send up his card to her room. She informed him that she had most of the Kelmscott books and had been getting the *Philistine* through her daughter from the beginning (HRHRC, Recip. Box K-Z, Folder S-T). Gladstone reports that he is showing his Roycroft books to his friends "with intent to prove that the world moves. . . . I cannot say you have improved on the Venetians, but you have nearly equalled them." Modjeska asked for a copy of everything in stock, and Zangwill admitted that he would be "proud" to have something of his own printed by the Roycrofters. The most interesting comment is this praise from Harold Frederic:

> Several Kelmscott books are mine and I am sure that Roycroft publications do not suffer in comparison. Your work shows a distinct personality, and the small imperfections I find, only add to their charm, like a patch on beauty's face.

It is possible that some bibliophiles who denigrate Hubbard's bookmaking ventures are familiar only with those editions he made of each publication for undiscriminating collectors, and not with the fine deluxe editions. Limited numbers (usually 20 to 100) were specially produced and bound, sometimes with hand-tooled leather, and sold for approximately $10, and sometimes for much more than that, while the others, selling for two dollars or so, were less painstakingly produced, and bound in plain boards. The deluxe editions are extremely rare and valuable today, whether for their quality or as Americana, and are to be found only in private collections.

In addition to his contributions to American applied arts, binding, typography and design, Koch argues that Hubbard must also be considered one of the principal founders of the Craftsman's Movement (1900-1915), which had a "profound effect on architecture and the decorative arts," including the work of Frank Lloyd Wright in the Midwest and in the many bungalows in the East (82). Even Mission-style furniture is indebted to Hubbard; the Roycrofters began making their chairs and other pieces of furniture before Gustav Stickley started making his, and Stickley's "Craftsman's Homes could never have had such a widespread vogue had not Hubbard paved the way with the printed word" (82).

Fame and Flamboyance

It was because of Hubbard's forceful and flamboyant personality that he was able to attract so many creative artists to his community, and so much attention to himself. One biographer has described Hubbard as a "combination of [P. T.] Barnum, Buffalo Bill, Mark Twain, Victor Hugo, [Robert] Ingersoll and Henry Ward Beecher," adding that he had the "common sense of Franklin, the synthetic reasoning faculties of Emerson, the simplicity of Thoreau, the acumen of Carnegie, the wit of Wilde--with just a touch of Cagliostro" (Balch, 145). Hubbard's idolators, thousands of whom made pilgrimages from around the world to the Roycroft Inn and campus, saw nothing of the Italian charlatan in Hubbard, while his enemies saw little else. People tended either to admire or despise him. As Champney notes in his biography of Hubbard,

> No two people--whether professional historians or literary figures writing their memoirs--seemed to see him

> in quite the same way. If there was a common element among the chroniclers and commentators who dealt with Hubbard, it seemed to be a flavor of emerging from shock--of having been brushed and shaken by some elemental force and being variously bemused, grateful, annoyed, and furious. (211)

Among famous Americans whose lives were influenced by Hubbard are Upton Sinclair, Hart Crane, Frank Lloyd Wright, and Carl Sandburg.

Sinclair abhorred Hubbard. In his critique of American journalism (*The Brass Check*, 1919), Sinclair complains that he and his expose of life in the Chicago stockyards, *The Jungle* (1906), had been attacked by a Hubbard pamphlet which was reprinted by "the Chicago packers, and mailed out to the extent of a million copies" (37). Sinclair devotes a chapter of *The Brass Check* to him, entitled "The Elbert Hubbard Worm" (Chapter 49). A sampling of Sinclair's venom:

> He is gone now, but . . . the corporations water his grave by free distributions of "A Message to Garcia . . . ." I am told that Hubbard got only five hundred dollars from the packers for his slashing of "The Jungle . . . ." The wage-slaves of the Copper Trust went on strike, and this poisonous worm crawled over them and ate out their eyes. And then came the Colorado coal-strike--and the poisonous worm crawled on its belly to the office of the Rockefellers, looking for more to eat. (314-315)

As documentation for the above vilification, Sinclair prints excerpts from a letter from Hubbard to John D. Rockefeller, Jr., which had appeared in *Harper's Weekly* (30 Jan. 1915, p. 112). In this letter (27 May 1914) Hubbard had proposed a special issue of his pro-business *Fra* (1908-1917) which would contain "a judicious and truthful write-up of the situation in Colorado" (316). He argued that one side of the controversy was receiving more than its fair share of publicity by muckrakers such as Bill Haywood, Charles Moyer, Mother Jones, Emma Goldman, Lincoln Steffens and Sinclair, and believed that an opposing viewpoint needed to be presented. He claimed to have "upwards of a million names of members of Boards of Trade, Chambers of Commerce, Advertising Clubs, Rotarians, Jovians, school teachers, all judges, members of Congress, etc." (316). Finally getting down to brass tacks, he notes that the price of extra copies of the *Fra* is $200 a thousand (317).

The letter excerpted by Sinclair is only one in a series of letters between Hubbard and Rockefeller regarding the Colorado strike which were reprinted in *Harper's Weekly*. Hubbard had written on 3 May 1914 to express his support of Rockefeller's stand; having visited the area, he reports that a

> good many of the strikers are poor, unfortunate, ignorant foreigners who imagine that there is a war on and that they are fighting for liberty. They are men with the fighting habit, preyed upon by social agitators. (112)

He promised to send a copy of the May *Fra* so that Rockefeller could read what he had reported about the copper strike in northern Michigan. Asking for financial help for his work "in the line of popular education," he stressed the urgency of "showing the country, if possible, that we are drifting at present in the direction of I. W. W. Socialism" (112). Rockefeller replied on 7 May, expressing an interest in reading Hubbard's article on "the Colorado situation." After receiving the letter of 27 May excerpted by Sinclair, Rockefeller replied with a short, noncommittal note, on 30 May, suggesting that Hubbard contact his publicity operators in Colorado. Responding on 8 June, Hubbard stated that he would visit Denver within a few weeks, and noted that he had enjoyed "a delightful game of golf with your father on Saturday." Writing to his publicity director the following day, Rockefeller advised him to assist Hubbard in his investigations, but to make it "distinctly understood that he is making this study entirely on his own initiative and at his own expense." If Hubbard then produced "something worth distributing," arrangements could be discussed (112).

The exchanges quoted above reveal Hubbard's fear of the "Wobblies," and his desire to counteract the influence of muckraking authors and periodicals. Sinclair's disgust with Hubbard's efforts for the "other side" is understandable, but it is puzzling to come across his earlier, polite letters to Hubbard asking for contributions to an anthology of socialistic writings. Sinclair wrote to Hubbard on 12 Aug. 1914 explaining that he has a passage written by him describing child labor conditions (undoubtedly the essay "White Slavery in the South," which appeared in the May 1902 [14.6:161-178] issue of the *Philistine*) and asking for his assistance in pointing out any other passages in his writings which "voice the protest against present-day economic evils." Five days later he thanks Hubbard for his "very kind" response, and then on 9 Dec. 1914 he reminds him of his promise to send a few passages for inclusion in his anthology of social progress (with the word socialism being understood *"in the broadest possible sense"*) (HRHRC, Box Recip. K-Z, Folder S-T). Perhaps Hubbard did not comply, or sent him instead a letter which made Sinclair angry enough to devote an entire chapter in *The Brass Check* to the libeling of Hubbard, who was no longer alive to defend himself.

At the same time that Sinclair was soliciting contributions from Hubbard, the teen-aged Hart Crane was living with the Hubbard family for several weeks during the summer of 1914, binding books in the morning and doing farm work in the afternoon (Weber, 9). He had all but run away from home, the first of his flights from his father; he had met Hubbard when Hubbard came to Cleveland to write a promotional pamphlet ("A Little Journey to Crane's Chocolate Studio," 1914) about the Crane chocolate business (8). One Crane biographer states simply that Crane became disillusioned with his pilgrimage to East Aurora, while retaining his enthusiasm for poetry (Horton, 28), but Brom Weber displays considerable bias in his Crane biography when he describes Hubbard's career as "one of the low points in American cultural history" (8), and implies that the boy's visit "speedily destroyed the illusion of the man as a literary genius" and undoubtedly encouraged Crane's decision to enter advertising as a profession; however, apparently not quite comfortable with his harsh assessment of Hubbard, Weber admits that Crane also owed "his familiarity, if not his initial acquaintance, with the works and ideas of America's classic poets" to this stay with Hubbard (9).

The connection between Hubbard and Frank Lloyd Wright is not well substantiated, but noteworthy. (The most recent Wright biographer, Brendan Gill, mentions Hubbard only a few times.) Hubbard and Wright, both admirers of William Morris, were friends who met on several occasions. In 1904 Wright was architect for the new Buffalo headquarters of the Larkin Soap Company, the company Hubbard had retired from in 1892. In addition, William Allin Storrer notes that all the Wright homeowners in Buffalo were officers with the Larkin Company; one of them replaced Hubbard upon his resignation from the firm, and another was the husband of Hubbard's sister Mary. The Roycroft Inn, as Koch notes, "with its peristyle connecting the several units, its exposed rafters, and its variety of purpose reflected in its plan, may well be a prototype of the several homes that Wright later built for himself" (77). Wayne Andrews, in his *Architecture, Ambition and Americans* (1955), raises the possibility that it was Hubbard who influenced Wright to wear long hair and flowing ties; moreover, he suggests that "Taliesin East" has "more than a little in common" with East Aurora, and that the Taliesin Fellowship is indebted to the example of Hubbard's community of Roycrofters (249).

This connection is further supported by Norris Kelly Smith in his *Frank Lloyd Wright* (1966), where he states that Taliesin was "inspired" by the example of Hubbard's Roycroft School, and that Wright emphasized in his first Taliesin prospectus his intention "to give instruction in just those crafts for which East Aurora was noted: typographical design, printing, molding, woodworking, weaving, and so on" (118). Even more intriguing is the transformation of Wright's attitude regarding mechanization. Just after the turn of the century, when Hubbard was preaching the virtues of handicraft, Wright was championing the "art and craft of the machine," and it was at this time that he designed the cathedral-like Larkin Soap headquarters, where even the furniture was made of metal (144). By the 1930s, however, he had become, as Hubbard had been, an outspoken opponent of the prevailing threats to the "human-element" in working life (144).

Because of Hubbard's complicated personality and his flamboyance, his reputation suffered, even as the circulation of the *Philistine* soared. Like many writers anxious for literary fame, he "created a public personality for himself to advertise his work" (Beisner, 106). His genius as an entertaining lecturer and his penchant for broad humor made many wonder if he was serious, if he was only a charlatan. This charge is refuted by a William W. Denslow illustration on the back cover of the October 1906 (23.5) issue. Three look-alikes dressed in black, apparently clergymen, are sitting on a rail fence observing a profusely perspiring Hubbard working in his garden. The caption asks, "Is he sincere?"

One contemporary writer, who would later become famous, believed he was. Carl Sandburg, who was still Charles when he discovered Hubbard, was a longtime admirer of Elbert Hubbard (Knox, 175). Sandburg had been led to Hubbard by Philip Green Wright, his professor at Lombard College, in Galesburg, Illinois. Professor Wright, like Hubbard, was a disciple of William Morris, and privately printed (in his basement) three booklets of Sandburg's writings in 1904 and 1905 (Jenkins, 311). Alan Jenkins describes him as Sandburg's "literary and spiritual mentor as well as first publisher" (311). Both Wright and Sandburg read John Ruskin, and both "found bracing the oracular moralizings" of Hubbard (Jenkins, 314). Armed with a letter of introduction from Professor Wright, Sandburg called on Hubbard one summer in East Aurora while selling stereoscopic views (314). (Perhaps Sandburg provided the impetus for Hubbard's use of a stereopticon on his 1908 lecture circuit.) Hubbard undoubtedly thought back to his own soap selling days as he and Sandburg talked, and the visit was a success; Hubbard published four of his caller's poems in early numbers of the *Fra*, one in 1908 and three in 1909 (Knox, 177), several years before Sandburg's association with Harriet Monroe's *Poetry*.

The earliest allusion to the Sandburg-Hubbard connection in Herbert Mitgang's *The Letters of Carl Sandburg* dates to 1901, sometime during the summer. In a letter to his sister Mary, "Charlie" mentions receiving a letter from "the Fra [Hubbard] containing fine bouquets and good wishes" (6). He trusts that she is "strong enough" to read Hubbard, adding cryptically, "I hope you get the full gist of Hubbard's meanings and that if a sadness comes over you in reading him, it is not tinged with bitterness" (5-6). Sandburg visited Hubbard again the following year, on Christmas Eve. Writing to Mary (26 Dec. 1902), he recounts his visit to the Roycroft shop. Hubbard had invited him to stay for supper, and presented him a deluxe Roycroft book. Sandburg, only 24, was greatly impressed with this reception, and we may excuse his youthful hyperbole:

> I went away from that place with a kind of a lump in my throat and a gladness in my heart, about it all, only this,--when future generations weigh in the balance the life of Elbert Hubbard, they will pronounce him one of the greatest men the world ever saw. (Mitgang, 7)

Two years later, in a letter to Professor Wright, Sandburg provided additional evidence of his esteem for Hubbard, stating that, in the category of essayists, he ranked Hubbard "highest among contemporary writers" (Mitgang, 35).

Sandburg publicized his veneration for Hubbard in several articles he contributed to the socialist periodical *To-Morrow*. In the first, "Subjugation of Elbert Hubbard" (October, 1905; 30-32), he reviews the condemnation of Hubbard that has been going on for several years (Knox, 166):

> Socialists have resented his socialism and individualists have ridiculed his individualism. For his methods in advocacy of the cooperative commonwealth, he is denounced as a spurious revolutionist; for his association with the common people and his defiance of conventionalities, he is condemned as dangerous to society. Big business men have adopted his "Message to Garcia" as the strongest vindication ever written for the employing class. Humanitarians have pronounced his "Consecrated Lives" one of the masterpieces of literature pointing toward that cherished possibility, "The universal brotherhood of man." (30)

Such a summary of conflicting assessments points to the inapplicability of simplistic labels to Hubbard and his writings. Sandburg explains that Hubbard speaks for "those more enlightened classes who recognize that civilization is yet at its dayrise," and that it is the "new truth so often thrown out by the *Philistine* boloist [sic] that scruffs the skin of the superior class" (30). Invoking a theory of conspiracy among contemporary journals, he asks why, even though the *Philistine* has a monthly readership larger than the annual readership of any American best seller during the previous decade, the "leading" magazines, such as the *Bookman*, *Munsey's*, and the *Critic*, maintain their policy of silence regarding the *Philistine* (31). He concludes that "the subjugation" of Hubbard is in a class with the suppression of Voltaire, Victor Hugo, and Emile Zola (32).

His later defenses of Hubbard in *To-Morrow* are "The Genial Fra Again" (June, 1906; 25-26) and "Elbert Hubbard's Idea of the Value of Human Suffering" (July, 1906; 59). In the former, a two-paragraph apologia, Sandburg admits that the labor unions have cause for wanting to tear "the Fra's reputation into little green ribbons" (25), but reminds his readers that Hubbard has also written "masterly and unanswerable analyses of some of the modern wrongs in society," such as child-slavery in southern cotton mills (26). In the May 1902 (14.6:161-178) issue of the *Philistine* Hubbard had written an essay titled "White Slavery in the South." The result of moving the cotton mills from Massachusetts to South Carolina, Hubbard claims, where there are no laws regulating child labor, is "child-labor of so terrible a type that African slavery was a paradise compared with it" (161). Blaming capitalists, politicians, and preachers alike, he denounces those who acquiesce in this "white slavery" as "good raw stock for missionary work" (168). It is particularly the clergy, however, who receive the brunt of Hubbard's anger. He charges that the "average clergyman will not champion an unpopular cause," and the "church has always sided with slavery . . . because she has thrived on the profits of slavery" (175). He can imagine nothing less Christian than "a partnership between grasping greed and religion" (175).

The latter contribution is signed "Valdemar Blad," perhaps because Sandburg did not feel comfortable as an "uncertain party-apologist" for Hubbard on the magazine, although Knox maintains that despite a growing personal skepticism he was still able "to subscribe to, and prescribe, a type of work philosophy sounding like 'Fra Elbertus'" (Knox, 175, 173). This one-page contribution is a summary of a talk Hubbard gave to the "intelligent" Roycrofters on the value of suffering in the evolution of thought. Sandburg avers that the quote, "all experiences are good, and the bitterest best of all--I feel sorry for the souls who have not suffered," comes from "one of the ablest and noblest thinkers of today," regardless of his many faults (59).

Sandburg was no stranger to Hubbard's community in East Aurora, delivering lectures at the Roycroft Chapel on Walt Whitman, George Bernard Shaw, and socialism. In a letter from East Aurora (6 July 1907), Sandburg gives Professor Wright a report on a presentation he gave to the Roycrofters:

> They are sort of crazy here about the lecture on Whitman I gave yesterday. . . . They drew out of me my best. Mr. and Mrs. Hubbard say I have "a world-beater." The crowd caught things right on the wing all the way through & when I was done & had seated myself & was talking nothings with somebody Hubbard grabs me by the arm & pulls me to the front again--they were clapping & yelling for an encore. . . . Hubbard tells me that an

> insistent demand for more of my stuff dictates that I go on for at least a half-hour talk tonight. (Mitgang, 49)

Hubbard also furthered Sandburg's career by publishing his poems in the *Fra*; these poems stem from his *Wanderjahre*, and were written while "Charles Sandburg was becoming Carl Sandburg and discovering his true metier" (Knox, 182, 185). George Knox concludes that "Hubbard's encouragement was essential to a growing confidence" in Sandburg's abilities, noting that his last item for the *Fra* was a short essay, "What Do You Think?" which embodies "a kind of poetic credo" (186). Sandburg's biographer, Harry Golden, suggests that Hubbard was to Sandburg's generation what H. L. Mencken was to Golden's, and what the *New Yorker* magazine was to that of the late 1950s (Golden, 59). As an indication of Sandburg's continuing esteem for Hubbard, he admitted to Golden, "Perhaps as long as I live I shall occasionally look into certain writings of Elbert Hubbard" (59).

The Hubbard Puzzle

The source of Hubbard's impact on contemporary Americans, and the most enduring accomplishment of this exasperatingly complex man, is the *Philistine: A Periodical of Protest*, the subject of this book. The wellspring of his fame and influence, his magazine provides the clearest expression of Hubbard's thoughts and impressions. He initiated his "little magazine" largely as a caustically satirical attack on those magazine editors, including William Dean Howells (*Harper's*), Richard Watson Gilder (*Century*), Edward Bok (*Ladies' Home Journal*), and S. S. McClure (*McClure's*), who had rejected his manuscripts, thereby thwarting his literary ambitions. Ever the successful entrepreneur, his publication was profitable from the beginning, and Hubbard derived intense satisfaction from its increasing competitiveness with established periodicals; following the appearance of "A Message to Garcia" in March, 1899, subscriptions escalated to 110,000 by 1904, peaked at 126,000 in 1906, and remained above 100,000 until its termination by Hubbard's son in 1915.[6]

The magazine's format varied over the years, but the thirty-two pages of a representative issue, sandwiched between a matching number of advertising pages (many of them for Roycroft publications and artifacts), begin with a quatrain, then one or two signed essays. The bulk of most issues, however, and often the entire thirty-two pages, are filled with Hubbard's "Heart to Heart Talks with Philistines by the Pastor of His Flock," a free-flowing compendium of short essays, reflections, travel notes, epigrams, literary gossip, satire, and risque jokes that an ordained pastor would never tell.

Although Hubbard wrote much, and sometimes all, of the magazine's contents, the 242 numbers of the *Philistine* contain also the work of approximately 200 writers, the most famous of whom is Stephen Crane. (See Appendix B for a complete list of contributors.) Although R. W. Stallman and other Crane critics have disparaged Crane's relationship with Hubbard, Hubbard and Crane were good friends who, at least in 1895, needed each other; Hubbard provided Crane his major periodical outlet (Katz, *Poems*, 42), and Crane's growing fame swelled the circulation of the *Philistine*. Ten of Crane's poems appeared in print for the first time in Hubbard's magazine; a total of 22 of his poems and prose pieces appear between 1895 and 1900. Among other writers of note represented in its pages (through contributions or reprints) are George Ade, Claude Fayette Bragdon, Gelett Burgess, Bliss Carman, Edward Carpenter, Benjamin De Casseres, Walter Blackburn Harte, Rudyard Kipling, Ouida, William Marion Reedy, Leo Tolstoy, and Eugene R. White.

In addition to its value as an American chapbook, Hubbard's magazine provides a record of a Midwesterner's search for a niche in American literary history. He wrote frequent and passionate protests against religion and the church, imperialism and war, and orthodoxy of thought in general. His acerbic observations over two decades regarding the Establishment (with considerable scorn for Harvard, where he enrolled as a "special student" for a short time, and was told by Professor Barrett Wendell that he would never be a writer), and the leading figures and publications of his time, make the *Philistine* valuable both to historians of this period and as necessary source material for a definitive biography. The longest-lived of the hundreds of "fadazines" which it spawned during the 1890s, with an extraordinary diversity of readers, ranging from avant-garde artists to United States presidents, the *Philistine* merits intensive study.

Despite its importance, however, no scholar has devoted more than a chapter to the *Philistine*. Because he was a businessman "with a literary attachment," and defended some of the targets of muckrakers, his integrity has been questioned, and his magazine and his literary relationships with Crane and others have been slighted. A thorough study of the *Philistine* does not yet exist, and the few monographs and scholarly articles devoted to Hubbard discuss the *Philistine* only in passing. The best single account is still the ten-page sketch by Frank Luther Mott in his *A History of American Magazines* (Vol. 4, 1957). A chapter misleadingly entitled "The Philistine" in Balch's biography is discursive and treats largely of events prior to the *Philistine*'s founding. While Stephen Crane's poems and short stories in the magazine have, of course, been noted in detail by Crane bibliographers, little has been said regarding Crane's relationship with Hubbard.[7] Even the few monographs devoted to Hubbard contain, at most, only a chapter on his magazine, and most of these works are not literary in scope; one is a sociological dissertation (Janice Gaus Crumrine, 1976), another is a library science dissertation (Bonnie Ruth Baker Thorne, 1975), and John Stephen Hopkins's M.A. thesis (1970) is an American Civilization study of Hubbard and the American business creed.[8]

This neglect of the *Philistine* by literary scholars is unfortunate, as this periodical served Hubbard both as an intimate log of his thoughts and experiences, and as a monthly "pulpit" (he facetiously referred to himself as "Fra Elbertus" and "The Pastor") for his "flock." Familiarizing oneself with the 242 numbers of the *Philistine* is a precondition for a full understanding of Hubbard and his work. Charles F. Hamilton demonstrates this point in his fine biographical study (*As Bees in Honey Drown*, 1973) which focuses on Hubbard's adulterous affair with Alice Moore, whom he later married. Using letters still being withheld by Hubbard family members, Hamilton shows that Hubbard, frequently away on national lecturing tours, would use the pages of the *Philistine* to speak to his lover; deciphering his codewords, she knew that his progressive and provocative thoughts on marriage, divorce, and love were written for her. Of all his avenues for literary expression, the *Philistine* was the most uninhibited, serving Hubbard almost as a diary. Hamilton describes the *Philistine* as "the best continuing source of insight to the temperament and philosophy of Elbert Hubbard" (*Roycroft Collectibles*, 33). The present book, while intended as a critical assessment of the *Philistine*, and not as a biographical work, will nevertheless serve as needed preparation for a definitive biography, one which can best be attempted after the complete Hubbard-Moore correspondence is released.

Biographical efforts to date have failed to rely sufficiently on the *Philistine*, and are, for this reason and others, flawed. In a foreword to Hamilton's biography, Hubbard's son, Elbert II, states his dissatisfaction with the efforts of the four previous biographers: Felix Shay (1926), Mary Hubbard Heath (1929), David Arnold Balch (1940), and Champney (1968). Champney elaborates on this dissatisfaction, noting that while Shay's book contains valuable material, the material is "scattered through a hodgepodge of impressionistic reminiscences" (216). In a review of Shay's biography quoted above, Joseph Wood Krutch notes that Shay was a Roycroft associate and disciple, and complains that his book is "weak in specific facts or figures and its chronology is far from definite" (107). Frederic Lewis Allen calls his biography "rapturous" ("Elbert Hubbard," 14), and Wolfe and McKenna confirm that Shay was Hubbard's "hero-worshipping disciple" (141). Hubbard's sister, Mary Hubbard Heath, was able to write authoritatively only about Hubbard's pre-Roycroft period. (Hubbard's granddaughter, Mary Roelofs Stott, contributed another familial testament in 1974.) Balch draws heavily upon Shay and Heath, provides little documentation, and is superficial (Champney, 215). Allen wrote that Balch is "over-kind" to his subject and never "quite solves the Hubbard puzzle. He puts the pieces on the table before us, as it were, without joining them in a coherent pattern" ("Fra Elbertus," 6). Balch's biography was, however, the only serious such attempt available for twenty-eight years, until Champney's *Art & Glory*. In addition to these flawed biographies, Brom Weber's biographical dissertation on Hubbard is one-sided and hypercritical; he later regretted his attempt to reduce Hubbard to a caricature and expressed to Hamilton a desire to collaborate with him on a fairer study of Hubbard (Hamilton, letter to the author, 23 Apr. 1985).

By far the best and most balanced biography of Hubbard is that by Champney, but even his is flawed. Though *Art & Glory* is acknowledged to be "the first to treat its subject in depth" (Braunstein, 9), Wolfe and McKenna, while conceding that Champney's is "the most useful" biography thus far, complain that it too, like the previous biographies, "contains many errors" (141). Immediately after the title page, for example, in a caption beneath a copy of a *Philistine* cover, Champney claims that the covers were "always brown paper, with black type and red decorations." In fact, some covers have other colors and some have green decorations. Champney himself admits that his work was "never intended· to be a detailed biography" (224), but more of a "do-it-yourself Elbert Hubbard kit" (212). Echoing what Allen had said about the Hubbard puzzle in his criticism of Balch's biography, Champney adds that Hubbard's life "had the same bits-and-pieces quality" (212). Students of the *Philistine* and other turn-of-the-century periodicals who read his incomplete biographical "kit" (which suffers from a lack of footnote and page numbers in the chapter notes) will find, for example, only a few allusions to Crane and other contributors; more disconcertingly, they will find only a four-page section on the *Philistine.* In sum, partly because of the lack of a comprehensive study of the *Philistine*, no satisfactory biography of Hubbard exists, and the present study of Hubbard's primary literary endeavor during the last twenty years of his life will address its significance to American literature and journalism, and help the next biographer piece the puzzle together.

Notes

[1] In 1973 the fourteen buildings of the Roycroft Campus won listing on the National Registry of Historic Places, and the Roycrofters-at-Large Association has been instrumental in establishing the significance of the Roycroft Movement.

[2] Thompson's superb book is extremely informative and helpful regarding the influence of Morris on American book design. What she has to say about Hubbard's importance as a printer is, however, beyond the scope of the present work; her chapter on Hubbard will need to be considered in a major biography of him.

Hubbard claimed that the Roycroft Shop was the first concern in the United States to "take up the hand-illumination of books as a business" ("An Interesting Personality," 314). Hand-illuminating was apparently the rage near the turn of the century, as Wallace Nutting (in Massachusetts and Connecticut) was also hiring young girls, to color his photographs of colonial interiors and rural scenes. One can visualize a parlor scene with guests admiring hand-illumined Nutting photographs on the walls and hand-illumined Roycroft books on the tables while they sit on Mission-style furniture, rather like a scene from Sinclair Lewis's *Babbitt*.

[3] Thomson sent Hubbard a note (on stationery of the U. S. Treasury Department) of transmittal and authority to publish Morris's letters on 8 Sept. 1906, adding,

> These Morris letters, heretofore unpublished, I send to you as the man so far as I know in America most likely to appreciate them kindly and most capable of presenting them fitly to such readers as may have hearts to enjoy them. The fact that they were addressed to me while sojourning in London in the years 1884 and 1885, is now of little significance and no general interest. They belong to mankind. I cordially authorize you to publish these letters in such form, with such "connective tissue" of comment or notation, in such "color scheme" as to you may seem fittest and best. (Harry Ransom Humanities Research Center, The University of Texas at Austin, Recip. Box K-Z, Folder S-T)

(This Center is the major repository of Hubbard manuscripts and correspondence, most of which were purchased from Elbert Hubbard II between 1964 and 1967. Hereinafter it will be referred to as "HRHRC.")

[4] In his autobiographical sketch for *Cosmopolitan Magazine* ("An Interesting Personality"), Hubbard gives high praise to Kinder, noting that he was the only skilled craftsperson to join the Roycrofters; all other skilled workers in the Roycroft Shop acquired their skills after arriving in East Aurora (314).

Paul McKenna is also the author of *A History and Bibliography of the Roycroft Printing Shop, 1895-1915* (1979).

[5] The Chautauqua movement, which began as a Sunday-school summer institute in Chautauqua, New York, in 1874, developed into a national network of progressive adult education resorts and activities. (One such resort was located in the author's hometown of Framingham, Massachusetts.) Hubbard met Alice Moore at a meeting of the East Aurora Chautauqua Literary and Scientific Circle (CLSC). Texts for Chautauqua study groups were provided by the CLSC Department of the Chautauqua Press in New York City. The approved *Outline Sketch of English Literature* (1886), for example, was by Henry A. Beers.

[6] *N. W. Ayer and Son's American Newspaper Annual* gives the following circulation figures for the *Philistine*: 1901--60,000, 1902--85,000, 1903--85,000, 1904--110,000, 1905--125,000, 1906--126,000, 1907--126,000, 1908--105,000, 1909--105,000, 1910--105,000, 1911--105,000, 1912--100,000, 1913--100,000, 1914--100,000, 1915--110,000. Circulation for the *Little Journeys* is listed as 30,000 for the years 1904-1907, and 60,000 for the years 1908-1912.

[7] Hubbard was extraordinarily appealing to American poets. In addition to Hart Crane, Stephen Crane, and Carl Sandburg, among the thousands of visitors to East Aurora was Robert Frost (Hamilton, *As Bees*, 200).

[8] Champney explains the paucity of scholarly work on Hubbard with characteristic wit:

> Even the frantic prospecting for doctoral-thesis material has largely passed up the Hubbard lode--understandably: it looks like a slag heap, and a generation of scholars trained to relate to respectable authorities is unlikely to see much profit in a subject so far outside the academic framework. (207)

He also blames Felix Shay's hagiography (1926), which sold 40,000 copies, for establishing much of the Hubbard mythology, thus encouraging historians to "consign the whole Hubbard story to oblivion" (206).

Chapter II

The Early Philistine and Contemporary Periodicals

The Founding of the Philistine

The only sustained discussion of the *Philistine* (and the founding of the Roycrofters) to appear in the magazine is in the June 1912 (35.1:1-11) issue, seventeen years after the magazine's debut. Hubbard explains that he started his magazine "as a sort of self-defense," as a "take-off on the popular periodicals" which had refused to accept his manuscripts (2-3). Ten years earlier, in his autobiographical sketch written for *Cosmopolitan Magazine* ("An Interesting Personality"), Hubbard stated that the first *Philistine* was undertaken following the success of his "Little Journeys" (begun in December, 1894) in order to publicize what he thought "about things in general, and publishers and magazines in particular" (311). He adopted the name "Philistine" because he was

> going after the 'Chosen People' in literature. . . . When you call a man a bad name, you are that thing--not he.

> The Smug and Snugly Ensconced denizens of Union Square called me a Philistine, and I said, "Yes, I am one, if a Philistine is something different from you." (312)

Hubbard has never been accused of not being different, and after he realized that readers wanted more of his refreshingly irreverent and provocative comments, he decided to continue with his little magazine. He was delighted to prove that the Eastern editors who had rejected his manuscripts had failed to realize that

> the country had got tired of soft platitudes, silly truisms and undisputed things said in such a solemn way. . . . The readers wanted brevity and plain statements--the editors said they didn't. . . . They failed to properly diagnose a demand. I saw a demand and supplied it--for a consideration. (318)

He continued to supply this demand, for very lucrative consideration, for the rest of his life.[1]

In the 1912 essay, the mature Hubbard, in the flush of his success and fame, is reflective and hopes that the "grouch, grump, and desire to get even" remain in his magazine only as a "chemical trace," if at all, for in a world of death, there is no time to hate (3). Realistic about the merits of his periodical, he admits that it will "hardly do to make a meal" of the *Philistine,* as some things published in it are "very good to forget" (8).[2] On the whole, however, he believes that his magazine has had a beneficial influence; it has "broken up ossified custom, and has done a little to destroy the ankylosis of orthodox superstition in medicine, theology and pedagogy" (7).

The founding and first year of the *Philistine* are shrouded in controversy and mystery. According to a retrospective account submitted in 1926 by Frank W. Noxon to Max J. Herzberg, president of the Stephen Crane Association in Newark, Harry P. Taber and one Bickford published "a Philistine" in Denver sometime in the early 1890s (Stallman, *Letters*, 337). As tantalizing as this tidbit is, Noxon, who admits to being a close friend of Taber, does not provide any supporting evidence, and is not to be relied upon with total confidence; for example, he states later in the same account that "years went by without the first annual dinner" (338) of the Society of the Philistines. In fact, the first issue of the *Philistine,* which solicited members (i.e., subscribers) for the Society, appeared in June, 1895, and the dinner for Crane was held in December of the same year.

Noxon's intimacy with Taber is significant, for Taber conducted a campaign of self-aggrandizement for many years after Hubbard's death at Hubbard's expense. Noxon states that Taber was the first of a series of editors Hubbard "took on" (338), and Taber is credited as editor in the July through December 1895 ("Edited by H. P. Taber"), and January 1896 ("H. P. Taber, Datary"), issues of the *Philistine,* and as the copyright holder in the September through January issues.[3] This claim of Taber's editorship is undisputed, but what happened in February, 1896, may never be knowable for certain. Here is what Hubbard had to say about the departure of Taber:

> One day in February, 1896, I went away on a lecturing tour, leaving Harry Taber in charge. I was gone just three days, and when I came back I found Master Harry had organized a stock company, with seventeen others of his ilk, including a pudgy poet known to the police as Dick White [probably Eugene R. White, of the *Buffalo News*], and this merry group had actually started another magazine with intent to either Bust the PHILISTINE or make me sell out cheap.
>
> I gave Harry Taber just one kick in the pants, and continued serenely on my way. (*Philistine,* January, 1899; 8.2:35-36)

William McIntosh, managing editor of the *Buffalo News*, and one of the original members of the Society of the Philistines, sheds additional light on this "rebellion" in his letters to Hubbard. In a letter dated 12 Feb. 1896, McIntosh prophetically predicts that though "the day of the little magazine is near an end," the *Philistine* "will attend the funeral of a good many of the little magazines." In view of this prediction, he feels that "the chief contributors to its success should share--taking the risks also. My notion is that a stock company might be formed. . . ." Three days later, upset with the religious views appearing in the *Philistine,* and with the use of a design symbolizing Dagon (the chief god of the ancient Philistines, represented as half-man and half-fish), he complains that the "present arrangement is unfair to the men who are supposed to be in the society." On 20 February he reiterates his call to form a stock company, and wishes to know what the terms might be. Hubbard, of course, would have had no desire to relinquish control of the enterprise, and apparently convinced McIntosh that he was out of line in his requests, for in a letter on 30 Mar. 1896, McIntosh admits, "I realize that I am beyond my rights entirely in addressing you concerning the management of the Phil." (This correspondence is among the Taber Papers in the Rare Book Room of the Buffalo and Erie County Public Library, hereinafter referred to as the Buffalo Rare Book Room.)

It seems reasonable to conjecture that Taber realized that Hubbard, having purchased the enterprise from him, would soon dismiss him. By attempting to form a stock company with his friends and journalist colleagues during Hubbard's absence, he apparently hoped to retain partial control over the *Philistine.*

Another clue to the causes of Hubbard's displeasure with Taber is provided in a letter from Hubbard to contributor Alexander Jeffrey (17 Feb. 1896):

> I've been away on a little lecturing tour, and on getting back this morning find the March Philistine on the press, with your beautiful poem ["Death the Doorway"] left out.
>
> I ordered it to have first place but Mr. Taber, splendid fellow that he is[,] has a most unfortunate thirst that defeats his best plans at times. (Whiskey, thy name is hell!) (Elbert Hubbard Museum)[4]

Hubbard was a teetotaler who often wrote describing the ills of drinking, and if Taber had a fondness for whiskey as alleged, then Hubbard would have orchestrated Taber's departure as soon as possible. Hubbard promised Jeffrey that his poem would have "first place" in the next issue, and instructed him to return the corrected proof directly to him, not to Taber. The poem appeared as promised in April, 1896 (page 153, opposite Stephen Crane's "To the maiden"), indicating that Hubbard assumed firm editorial control after his return from his lecture tour.

Taber sorely rued his ouster, and would have felt vindicated by the partisan treatment he received in the pages of R. W. Stallman's *Stephen Crane: A Critical Bibliography* (1972), with Stallman apparently accepting all of Taber's grievances and statements at face value. Stallman calls his inclusion of the Tom Daly (1916) material, which is Taber's version of his clash with Hubbard, "an important eye-witness report," and Stallman's sympathy for the (to him) sadly abused Taber is in inverse proportion to his distaste for Hubbard, a topic that will be discussed in Chapter III.

The Daly material is two columns which appeared in the *Philadelphia Evening Ledger* on July 27 and 28, 1916, under the byline "Tom Daly's Column." The first of these columns begins by noting that while it is not well to speak unkindly of the dead (Hubbard and his wife had gone down with the *Lusitania* the year before), "there are things that must be told," and although it would have been better had these "things" been "brought out while the chief actor was still alive," they could not be published during Hubbard's lifetime (Stallman, 298). No reason is given for the dramatic urgency of Taber's wanting to set the record straight after Hubbard's death, but dispassionate reflection will lead one to suspect that it was because Hubbard was no longer alive to sue Taber for libel.

What appears in the Daly columns (given entirely in quotation marks, with Daly apparently publishing Taber's script verbatim) is a description of the founding of the *Philistine.* Not surprisingly, Taber's hand in its founding receives expansive discourse. His "fatal mistake," as he realizes in hindsight, one illustrating his lack of business acumen, was sending the magazine out to individual newsdealers across the country instead of going through the American News Company; this resulted in more than a thousand uncollectable accounts, ranging from 50 cents to $5 each, and by late August, 1895, the publishers were at "the end of their financial rope" (299). When fellow townsman Hubbard was approached for financial help, he agreed to "take the affair over" if he could become the sole owner of the periodical, "agreeing that Taber was to remain as editor-in-chief and keep a half interest in the business" (299). The split between them came, as stated before, in February, 1896, when Taber refused to print an objectionable essay of Hubbard's. In a column in the Wilmington, Delaware, *Star* (Taber worked for the Department of Ordnance at duPont during World War I), Taber claimed that Hubbard, "the solid burgher who put some $16,000 into the venture," had written something "dangerous" ("I think it was on free-love"), and Taber rejected the submission. When Hubbard "stormed" about his being the owner, they agreed to dissolve the partnership.

After a digression explaining how Hubbard also "destroyed" Walter Blackburn Harte and "drove" Michael Monahan from East Aurora, Daly/Taber continues with his own version of the Stephen Crane dinner (see Chapter III) before returning to his dispute with Hubbard. Taber and former associates in newspaper work in Buffalo asked Hubbard to name his price for his interest in the Roycroft Printing Shop and the *Philistine.* When Taber presented Hubbard with a certified check for his specified price, Hubbard said he had changed his mind and refused to sell any part of his interest. Because "it would have cost an interminable legal battle, the new company gave up" (301).

Stallman was proud to have published Taber's "expose of Hubbard" (301n.) and also included two subsequent, related items by Taber (1923 and 1940) in his Crane bibliography. The 1923 item was a letter to Thomas Beer, Stephen Crane biographer, and the 1940 item was a letter to David Balch, a biographer of Hubbard. The letter to Beer is ostensibly about Taber's dealings with Crane, but Taber cannot refrain from discussing his clash with Hubbard. After noting that his name did not appear in the first *Philistine,* he explains that in "an evil moment I had asked Elbert Hubbard to become associated with the enterprise," and refers Beer to the Daly columns (311).

In the letter to Balch, Taber explains that his name was left off the masthead of the first number of the *Philistine* because of "an error on my part in making up the type pages" (356). Going into detail regarding his business affairs with Hubbard, he states that he sold the *Philistine* and the Roycroft Shop to Hubbard on November 29, 1895, but was, according to the terms of the contract, to remain editor and receive one-half the net profits, "payments to be made every six months" (357). He notes that that contract is, after forty-five years, still in his desk, and compares Hubbard's behavior regarding contracts to Hitler's. Again, he claims that he could not go into court and fight, but does not explain why. After correcting Balch's biography on several counts and accusing Balch of slighting his part in the magazine's founding, he concludes lamely that he has "no grievance now" against Hubbard, nor against Balch for the "rather contemptuous treatment of my part in the play" in his biography of Hubbard (358). He notes sadly that the spirit of the *Philistine* and the Roycroft died when the "Great Showman took control" (358).

As Stallman emphasizes a second time in a note on page 358, these letters and the Daly article were published for the first time in his bibliography. What is puzzling, however, is Stallman's prima facie acceptance of Taber's claims. To be sure, it does appear that Hubbard, being the experienced businessman that he was, and zealous of a chance to make a name for himself in literary circles, astutely drove a hard bargain when he agreed to assume Taber's debts and save the *Philistine* and the Roycroft Shop. What is suspicious, however, is Taber's reluctance to sue, especially if, as he claims in his letter to Balch, he had a written contract sitting in his desk. This suspicion is shared by Hubbard's most recent biographer, Charles F. Hamilton, who observes, "From what the old Roycrofters (who knew them both) told me about both Hubbard and Taber, I suspect some wishful thinking motivated Taber" (letter to the author, 23 Apr. 1985). We can conclude that perhaps he did not have a written contract, in which case litigation would indeed have been an expensive gamble. His caving in so abjectly in February, 1896, when he had such great dreams and so much invested in their realization, together with his attempts to rewrite history only after Hubbard's death, do nothing to encourage an uncritical reliance upon only his version of his altercation with Hubbard. However much Stallman despised Hubbard, and even if Hubbard was "an egocentric ass," as he claims (615), Stallman simply had no convincing justification to give the prosecuting Taber his day in court without at least some critical cross examination.[5] The editors of the *Saturday Review* had been much more cautious than Stallman about publishing Taber's charges when he submitted a review of Felix Shay's 1926 biography of Hubbard. Amy Loveman wrote Taber (12 Aug. 1926) to make sure it was "absolutely certain that if any question of libel comes up" he could produce the documents that would support his charges. In a follow-up letter on 10 September, Henry S. Canby repeated Loveman's concern that the article was "of course open to a suit for libel"; he subsequently published an edited version of Taber's submission (in the October 16 issue) not as a critical review of Shay's biography but as a "Points of View" column (Taber Papers, the Buffalo Rare Book Room).

Contemporary Journals and Parodies

One of the more valuable features of the *Philistine* is its being a record of comment regarding contemporary periodicals and journals. Hubbard, in addition to his numerous subscriptions to a great variety of publications (including several German trade publications for the benefit of his printing staff), undoubtedly subscribed to a clipping agency, an inexpensive service used by many at the time (including Stephen Crane, who collected clippings to keep track of what his critics said regarding his works); such a subscription could be had for as little as $1.00 per month from the Chicago Press Clippings Bureau (1.1:bap).[6] Whether he read all the publications he mentions in his magazine or whether he relied in part on clippings, his "filler" items in the pages of the *Philistine* often have to do with the publications of his literary colleagues. His comments are colloquial and usually derogatory, and must have provided his readers consistent entertainment. He truly believed that the articles in his magazine provided superior reading compared to those in other publications, saying, for example, that they were "better than anything to be found in Harpies or the Eighteenth Century" [*Harper's* and *Century*] (January, 1899; 8.2:33).

Praise from contemporaries for the *Philistine* was frequently displayed in filler pages. The following testimonial, from Frank Putnam, editor of the *National Magazine*, appears several times:

> Elbert Hubbard is one of the three greatest writers in the world to-day. He uses as many words as Shakespeare. He has ease, facility, poise, reserve, sympathy, insight, wit, and best of all--commonsense. He is big enough and great enough to laugh at himself: his enemies he regards as friends who misunderstand him, and his avowed friends cannot turn his head by flattery. (November, 1906; 23.6:cap)

These comments begin with the first volume (June through November, 1895). In the June number he reports that Mark Twain is writing "Joan of Arc" anonymously in *Harper's* because Twain is "convinced if he signed it the people would insist the stuff was funny." He reassures his readers, however, that "Mr. Twain is worried unnecessarily. It has been a long time since any one insisted the matter he turns out so voluminously was or is funny" (1.1:22). In the September number he admonishes him thus: "I am awfully sorry you have lost all your money . . . but let's not talk about it all the time" (1.4:123). In an equally malicious gibe at another target, Hubbard notes that the editors of the *Chip-Munk* are "a bit slow in reading their exchanges," for they printed an item in their May 1895 issue which had appeared in one hundred and forty-nine newspapers in 1894 (1.1:25). Other publications cited briefly (sometimes only epigrammatically) in the remaining pages of this inaugural issue are the *Baseburner*, *Current Literature*, Hubbard's own *Little Journeys*, the *Bibelot*, *Chips*, *Town Topics*, the *Buffalo Courier*, *Kate Field's Wash*, the *Arena*, *Humanitarian*, *McClure's*, *Scribner's*, *Godey's*, *Basis*, the *Century*, and *Peterson's*.[7] Comments regarding the last nine are grouped under the heading, "The Magazines" (1.1:30-31), and Hubbard's caustic lines are incisive.[8] For example, he makes the deadpan observations that *Scribner's* has a "thrilling article on 'Books We Have Published,'" and the *Century*, "it is said, will insert a page or two of reading matter between the Italian art and the ads." Two additional publications, *Footlights* and the *Echo*, are advertised in the back pages.

One of the leading figures of American journalism whom Hubbard excoriated was Edward W. Bok, who edited the very influential *Ladies' Home Journal* for thirty years, from 1889 to 1919. Bok was even more of an "outsider" than Hubbard was, having been born in Holland, but he reached a level of popular success and acceptance in the Establishment that even Hubbard could not hope to attain.[9] Bok receives his first mention in the *Philistine* in a bogus bill for the amount of $11.70 from Bok to W. D. Howells (1.1:32). The bill was for the following items: "42 sq. inches in Boiler Plate . . . on What I Know of Howells's Modesty" ($4.20); mentioning Howells's name 730,000 times "in same" ($7.30); and, for twenty cents, "Cussing *Trilby* [by George du Maurier] (your suggestion)." Howells had the option of obtaining a two per cent discount if he paid cash.

Hubbard attacks both Bok and Howells again in the next issue. One gets an idea of the nature of Bok's magazine by the following:

> *How to Carry a Cat in a Basket* is the attractive title of

> an article to appear in the forthcoming *Ladies' Fireside Fudge*, from the pen of its gifted editor, Mr. E. W. Sok.

His attack against Howells is through his daughter:

> It runs in the Howl family. W. Dean has a daughter who puts her poems under display ad heads in *Scribner's*. The decorative head is the thing. The poem just belongs.

Among other targets of his satire and venom in this second issue of the *Philistine* are the Chicago publishers [Herbert] Stone and [Hannibal] Kimball ("Rock & Bumball"), Lew Wallace, Ida Tarbell (the contributor of "muckraking" articles to *McClure's*, whose future "expose" of Standard Oil Hubbard would contest), and the publications *Basis*, *Overland Monthly*, *Budget*, *Mid-Continent*, *Century*, *Atlantic* (which is "very pacific--not to say mild"), *Chautauqua*, and the *San Francisco News-Letter* (1.2:65-70). Page 72 of this issue contains six brief advertisements, and it takes a moment to realize that they are all bogus. One is for "Rock & Bumball," who are "Literary Undertakers" whose specialty is "Peacock Feather Caskets." Another advertises the Canadian poet Bliss Carman's "Condition Powders," which make poets "lay." And a third is from a literary analyst at Columbia College, who will interpret Ibsen "while you wait."

Hubbard conducts a much more sustained criticism of the failings of contemporary journalism in an essay decrying a sensational and prurient *Ladies' Home Journal* ("Ladies' Hum Journal") article which expounded upon the effects of syphilis while managing never to mention the topic explicitly (December, 1908; 28.1:3-13).[10] Hubbard has no patience with Bok's timidity:

> What is this Awful Something that Brother Bok so mysteriously sidesteps and avoids mentioning--out with it--tell us about it, illustrate it, picture it, throw it on a screen!
>
> But the bully Bok is an editorial ink-fish--he shoots his headlines and then escapes under cover of the smoke, leaving us in a maze, a fog of doubt. (5)

He admits that the shrewd Bok knows what he is doing, however, for Bok is a businessman, or at least "one kind of a business man," who knows that the average bourgeois female mind is "undeveloped, inexperienced . . . shut in, repressed, suppressed, [and] hedged around" (8).[11] Still, "she is a woman and sex is strong in her head, at least," so Bok cunningly "excites his flock with his stentorian cry of 'Disease!'" (8). Under the "specious excuse" that he is serving the interests of science Bok "gives glossed pornography. It is a sort of cantharides literary libidinous lotion" (10). And although Hubbard wants Bok to be deposed and replaced by an old woman who will not merely try to "titilate [sic] the curiosity" of her subscribers, but tell the truth once in a while (13), Hubbard is fair in assessing where the trouble really lies: it is not so much with Bok as it is with "the society whose mouthpiece Bok essays to be" (8).

Bok could well have responded by accusing Hubbard of hypocrisy, for Hubbard never mentions the word syphilis either. Moreover, Hubbard was occasionally guilty of titillating his own readers. An amusing allusion to the magazine's "scorching" reputation is a "silly and slanderous story" ostensibly received from Reno, Nevada, and included in one of the installments of "Heart to Heart Talks." In this hoary joke, a young woman, while reading the *Philistine,* takes off her shoes and stockings and then puts the stockings on again wrong side out. When asked by the gaping passengers what she is doing, she replies, "I found the text such hot stuff that I felt compelled to turn the hose on myself" (July, 1909; 29.2:64). In a similar vein, the cover of the March 1905 (20.4) issue has this warning printed in red from top to bottom: "This number is Printed on Asbestos and is Intended for Neither Children nor Fools." (With some justification, as it contains Hubbard's scathing essay, "Theology vs. Social Science," in which he argues for civil marriages and the right to dignified divorce proceedings. See Chapter V for a discussion of this essay.)

Hubbard and the *Philistine* received a great deal of attention, and imitation being the sincerest form of flattery, Hubbard must have been gratified by the fact that his magazine spawned a host of both imitations and parodies. According to Frank Luther Mott, the "success of Hubbard's little magazine called forth a horde of imitators about the turn of the century, as well as some parodies and an *Anti-Philistine* in London" (647). Hubbard claims that his magazine inspired more than two hundred imitators. In the August 1899 (9.3) issue he complains that "if this thing continues I 'll start a Pillory for the benefit of Rogues who are stealing my Good Stuff" (94), and cites three examples. The first is the *Anti-Philistine* (see text below). The second, the "most brazen bit of kleptomania," is the *Crockery Journal*, published in New York City by Whittemore & Jaques, which printed his "A Message to Garcia" in its June first issue without giving credit (95). Finally, a Mr. H. Gaylord Wilshire, of Los Angeles, had recently issued the first number of a magazine called *The Philistine: a journal devoted to the demolition of preconceived ideas* (95).

If the following claim by Hubbard is true, it is a cruel note for bibliographers and scholars of American periodicals:

> For several years we kept copies of these new magazines that were continually springing into being, started by the sophomorish mind and occasionally by those who had a lust for lucre. Finally, however, the index of these grew too big and bulky to continue; and the imitators no longer interested us. (June, 1912; 35.1:11)

Hubbard clearly enjoyed keeping track of his competition (and plagiarists), and would announce the death of a contemporary magazine from time to time with unabashed pleasure. For example, after ten allusions in various issues of the *Philistine* to the *Chap-Book*, founded in 1894, he makes the following droll announcement regarding its demise:

> Will the Philistines please observe that altho the "Chap-Book" is dead, very dead, thro fatty degeneration of the cerebrum, I have not once said, "I gloat, I gloat! (September, 1898; 7.4:115)

He said it twice, that is, and his exuberance at his own success is manifest. He was no doubt justified in gloating over the extraordinary phenomenon of a literary publication in East Aurora, edited by a former soap peddler, outlasting the Chicago enterprise of Herbert Stone, a professional publisher.

Actually, Hubbard need not have felt insecure about the quality of his magazine in comparison with that of the *Chap-Book*. As John Stephen Hopkins reports in his thesis, there was not a "great deal to choose between their respective literary qualities" (52). Hopkins notes that Hubbard was able to get contributions from many of the authors who wrote for the *Chap-Book*, including Stephen Crane, who appeared in the *Chap-Book* four months after his first appearance in the

Philistine (52).

A comparative study of the list of contributors in Wendy Clauson Schlereth's *The Chap-Book: A Journal of American Intellectual Life in the 1890s* (1982) and the author's list of contributors to the *Philistine* (see Appendix B) reveals that the *Chap-Book* and the *Philistine* have these twenty-five contributors in common: Irving Bacheller, Katherine Bates, Neith Boyce, Claude Fayette Bragdon, Gelett Burgess, Eleanor B. Caldwell, Elizabeth C. Cardozo, Emma Carleton, Bliss Carman, Stephen Crane, Nathan Haskell Dole, Philip Becker Goetz, Louise Imogen Guiney, Thomas Wentworth Higginson, Tudor Jenks, Frank W. Noxon, Charles Roberts, Clinton Scollard, John B. Tabb, Gardner Teall, Vance Thompson, O. L. Triggs, Carolyn Wells, Eugene R. White, and Jean Wright.[12]

Intriguingly, Stone and Hubbard were students at Harvard at approximately the same time (neither staying long enough for his degree), and it is likely that Hubbard knew of Stone's publishing ambitions, and may have been jealous of them. Hubbard may also have resented Stone's social status (he was of colonial Massachusetts stock); though both of them were from the Midwest, Stone traveled in the best collegiate and Cambridge circles, while Hubbard, much older and a self-made business success, was considered a misfit. It is, however, possible that Stone may have been jealous of Hubbard. As Sidney Kramer points out in his study of Stone & Kimball, in the July 1, 1895, issue of the *Chap-Book* Stone avers that the *Philistine* has Hubbard's "usual overwhelming dullness and paucity of idea, while the style has all that deftness which we have learned to know as peculiarly his own, a delicacy of touch as of a hippopotamus on a tight rope or a Nordau forging *vers de societe* (44)." Surely he protests too much, and such hyperbolic vitriol would be engendered either by personal animus or jealousy.[13]

Bilioustine: A Periodical of Knock

According to Mott, the best parody of the *Philistine* was the *Bilioustine: A Periodical of Knock*, which appeared in only two numbers, May and October of 1901 (647). The motto on the first number is "Love One Another and Knock," and the cover announces, "Printed whenever we need the money by the Boy Grafters at East Aurora, Illinois." As Mott explains in a footnote, however, the material in the *Bilioustine* was originally published in the *Chicago Tribune*, in Bert Leston Taylor's "A Line-o'-Type-or-Two" column, and "done into a book" (26 pages each) by William S. Lord, Evanston, Illinois, with each number costing 25 cents. (The copy in the author's collection was sent to a subscriber in Pawtucket, R.I., with a one-cent stamp.) Taylor later did more of this satire for *Puck* (Mott, 647). Hypocritically, both numbers, which satirize Hubbard's advertising methods, carry ads promoting Lord's own little magazine *Noon*.

The burlesques of *Philistine* material are well done. The "Tribe of Knock" is "an association of clever persons who paint, pose and preen, for the benefit of women that adore long hair and soft eyes" (1.1), a burlesque of the language from Hubbard's invitation to join the "Society of Immortals": "An association of Book Lovers and Folks who Write and Paint." And in making fun of the many Roycroft limited editions, a "limited edition" of 984 copies is explained to be an edition of 984 copies for the Chicago area, another 984 copies for the Denver area, and so forth (1.2). Hubbard's *Little Journeys* are parodied by the following: "Little Journeys to the Scenes of Famous Explosions, Series of 1901: The Explosion in Lake Michigan. The Explosion in the Chicago River. The Explosion of the War Ship on the Drainage Canal. Each bound in Burlap, lined with wall paper, with author's autograph and lock of his hair. Single copies, $13.00" (1.3).

Instead of Hubbard's "Side Talks" (which itself was a mocking allusion to a column by Ruth Ashmore in the *Ladies' Home Journal*), we have "Side Wipes," and the lead quatrain of the first number is entitled "Fame":

> If you would strike the road to fame
> Just print a lot of rot;
> And if you make it strong enough
> You'll win, as like as not.

The first sentence of the article is biting:

> I took a trip to Denver recently over the P. D. & Q. [i.e., the Pretty Damn & Quick] railroad, the best road in the country (I have an annual pass over it), and in the smoking car I noticed a wreck of a man, who confessed

> to me that reading essays printed on ordinary paper with ordinary ink, and bound in ordinary cloth covers, had impaired his eyesight and general health.

For many years Hubbard enjoyed free train passes, either because of his alleged status as "pastor" or because he gave so much good press to the railroads in the *Philistine,* and his publications were distinguished by their unusual appearance.

Just as the readers of the *Philistine* enjoyed being on the "in" and prided themselves on getting the jokes and catching the allusions, the *Bilioustine* expected the same from its readers. For example, this item appears in a section headed "Little Liver Pills": "Fra McGinnis [for Fra Elbertus] is preparing a preachment, which he will shortly do into hot air in Chicago." It is entitled, "The Gentle Art of Making an Ass of One's Self," and alludes, of course, to Whistler's *The Gentle Art of Making Enemies* (1890). Similarly, the following quatrain, entitled "The Pale-Blue Ass" (and attributed to Fra McGinnis) is a parody of "The Purple Cow" verse by Gelett Burgess that appeared in the *Lark* in 1895:[14]

> I never saw a pale-blue ass--
> I've always wished to see one.
> Meanwhile I do my level best
> Endeavoring to be one.

Other examples of spoofing abound. Hubbard's "Those who really do not know how to take this Magazine, had better not" (the cover motto for February, 1898; 6.3) becomes "People who cannot understand the *Bilioustine* would better not try" (2.11). Hubbard's "Every Knock is a Boost" (illustrated by W. W. Denslow for the back cover of the February 1906 [22.3] issue) becomes "Every Boost is a Knock" (2.15). And in place of the Roycroft "Articles of Faith" is the following burlesque of Hubbard's creed:

> I believe in Fra McGinnis. I believe he is hot stuff.
>
> I believe in the Body Beautiful, and the Saturday night bath.
>
> I believe in Watt'ell [what the hell, for Whatman] paper and Japan vellum, in long hair and hand-painted initials.
>
> I believe they are good for the race.

> I believe that Walt Whitman was a good hobo, and that Henry Thoreau knew beans [an allusion to *Walden*].
>
> I believe that the best way to prepare for a Future Life is to get born, and to finish Monday before beginning Tuesday.
>
> I believe that I am here today and may be gone tomorrow. Such things have happened.
>
> I believe that I may believe something entirely different next week, if I happen to take a notion. (2.20)

The *Bilioustine* received plaudits from periodicals in a limited geographical area, such as the *Denver Republican*, the *Chicago Journal* ("Not only is 'The Bilioustine' a faithful copy of the original pamphlet both in style and appearance, but in many cases the imitation is an improvement upon the original"), the *Chicago Post*, Reedy's *St. Louis Mirror* ("One of the best parodies perpetrated in the last twenty years"), and the *St. Louis Republic* (2.inside front).

Hubbard himself was probably not displeased with this imitative flattery, for a poem by Taylor appeared in the *Philistine* in June, 1913 (37.1). Hubbard no doubt relished printing it as the lead verse, as it is an invocation to the Comic Spirit to "instruct and guide me in the gentle art/ Of thoughtful laughter." The last stanza pleads,

> Am I inspired to mirth or mockery,
> Grant, Spirit, that it be not overdrawn;
> And am I moved to malice, let it be
> Only "the sunny malice of a faun."

Anti-Philistine

If the *Bilioustine* was a burlesque of the *Philistine,* and lasted for only two issues, the much more substantial *Anti-Philistine* made many parodic allusions to the *Philistine,* and lasted for four issues, from June 15 through September 15, 1897. Hubbard refers to the demise of the *Anti-Philistine* twice, in April, 1898 (6.5:137-138), and in August, 1899 (9.3:94-95). In the former citation he notes that this latest of the "chip-munk" magazines to die was "grabbed by the bloomin' bailiffs" in London after only four issues. Actually, he argued, it was never alive, as it was "just a wax-wurx [sic] dummy, made in imitation of the Philistine. Its editor stole my cover, stole my motto & annexed my jokes, first diluting them to fit the large British ears. Then he sent a copy of his periodical to me asking to exchange" (137). Being, as Hubbard adds in the latter citation, "perfectly familiar with the stuff, it was of no use to [him]" (95). Hubbard is hyperbolic about the extent of the borrowings, but his charge that the *Anti-Philistine* (*A Monthly Magazine and Review of Belles-Lettres, and also a Periodical of Protest*) was made in imitation of the *Philistine* is incontrovertible.

The supposed conducters of the *Anti-Philistine* were John and Horace Cowley, of London (Granville House, Arundel Street, Strand), and the magazine was printed in Edinburgh.[15] But as Frank Luther Mott explains in his *History of American Magazines*, the publisher was in fact a Chicagoan, Cowley Stapleton Brown (390). Despite its title and parodic elements, the *Anti-Philistine* is not, as Jerold J. Savory contends in his article cataloging the comic collection of the Newberry Library, a "comic journal." Savory defines a comic periodical as being characteristically an illustrated weekly, selling for no more than three pennies (96). The unillustrated *Anti-Philistine* was a monthly, as was the *Philistine,* and sold for six pence, with the September issue price doubling to a shilling. (The *Philistine's* price of ten cents a copy, or one dollar a year, never varied.) In his annotated list Savory notes that the *Anti-Philistine* was proposed to serve a spirit of 'innocent friskiness' to counter [the] corrupt state of current fiction" (97). Friskiness there is (or at least "a certain Yankee smartness," according to the *Dundee Advertiser*, as quoted in the July number, p. 94), but it serves a serious cause, and bantering matter appears only in a few pages of Notes in each number. And Hubbard would have argued that the *Anti-Philistine* was itself corrupting literature with its contributions by American Decadents, including Bierce's macabre and decadent fiction, which constitutes nearly half the pages of the August and September numbers. Savory is not alone in missing the nature of the *Anti-Philistine* and its relation to Hubbard's magazine. The curator of the Rare Book Room at the Buffalo and Erie County Public Library, in Buffalo, which has a special collection of Roycroft materials, was unaware of the connection, and moved its rare volume of the *Anti-Philistine* (which, unfortunately, is no longer available at the Library of Congress) from the general collection to the Roycroft collection after a visit from the author.

The most graphic tie between the two periodicals can be seen by comparing page 138 of the July issue with the advertisement for subscribers found in many issues of the *Philistine.* The *Philistine* refers humorously to the "American Academy of Immortals, Otherwise THE SOCIETY OF THE PHILISTINES," which is described as "An association of Book Lovers and Folks who Write and Paint. Organized to further Good-Fellowship among men and women who believe in allowing the widest liberty to Individuality in Thought and Expression."[16] The *Anti-Philistine* steals most of this:

> The British Academy of Immortals, otherwise the Honourable Society of the Anti-Philistines. An association of Book Lovers and Discontented Folks who Write and Paint, and are naked under their clothes. Organized to further Good-Fellowship among Men and Women who believe in allowing the widest liberty to individuality in Thought and Expression.

Hubbard was clearly responding to the *Anti-Philistine* when he altered the advertisement in his July issue, adding "and Dream" at the end of "An association of Book Lovers and Folks who Write and Paint."

As additional proof of this transatlantic interchange, the subscription advertisement in the *Philistine,* which appeared in the first issue (June, 1895), contains two "excerpts" from imaginary by-laws, namely Article XII. SEC. 2 and Article XIX. SEC. 4. The first states that the "annual dues shall be one dollar. This shall entitle the member to all the documents issued by the Society, together with one copy of the incomparable PHILISTINE Magazine, monthly, for one year." The second states that the "duties of each member shall consist in living up to his highest Ideal (as near as possible) and in attending the Annual Dinner (if convenient)." The *Anti-Philistine*'s "by-laws" also contain just two articles, which have identical numbers. And the only differences in the language are slight: the annual dues are 7s.6d., payable in advance, and "Supper" is substituted for "Dinner."

The only significant display of originality by the London

imitator is in a sensuous description of the proposed decadent "Supper":

> The inaugural Supper will be given in August next. . . . The guests will recline on couches, and will be fanned by young children, whose curly hair they will use for napkins. The menu will be embroidered on the table-cloth--not the mere list of dishes, but pictures, drawn with the needle, of the dishes themselves. At this stage in the proceedings, from panels in the ceiling, such masses of purple roses will fall, that many guests will be smothered. Those that survive will have set before them glass game and sweets of crystal. . . . As the cups circulate, choirs will enter, chanting sedately the last erotic song; little virgins, their bodies rubbed with oil, will wrestle like athletes at the Inter-'Varsity spate . . . It will begin at twelve midnight, and will end at twelve noonday. It will be a modern edition of the feast given by Heliogabalus.

Prospective subscribers were urged to send in their names at once, as the number of members in the Academy was "strictly limited." The President reserved the right to reject undesirable candidates, all of whom must "speak fluently in English (*not United States*), and must enclose a genuine certificate of good moral character."

This "nicely printed" (though on acidic paper which is now yellowed and brittle) periodical was praised by the *Brighton Society* and two dozen other contemporary periodicals, whose comments were printed, many of them twice, in three lines of small type at the foot of each page, beginning with page 65 in the July issue. The few disparaging comments were either humorous ("a sad, mad, bad, degenerate, decadent, disagreeable, bibelot magazine") or harsh and responded to in kind; when *The Sketch* noted that "Collectors of the curious will get it; but one swallow doesn't make a summer," the editor added a parenthetical description of that periodical: "the pictorial weekly which takes 'all the tarts, and puts them into pictures.'" (This audaciously clever phrase was not included when the excerpt appeared a second time.)

The manifesto of the *Anti-Philistine* appears in the Notes of the first issue, where the editor cries that there should be a "place in London for an independent literary journal conducted by men and women for men and women" (51). It was to be "a pamphlet periodical of carefully selected Literature from some of the best Wits, the strongest, most robust and masculine minds amongst the Younger Writers in the Modern Movement" (64). How this last prescription made room for women is not clear, though the tenor of this and other assertions by the editor is illustrated by the admission that "good-natured relatives have already assured us that it will at any rate be to us a pleasant reminiscence to have edited a literary journal" (53).

What makes this British periodical so unusual is that its pages are largely filled by, and devoted to, American writers. The June issue has contributions by Ambrose Bierce, Eugene Field, Edgar and Francis Saltus, James Whitcomb Riley, Joaquin Miller, and Opie Read, and the July issue has contributions by Stanley Waterloo, Edgar Saltus, Percival Pollard, and Walter Blackburn Harte. The August issue has three stories by Bierce, yet another Francis Saltus poem, and a Miller poem. Finally, the September issue has three more Bierce stories, a story by Gertrude Atherton, two poems by Francis Saltus, one by Ernest M'Gaffey and another essay by Harte. With the exception of Harte, none of these authors contributed to the *Philistine,* and Hubbard had little sympathy for any of them.

Ambrose Bierce is one of the few contributors to the *Anti-Philistine* who receives laudatory mention in the *Philistine* (see 17.3:69 and 20.1:21). Perhaps Hubbard admired his *Devil's Dictionary*; Hubbard sprinkled the pages of the *Philistine* with his own cynical definitions, such as this definition of a bard: "Anciently a poet; now a Poet-Laureate" (July, 1912; 35.2:69). Bierce once pleaded (unsuccessfully) with Hubbard to publish the poetry of an acquaintance, thus testifying to the significance of the *Philistine* in American belles-lettres. In a letter (28 Jan. 1901) from Washington, D.C., Bierce enclosed some verses by his "young friend Herman Scheffauer, of San Francisco," hoping that Hubbard would publish them in the *Philistine* (HRHRC, Box Recip. Uniden.-J, Folder B-Bz).

Regarding Stanley Waterloo, who was editor of the *St. Louis Republic*, and subsequently of the *Globe*, the *Democrat*, and the *Chicago Mail*, Hubbard reported that he had been one of the applicants to join his "colony," but that he had told him to "rub [his] head against the vest front of B. O. Flower," who was the editor of the Boston muckraking periodical *Arena*

(8.2:39).[17] And in a poor pun, Hubbard noted that at one lecture he gave, "In the box with Stanley Waterloo was Ethelyn Leslie Huston (who has not met her Waterloo)" (8.5:154). (Huston was a contributor to the *Philistine.)*

The *Anti-Philistine* waxed ecstatic over the poetry of Joaquin Miller, but Hubbard was more reserved. In the March 1896 issue of the *Philistine* he quotes praise for Miller from a recent article in the London *Athenaeum*: "In point of power, workmanship and feeling among all poems written by Americans we are inclined to give first place to the *Port of Ships* [otherwise known as 'Columbus'] . . ." and adds that "this is high praise, and whether deserved or not I leave to my readers to determine" (2.4:114). It is not until 1903, when Hubbard writes his "Little Journey" to Miller's California home, that he commits himself to seconding this praise.

Hubbard berates Edgar Saltus for fifteen pages in the October 1907 (25.5:129-143) number of the *Philistine.* Calling him "the Lord of Language, if not the Crown Prince of Ideas," he claims that he is a "writer's writer, and writers read him not for what he says, but for the way he says it" (141). Being academic and bookish, Saltus is a "titled exile" from "all the plain, simple, necessary knowledge of the common people," a "mental derelict with a university degree" (141). Introducing a choice sample of his writing, he denounces it as "the basest of Crapseyism, yet you could read it aloud at a Methodist prayer meeting and no one would suspect it was loaded. You could intone it in a church dedicated to episcopopogy [sic], and with a soft pedal accompaniment bring tears to the eyes of a bronze griffin" (129-130).

Percival Pollard is also slighted several times in the *Philistine.* In the May 1899 (8.6:188-189) number, for example, Hubbard calls Pollard a "hack writer for 'Town Topics,' the 'New York Journal' & the 'Utica Globe'; and general pessimistic, pistareen, pismire poet cheap for cash" (188-189). Pollard's reputation as an American "decadent" (see Schlereth's *The Chap-Book*, page 106) was cause enough for Hubbard's antipathy, but he adds that Pollard "starts magazines, newspapers, periodicals, and when they bust (for [his] name is failure) there is left behind a train of victimized creditors"; his "idea of a friend is one whom he can touch for a five" (189). What especially galled Hubbard about the "failure" Pollard was Pollard's audacity in sneering at "the disgusting commercial tendencies of America" (189); concluding his attack, Hubbard points to the moral that "the man who sneers at commerce is the one who has just been prodded by his landlady and turned down by his tailor" (190).

Hubbard's antipathy toward Walter Blackburn Harte (whom he called Walter Blackhart Burne and Walter Hurt) is well documented. Harte had contributed two essays (see Chapter IV) to early issues of the *Philistine,* "An Interview with the Devil" (1.2:55-59), and "Shakespeare's Borrowings" (2.6:184-187), but he and Hubbard had a falling out. Perhaps the canny Hubbard used a portion of a letter from William McIntosh to justify reneging on whatever business arrangement he had promised to Harte. In the letter of 30 Mar. 1896 quoted from earlier in this chapter, McIntosh informs Hubbard that he has just seen the latest issue of the *Fly Leaf*, the principal article of which is Harte's "The Apotheosis of the Harlot," and warns, "I write you protesting against what I believe is in store for the Phil" (Buffalo Rare Book Room). If this article is similar to (or an earlier version of) Harte's "The Ubiquitous Fille De Joie," which appeared in the July 1897 issue of the *Anti-Philistine* (87-94), McIntosh's trepidation is understandable. While Harte clearly is disgusted with "the triumph of the Harlot," his topic is shocking and his language inflammatory. For example, he hyperbolizes (with calculated alliteration) that the "fame and name of every fresh bawd from the canaille is now cabled to the four corners of the earth" (93).

In January, 1899, Hubbard avers in his "A Manifesto!" that Harte "remained in East Aurora two weeks . . . & did n't do a thing . . . but tie fire-crackers to my coat tail" (8.2:36). Harte "towsled his hair like a boofay artist, curst in falsetto, & rusht into 'Footlights' and another sheet like it, called 'The Critic [23 May 1896],' telling why East Aurora was no place for a man of genius, and declaring I was a big What-D'ye-Call-It" (36). What Hubbard neglected to add was that Harte felt that Hubbard had "murdered" his Boston periodical, the *Fly Leaf*, after extending his offer in 1896 to combine the two periodicals. Just as Hubbard's business acumen had gotten the better of Harry Taber, so too did an embittered Harte learn that Hubbard merely wanted to narrow the field of little magazines (Mott, 389). Hubbard was a "business man with a literary attachment" (Balch, 103), and Harte was no match for him in a business undertaking. It is not surprising, then, to find both Harte and Percival Pollard, a contributor to Harte's *Fly Leaf*, published in a magazine called the *Anti-Philistine*.

Notes

[1] According to Hubbard, all the revenues from writing, lecturing, and book publishing went into the common fund of the Roycrofters: "[T]he benefit is for all. I want no better clothing, no better food, no more comforts and conveniences, than my helpers and fellow workers have" ("An Interesting Personality," 319). As photographs of him prove, he certainly dressed in plain clothing (though eccentrically), and there is no evidence that his life style contradicted the above assertion. The Roycrofters were not, however, a socialistic commune in the sense of common ownership of property, but rather a superbly-managed business corporation owned by members of the Hubbard family.

[2] Hubbard was equally realistic about himself. Encouraging those writers who receive rejection slips, as he himself had before he became his own publisher, he says that every man is a "dam fool for at least five minutes every day, and if he has three days out of a month when he is filled with insight and great love, he does remarkably well"; even the genius is a genius only occasionally, as most of the time he is "deadly commonplace" (January, 1910; 30.2:57).

[3] The June 1895 issue in the author's collection has "Copyright, 1896, by B. C. Hubbard." B. C. Hubbard was Hubbard's first wife, Bertha, and this copyright notice may have been added to the front matter of the first issue when the first volume was bound. The attribution of the copyright to Bertha Hubbard reappears with the February 1896 (2.3) issue, and continues through the July 1897 (5.2) issue, after which it is assigned to Elbert Hubbard. Frank Luther Mott points out that the format of the first three issues was larger [4 3/4 by 6 1/4 inches as opposed to 4 1/2 by 5 3/4 inches] than that of subsequent issues (640), and the first issue bound in the author's copy of the first volume is smaller than the next two issues and the same size as those beginning with issue four, evidence that copies of the premier issue may have been reprinted in order to fill orders for binding the first volume. And in support of Hubbard's claim that the *Philistine* was an impromptu venture, the second through sixth numbers in the author's collection do not have any volume number printed on the covers. (In his dissertation on the *Chap-Book*, Jack

Patnode accuses Hubbard of imitating the *Chap-Book*'s size; he apparently never measured a copy of the *Philistine,* for the *Chap-Book* measures 4 1/2 by 7 1/2.)

After gaining sole possession of the *Philistine* Hubbard, of course, never relinquished control of the magazine. Sixteen years later the copyright holder is given as "Elbert Hubbard, Editor & Publisher," and, according to the statement of ownership, Hubbard is Editor, Managing Editor, and Business Manager, with the Roycrofters listed as Publisher; the owners are Hubbard, Elbert Hubbard II, Miriam Hubbard, Alice Hubbard, and C. Hubbard (December, 1912; 36.1:inside front cover).

[4] In this letter Hubbard reveals that he was thinking about changing the name of the magazine to *The Philistine: a Periodical of Progress* (instead of "Protest"), explaining to Jeffrey that "I do not want to pose as a pure destructionist. Negation is death. We will strike[,] to be sure, but what I desire is more affirmation--in line with your poem." (Jeffrey's poem concludes with the line, "all life is only the germ of better things.") Twelve years later, in March, 1908, Hubbard incorporated this mood of affirmation into a magazine he started publishing for businessmen. In his prospectus for the new venture, he announced that it would be called "*THE FRA*--not for Mummies--a Journal of Affirmation" or "A Periodical of Progress, I have forgotten which" (26.4:97). (The actual subtitle was "A Journal of Affirmation.") He admits that in the *Philistine* he has been "flippant, slangy, rude and crude," and states his intention to continue producing it "in the good old butcher's paper" (97), so that he will be able to continue to make his readers think (98). Nevertheless, alluding to muckraking journalism, he feels that there has been "enough of the literature of depreciation and defamation" (98), and thus offers *The Fra*, which will "stand for beauty in typography and ornament, as well as beauty in spirit" (98), as antidote.

[5] Stallman even goes so far as to assert, without a shred of evidence, the preposterous claim that Taber, not Hubbard, wrote "A Message to Garcia" (*Bibliography*, 243). The only evidence which may support the contention that the "Message" was not original with Hubbard is a letter (2 Mar. 1900) from the Rev. Edward Everett Hale, author of *The Man Without a Country*, in which this friend of Hubbard and Life Member of the Society of Philistines writes,

> It was I who sent you that old sermon on the Shiftless. I had forgotten it for twenty years. But when I read the Garcia I remembered that I had handled that difficult subject in my poor way. . . . (HRHRC, Box Recip. Uniden.-J, Folder H-J)

[6] The abbreviation "bap" stands for back advertising pages. Future use of "cap" and "fap" will signify center and front advertising pages.

[7] In his autobiographical sketch for *Cosmopolitan* (1902), Hubbard professed, both sarcastically and resentfully, not to be a popular writer, since his name has never been mentioned in the *Atlantic*, *Scribner's*, *Harper's*, *Century*, or the *Ladies' Home Journal* (309).

[8] In addition to the competing magazines which received "free" (if unflattering) advertising, the *Philistine* carried paid advertisements for many periodicals during its first few volumes. They include the following: *American*, *Bachelor of Arts*, *Bibelot*, *Bookman*, *Conservator*, *Echo*, *Fly Leaf*, *Footlights*, *Humanity*, *Intelligence*, *Literary Review*, *Lotos*, *Lotus*, and *Modern Art*.

[9] Whatever relationship Hubbard had with Bok during the first years of the *Philistine* seems to have subsequently dissolved. Bok wrote to Hubbard (5 Dec. 1899) about an unspecified project he wanted Hubbard's help with, and again (8 Mar. 1900) inviting him to dine with him and Mrs. Bok before they attended one of Hubbard's lectures (HRHRC, Box Uniden.-J, Folder B-Bz). However, Bok's Pulitzer Prize winning autobiography, *The Americanization of Edward Bok* (1920), contains not a single reference to Hubbard.

[10] Perhaps the most notorious instance of prissiness among the leading magazine editors of Hubbard's time was the refusal of Richard Watson Gilder, editor of *Scribner's* and then *Century*, to receive Robert Louis Stevenson. Gilder apparently had reservations regarding Stevenson's respectability.

[11] Highlighting the commercial nature of Bok's magazine, Hubbard, in an essay defending the Mormons, insists that the *Ladies' Home Journal* (and *Munsey's*) is not an inspired publication, but is produced "for pelf" (August, 1903, 17.3:70). In contrast, the Bible, the Book of Mormons, the *Philistine,* and all things that "leap hot from human hearts are inspired," for they reveal a person's point of view and contain elements

of truth.

[12] Schlereth's study focuses on the intellectual climate of Harvard and the life and thought of Herbert Stone, and gives very little attention to contemporary magazines. Hubbard and the *Philistine* are not mentioned, but neither are any other contemporary mass circulation magazines. She does not even provide any circulation figures for the *Chap-Book*. Fred Lewis Pattee, in his *The New American Literature 1890-1930*, states that the *Chap-Book* claimed to have had a circulation of 15,000.

[13] In an extraordinary coincidence, Stone also went down with the *Lusitania* (Schlereth, 152).

Hopkins adds that "even more than *The Chap-Book*, *The Philistine* came across as a place where previously undiscovered talent might at last be recognized" (54). His thesis, "Elbert Hubbard and the American Business Creed" (M.A. in American Civilization, Brown U., 1970), despite its inexcusable lack of proofreading ("Journies" for "Journeys," "Mackintosh" for "McIntosh," "amatures" for "amateurs," etc.), has helpful background material on the *Philistine* and contemporary periodicals in his Introduction and in Chapters III and IV.

[14] Claude Fayette Bragdon recalls in his reminiscent article about the "dinkey magazines" that Burgess, a year or so after the appearance of this famous verse, published the following "retraction":

> Ah yes, I wrote The Purple Cow,
>   I'm sorry now I wrote it,
> But I can tell you anyhow,
>   I'll kill you if you quote it! (475)

[15] The *Philistine* had a truly international following. In the Elbert Hubbard Museum is a request (23 Dec. 1895) for a subscription from an A. Kersha, of St. Petersburg, with a 60-ruble note attached. Hubbard's sales agents abroad were Brentano's in Paris (37 Avenue de l'Opera) and G. P. Putnam's Sons in London (24 Bedford Street, Strand).

[16] Hubbard would occasionally fill portions of advertising pages with announcements regarding who were members and who were not. In the May 1903 (16.6) issue he insults Grover Cleveland, "ex-Sheriff of Erie County," by divulging why he is not a member of the American Academy of Immortals: "We accept no man who acknowledges that he weighs over two

hundred pounds." (Cleveland had twice been president, of course, after being sheriff.)

Eighteen years after facetiously establishing the American Academy of Immortals (that is, all paid-up subscribers to the *Philistine),* the American Academy, organized in 1913, chose the first members of the American Immortals. Hubbard's name is not among them (Pattee, 16).

[17] Hubbard worked for Flower briefly at the end of 1893 and early in 1894, and two of his essays appeared in the *Arena*, which lent its voice to the William Jennings Bryan presidential campaign and the muckraking movement (Champney, 49). Flower published both Hubbard's *One Day* (1893) and *Forbes of Harvard* (1894) (Hamilton, *As Bees*, 49).

Chapter III

Stephen Crane and the Philistine

The personal and literary relationships between Stephen Crane and Elbert Hubbard were important to them and their careers. Most Crane scholars, however, have consistently failed to acknowledge the extent and influence of these relationships. Thomas Beer gives misinformation regarding Crane's contributions to the *Philistine,* and mentions Hubbard only once in his slighting of the Philistine Society dinner (Stallman, *Letters*, 62n.; hereinafter *Letters*). John Berryman dismisses Hubbard in his biography of Crane as "the busy, banal former soap salesman" (Katz, *Stephen Crane Newsletter*, 2.3:8; hereinafter *SCN*). R. W. Stallman, continuing in this vein, compounds factual errors and animosity, and gives weight to testimony from only Hubbard's enemies.[1]

It appears that those scholars who consider Hubbard a blight in American belles-lettres are not comfortable with Crane's association with Hubbard. Amy Lowell lamented that Crane's best work first appeared in the *Philistine,* that he became an "unexpected star . . . proud to shed its light upon East Aurora" (Hoffman, 29); she seems to have judged this fact an inexcusable indiscretion on Crane's part, a sin of literary "slumming," if you will. Given the implied assumption that Crane somehow burst forth miraculously in full flower (like his Maggie, who "blossomed in a mud puddle"), it is not surprising that Crane's debt to Hubbard has not been explored or appreciated. It is convenient to forget that in the closing months of 1895 Crane was so destitute and insecure about himself and his work that he had to be outfitted and coaxed by his friend Willis B. Hawkins to accept Hubbard's invitation to attend a dinner in his honor. As David H. Dickason, the first scholar to argue for the importance of the Hubbard-Crane relationship (1943), has pointed out, when Hubbard sent his invitation Crane was still largely unknown; *Maggie: A Girl of the Streets* had been languishing on the shelf for more than two years. *The Black Riders* had been ridiculed for six months, and sales of *The Red Badge of Courage* were barely more than one thousand copies (279). Regardless of one's opinion regarding Hubbard and his work, he nevertheless possessed the literary acumen to be "one of the first to detect Crane's growing importance" (Katz, *Poems*, xxxvii); and while the charge that Hubbard exploited his relationship with Crane is valid, a charge that could be made generally against publishers regarding their contributors, the fact remains that the *Philistine* provided Crane his major periodical market (xlii). In short, the Hubbard-Crane relationship was mutually beneficial.

Hubbard learned of Crane through a review copy of *The Black Riders* in April, 1895. In a letter thanking the publishers for the copy, he noted that he intended to pay his compliments to the book in the *Philistine* "in a way that will hurt no body [sic] and possibly help a bit" (*SCN*, 2.3:8). These jocose comments appear in the maiden issue of the *Philistine,* June, 1895, under "Side Talks":[2]

> Messrs. Copeland & Day of Boston recently published for Mr. Stephen Crane a book which he called "The Black Riders." I don't know why; the riders might have as easily been green or yellow or baby-blue for all the book tells about them, and I think the title, "The Pink Rooters," would have been better, but it doesn't matter. My friend, The Onlooker, of *Town Topics*, quotes one of the verses and says this, which I heartily endorse: [Crane's "I saw a man pursuing the horizon"--see below for text.] This was Mr. Howells proving that Ibsen is valuable and interesting.

> It is to be hoped that Mr. Crane will write another poem about him after his legs have been worn off. (1.1:26-27)[3]

On June 11 Hubbard sent a copy of these so-called "compliments" to Crane, hoping that he would not "take to heart the little stunt on The Black Riders. We will take it all back in the next issue" (*SCN*, 2.3:8). Hubbard asked for "a bit of ms," saying that they could help each other; Hubbard was courageously embarking on his own literary journey, having sold out his interest (and all but certain lifelong wealth) in the Larkin Soap Company, and he saw in Crane another "coming man" (*SCN*, 2.3:8). Crane must have agreed, for he complied with the request for additional material, probably sending "The chatter of a death-demon from a tree-top" and "Each small gleam was a voice," which appear in the August and September issues of the *Philistine.* Crane would continue to comply for five years, even without payment (*SCN*, 2.3:9), although Hubbard had allegedly paid for two articles from Crane in 1894, one on slum charities and the other on social theory, both of which were lost on a train (*Letters*, 62n.). Two dozen of his poems and prose pieces appear through September, 1900, with most of the poems appearing in print for the first time.

There is ample documentation regarding the extent of their literary relationship. As evidence of Crane's trust in Hubbard's editorial guidance, at the end of a letter containing the thirteen-line poem, "What? You define me God with these trinkets?" (1896 or 1897) Crane wrote, "Oh, Hubbard, mark this well. Mark it well! If it is over-balancing your discretion, inform me. S.C." (Cady, 76) As an indication of Crane's respect for the elder Hubbard's advice, Hubbard was able to convince Crane to read *Huckleberry Finn* before Crane traveled to the American West (*Letters*, 51). And as an instance of Crane's admiration of Hubbard, in a letter to Hubbard on 18 Nov. 1895 (after receiving the dinner invitation, that is, so that flattery was not required on Crane's part), Crane thanked Hubbard for his photograph and admitted, "I am quite an old reader of your Little Journeys and I think them the best things that have been said" (*Letters*, 75).[4]

Frank Noxon suspected that when Crane and Hubbard parted company in 1896, it was because, as with other contributors to the *Philistine,* of "the Fra's democratic prejudice against royalties" (Cady, 69), although Noxon is being harsh in singling out Hubbard for an editorial practice that was common, particularly regarding the printing of foreign works in American periodicals.[5] Moreover, the break between Hubbard and Crane was far from complete. In a letter from England Crane complained, "I must have Egyptian blood in me. Mummies rise from the tomb and come to pay calls that last for days" (*Letters*, 200, quoting Beer, p. 372). In 1897 Crane wrote from London apologizing for being a poor correspondent: "I am glad you wrote to me because I have been believing myself an ass in your respect and now I have opportunity to say so" (Stallman, *Bibliography*, 585). Hubbard had apparently sent Crane a calling card for friends in London, but Crane had lost it and asked Hubbard for another. He adds that he had sent a submission to the *Bookman*, with instructions that if "they could not use it ($), they should forward it to The Philistine," and closes by asking Hubbard to remember him "vividly to Mrs. [Alice] Hubbard, to the doctor [Hubbard's father Silas] and his wife and to Marie [Alice and Elbert's daughter Miriam] and to the hoodlums who played Indian on your lawn" (Stallman, *Bibliography*, 585). On May 1, 1899, he sent Hubbard two articles which had appeared in the *Westminster Gazette*, and repeated his request made two years earlier that Hubbard reprint them, adding, "if you are not a duffer you will consider them good and human enough even for your blinding *Philistine*. Send me the *Philistine* or I will set fire to East Aurora by cable." (Hubbard proved to be a "duffer" in this case.) This letter concludes, "When I think of you I rejoice that there is one man who can keep up a small independent monthly howler without either dying, going broke, or becoming an ass" (*Letters*, 220). And in a letter to Hubbard from England (date not given) Crane praised a "magnificent" paragraph by Hubbard, identified by Champney (219) as the conclusion of his novel *No Enemy*, that he had felt "in the roots of [his] hair." "Hell and Blazes," he continued, "I do envy you that paragraph! . . . The book strengthened me and uplifted me" (Shay, 508). After Crane's death Cora Crane informed Hubbard (17 Oct. 1900) that his photo had always graced Crane's study at Brede Place (Sorrentino, 236).

Although Hubbard valued Crane's friendship and championed his genius, he was understandably ambivalent about some of his verse. In the August 1895 issue of the *Philistine* Hubbard quotes the London *Athenaeum* on Crane's verses and ends by defending them:

> "Stephen Crane is the coming Boozy Prophet of America; his lines send the cold chills streaking up one's spine, and we are in error if his genius does not yet sweep all other literary fads from the board." All of which strikes me as a boozier bit of cymbalism than any of Mr. Crane's verses. (1.3:99-100)

In the October 1895 *Philistine* Hubbard is more ambivalent, joking that the poetry of Bliss Carman is worse than Crane's, for Crane "at least has a vague idea somewhere, though he rarely does us the favor to express it in a seemly manner" (1.5:157-158). In the following month's issue he wittily explains why Carman and Crane do not write for *Lippincott's*: "Some of their verse is bad enough. But the secret is out. They have only two names apiece" (1.6:200). Nevertheless, the fact remains that Hubbard recognized Crane's originality, was supportive of his individuality, and intuited the importance of his work. In a letter to Crane (July, 1895) he frankly admits,

> I do not confess to an unqualified liking for your work. When you hand me the book I am grown suddenly blind. It rather appeals to my nerves than to my reason--it gives me a thrill. Your work is of a kind so charged with electricity that it cannot be handled. It is all live wire. It eludes all ordinary criticism and it escapes before one can apply his Harvard Rhetorical Test. What is left? I'll tell you, we can stand off and hoot. Your lines show too much individuality to pass by and so we laugh and make the feeble joke. (*SCN*, 2.3:9)

Crane's "lines" were so individual, in fact, that they prompted over one hundred parodies between 1895 and 1900 (Hoffman, 25), some of them published by Hubbard. For example, "I saw a Man reading an Invitation," by Hayden Carruth, appeared on the Crane dinner menu folder, and "I Saw a Man Tugging at His Boot Straps" appeared on the back cover of the February 1899 *Philistine,* with an illustration by W[illiam] W[allace] Denslow (see below for the text of this parody). "The Spotted Sprinter," yet another parody of Crane's "I saw a man pursuing the horizon," appeared in the July 1895 (1.2:70) *Philistine.*[6] Subtitled "After the Manner of Mr. Steamin' Stork" [Stephen Crane], this delightful parody is given here entire:

I saw a man making a fool of himself;
He was writing a poem,
Scratch, scratch, scratch went his pen,
"Go 'way, Man," says I; "you can't do it."
He picked up a handful of red devils and
Threw them at my head.
"You infernal liar," he howled,
"I can write poetry with my toes!"
I was disquieted. I turned and
Ran like a Blue Streak for the Horizon,
Yelling Bloody Murder.
When I got there I
Bit a piece out of it
And lay down on my stomach and
Thought.
And breathed hard.[7]

One of the contemporary periodicals taking jabs at Crane was the *Lotus* (Kansas City, November 1895-November 1897), which was similar in format to the *Philistine.* Walter Blackburn Harte became its second editor in 1896, after losing his *Fly Leaf* in a bitter business deal with Hubbard, so it is little wonder that the *Lotus* satirizes Crane's writings and attacks his friendship with Hubbard (Weatherford, 2-4).

Many of the readers of the *Philistine* also recognized Crane's originality; Hubbard reports to Crane (26 Aug. 1895) that the appearance of "The chatter of a death-demon from a tree-top" in the August issue "brought us more notices than all the other articles combined. Several very complimentary, but others mystified of course" (*SCN*, 2.3:10). Hubbard had done what every literary editor dreams of doing, he had "discovered," Hamlin Garland and William D. Howells conveniently forgotten, of course, a new and marketable author, and in a postscript he invited Crane to visit with him in East Aurora. Crane did not accept this first invitation, but would visit later, first for the famous dinner in his honor, when he stayed in East Aurora for several days, and on subsequent trips.

The dinner was held on December 19 at the Genesee House in Buffalo, and Hubbard arranged for railroad passes to be sent to the impoverished Crane in Hartwood, N.Y., approximately 250 miles from Buffalo, and sent him money in case the passes did not arrive (*SCN*, 2.3:10). He thanks him for the two "charming" poems received, most likely "A slant of sun on dull brown walls" and "I have heard the sunset song of the birches," which appeared in January and February, 1896. In a follow-up note he reports, "I see the papers all over the country are 'chewing' about the Dinner!" (*SCN*, 2.3:11)

In his invitation Hubbard told Crane that Crane represented a "cause," and that he wished to recognize that cause (16 November; *Letters*, 75). When Crane got the invitation he was "delighted and charmed," but he also fretted about it to Willis B. Hawkins on 17 November: "I am getting frightened already. Imagine me representing a 'cause'" (*Letters*, 75). In a letter to Hawkins a few days earlier, he had admitted that he wanted to "whoop it up to somebody," but he also wondered, "What do you suppose made the Philistines do this dinner thing? Was it because I wrote for their magazine? You could have knocked me down with a gas-pipe when I got their bid" (*Letters*, 73, 74). He was clearly distressed by his lack of wardrobe. He complained to Hawkins (8 November) that his dress suit "took to the woods long ago," and that he had not had patent leather shoes in three years (Columbia, 27). The reassuring Hawkins reminded Crane that there was "a business side of life that must not be wholly ignored," and told him to send his chest and leg measurements, promising that he would be "togged properly" in time (11 November; *Letters*, 72). On 12 November Crane wrote rather poignantly to Hawkins about his mixed feelings:

> The dinner scheme mingles my emotions. In one sense, it portends an Ordeal but in the larger sense it overwhelms me in pride and arrogance to think that I have such friends.
>
> By the way, you ought to see the effect of such things upon my family. Aint they swelled up, though! Gee! I simply cant go around and see 'em near enough. It's great. I am no longer a black sheep but a star. (*Letters*, 73)

A few days before the dinner Crane, in another display of insecurity, wrote to Hawkins, "[W]hile I look forward to it as probably the greatest pleasure of my life, I feel as if I were astride of your shoulders. And if I could stop the thing now I would" (ca. 15 December; *Letters*, 81). Crane's dependence upon Hawkins is extraordinary; he seems to be nearly helpless without his assistance. This is excerpted from a letter he sent

Hawkins on 18 Aug. 1895:

> The Philistine people [Hubbard and Taber] have written to me about the notice of *The Red Badge of Courage* which they wish to bring out in their September number. What shall I say in it. I dont know how to write those notices. Can you advise me concerning a little notice. (I meant to say *will* you.) . . . (*Letters*, 62).

(No such notice ever appeared.)

Hawkins, in marked contrast to Crane, was clearly relishing all the excitement; writing back on 18 December, he explained, "It's one poor devil [Hawkins] faking up a way for another poor devil to get his fingers into pie. I haven't had any fun at all lately, and this is a real enjoyment. We'll have a bully time" (*Letters*, 81). In addition to indebting himself to Hawkins, Crane worried about having given Hubbard "a hideously long list" of guests to invite, including William Heinemann, the English publisher of *The Red Badge of Courage*" (Sorrentino, 233).[8] Crane asked Hubbard how it was possible to repay him for his trouble (Sorrentino, 233), but he need not have worried. Hubbard, without Crane's knowledge, had released Crane's acceptance of the invitation to the Buffalo newspapers (*Letters*, 74n.), had three souvenir pamphlets prepared to commemorate the event, and was eagerly looking forward to the dinner and its ensuing publicity as much as Hawkins was (Sorrentino, 235).[9]

The dinner turned out to be a roast of Crane, a "drunken" one, according to some; Hubbard's Roycroft enemy H. P. Taber sniped that Hubbard had little to do with the dinner "except to talk somewhat discursively upon his favorite topic: Love and Himself" (Sorrentino, 236). Stallman contends, without any convincing evidence, that this dinner was to Crane what war was to Henry Fleming, that afterward Crane saw himself as "the deluded hero"; he further argues that the dinner is responsible for a major "change of vision," a "turning point in Crane's outlook" (*Letters*, 73n.). In fact, Crane, though unsure of himself and not at ease, seems to have weathered the experience without trauma; in a letter to Hawkins on 31 December he wrote that he was "very anxious to hear wether [sic] you are satisfied with the dinner. I did not drink much but the excitement soon turned everything into a grey haze for me and I am not sure that I came off decently . . ." (*Letters*,

84). On that same date he bragged in a letter to Nellie Crouse that he had "had a good time and caused them considerable trouble in inventing nice things to say to me" (Cady, 29), and on 6 January he wrote Crouse again to say that the *Philistine* would have "something" of his in every number in 1896" (Cady, 31).[10] Thus it is apparent that the dinner, despite the discomfort it caused the young Crane, did not prevent him from looking forward to his continued relationship with Hubbard. The only dinner guest who clearly failed to enjoy himself was Claude Fayette Bragdon, who almost spoiled the evening by walking out before being mollified by Hawkins.

In a letter dated 7 Dec. 1926 to Max J. Herzberg, of the Stephen Crane Association, Frank Noxon, Crane's fraternity brother at Syracuse, who became an intimate friend of Hubbard's nemesis H. P. Taber, gives his version of the dinner, making the petulant and foolish charge that "Crane was one of the series who were driven from Elbert Hubbard by what they believed was Hubbard's abuse of them" (Cady, 67); Crane was temperamentally unsuited to settle down as a member of Hubbard's or anyone else's community. Noxon's account of the dinner differs from Bragdon's. Bragdon comes off rather priggish in admitting that the dinner is "still a distressing memory--like the sight of a young ox led to the slaughter" (*Letters*, 85n.). Noxon's account seems more balanced, and confirms Bragdon's stuffiness: after suffering through the "roast" Bragdon announced, "I came here to do honor to Stephen Crane, not to ridicule him. I regret to take this step, but I cannot longer remain in the room" (*Letters*, 338). Noxon recalls that there were 15 or 20 guests there, "most of us freaks or near-freaks" (338). When Taber began his speech he got only as far as "Probably the most unique . . ." when a voice called out, "Can 'unique' be compared?" (338). From there the dinner party got better (or worse, depending upon one's taste), in what Noxon describes as "the best Clover and Gridiron manner," and Taber and all the other speakers were "guyed and ragged from start to finish" (338). Of most interest is his recollection that Crane was "having the time of his life" (338); additionally, when Hawkins mollified Bragdon by convincing him that Crane would much prefer "the spirit of the meeting" than "solemn eulogies" Crane "was nodding his head off" (339).

In his "Purple Cow Period: The 'Dinkey Magazines' That

Caught the Spirit of the 'Nineties," Bragdon concedes that Hubbard was sincere in admiring Crane's talent, but complains that the dinner was "dominated by a lot of drunken pseudo-reporters, who had come there with the evident intention of turning the whole affair to ridicule by their ribald and irrelevant interruptions" (478). When these men were "finally cowed into some semblance of order" Crane responded as follows, as reported in the next morning's *Buffalo News*, to Taber's tribute to "the strong voice now heard in America":

> Mr. Crane responded modestly and gracefully, saying he was a working newspaper man who was trying to do what he could "since he had recovered from college" with the machinery which had come into his hands--doing it sincerely, if clumsily, and simply setting forth in his own way his own impressions. (478)

Hawkins provides his version of the dinner as well. During the twenties Hawkins wrote a column entitled "All in a Lifetime" for an unidentified newspaper, and a few of these columns are devoted to Stephen Crane. In one ("Stephen Crane's Struggles") he recounts how Crane, after receiving the dinner invitation at Hartwood, begged Hawkins to "invent a decent form of refusal for him" (*SCN*, 1.3:5). In another column ("Stephen Crane Flinches") Hawkins goes into more detail regarding Crane's anxiety regarding the dinner. He sat next to Crane during the dinner (on his right, according to Noxon) and observed how "ill at ease" he was. His insecurity made it impossible for him to accept any of the praise being bruited as anything other than "kindly-intended bosh" (*SCN*, 3.1:6). When Hubbard, after praising Crane as a man and genius, called upon him to speak, Crane was at a loss. When he could at last find his tongue "he could say only that he had done nothing in a literary way but to tell in his own poor words what he saw as he saw it" (*SCN*, 3.1:7); according to Stallman, this was the only time in his life Crane made a speech (*Letters*, 34). Hawkins takes exception to Hubbard's description of the dinner in the first issue of the *Roycroft Quarterly*, in which Crane is praised for being "well poised"; in fact, says Hawkins, Crane "was in a blue funk" (*SCN*, 3.1:7).[11] 'Perhaps Hawkins's column is what prompted Stallman's ominous interpretation of the dinner. However, this account appeared 30 years after the event, and was written by Crane's former confidant and protective custodian, so Hawkins may be exaggerating Crane's distress.

On 7 Jan. 1896, Hubbard alluded to the dinner in a letter to Crane:

> Noxon is all right! I'm glad he knows I was sincere. . . . I can joke all day long, but there are times when I am in dead earnest. I have faith in you; and if you never wrote another page I have faith in you. That one last Poem you sent us [possibly "What says the sea, little shell?"] is a masterly little thing and worth all the school-girl jingles ever pasted in yer granny's scrap book. That fourth stanza is sublime in its gentleness and strength!" (*SCN*, 2.3:11)

And in the *Philistine* for February, 1896, Hubbard responded to some criticism of the Society of Philistines by the New York *Tribune* by saying, "I don't think it's necessary to defend Mr. Crane against the Serious Critic, but one thing may be said in his favor by way of contrast: he knows a joke at sight" (2.3:104).

In his next letter, also 7 January, according to Katz, Hubbard complains about the Roycroft revolt (led by H. P. Taber) taking place at East Aurora and tries to persuade Crane not to accept the "opposition's" offer to publish his book:

> I do not think you would be o'er wise to let *me* publish a book for you much less these experimenters. You have fame enough to catch the big publishers and I believe if you stick close to Appletons they will do you mighty good service. (*SCN*, 2.3:11)

Turning to a more congenial topic, he tells Crane, who was an excellent horseman, that Peanuts, the horse he is coming to purchase, is "as fine as silk," and that he does not have to pay for him in advance. Finally, Hubbard asks for "a bit of a Poem . . . or a short prose sketch or something" for the May *Philistine* (*SCN*, 2.3:11). (There is no Crane piece in this issue, but the June issue has "Fast rode the knight.") In mid-February Crane wrote to "Hub" to apologize for his "curious silence" and to say that he planned to be back in East Aurora in about two weeks to "chew the rag at great length" and to purchase "that noble horse" (*Letters*, 118). Hubbard supposedly told Felix Shay that Crane left East Aurora because of restlessness: "I gave him a horse--a big, fine, strong horse [Peanuts], and he rode away, over the horizon and was gone! I never saw him again!" (Shay, 285) Hubbard also opined in the December 1896 *Philistine* that "as long as Steve Crane remained in East Aurora he was all right" (4.1:19).

It is not so surprising that Crane and Hubbard enjoyed a good relationship. They were both iconoclasts, with particular hatred for sanctimony, hypocrisy, and imperialism. Though their fathers were professional men (Hubbard's father was a doctor), both sons failed to complete college, and were "special students" during their brief college tenures; they were graduates of the "school of hard knocks," and proud of their bohemianism. They were well read, nonetheless, especially Hubbard, and shared enthusiasm for Emerson (Holton, 92). Both were horsemen, inveterate travelers and observers, with a passion for life, and a fascination for journalism (both worked for Hearst) and the crisp directness of journalistic prose. Both shared a morbid fascination for ship-wrecks (Holton, 314, n.6), and both were capable of enjoying broad humor.[12] The serious, jesting author of the motto, "Life consists in moulting one's illusions" (printed in capital letters on the cover of the March 1905 *Philistine),* shared important affinities with the young master of irony who was obsessed with his "cylinder of vision," who "directed his irony at self-delusion . . . at refusals to see" (Holton, 284).

Crane's Poems in the Philistine

Joseph Katz notes that Hubbard published twenty-one of Crane's poems, many of them more than once (*Poems*, xlii). Fifteen of these poems appeared in the *Philistine* (one of them, item 10, twice), and of the twelve that were contributed by Crane (three of the fifteen, items 1, 9, and 15, were reprints), ten of them (items 2, 3, 4, 6, 7, 10, 11, 12, 13, and 14) saw their first appearance in the *Philistine,* with the other two (items 5 and 8) appearing first in other Hubbard publications. Items 1, 9, and 15 are from *The Black Riders and Other Lines*, and items 13 and 14 are in *Uncollected Poems*; the remaining ten are collected in *War Is Kind.* They are given below, exactly as they appear in the *Philistine,* in the order of their publication:

1. I saw a man pursuing the horizon
   June, 1895 (1.1:27)

I saw a man pursuing the horizon;
Round and round they sped.
I was disturbed at this;
I accosted the man.
"It is futile," I said,
"You can never"----
"You lie," he cried.
And ran on.

Second appearance. Katz #24; 26. VA #24; 14, 245. Stallman, 187. This cannot be considered a contribution, as it is an excerpt from *The Black Riders*. ("Katz" refers to his *Poems*, "VA" refers to the Fredson Bowers [University Press of Virginia] edition of Crane's collected works, and "Stallman" refers to his *Critical Bibliography*.)

Following is the parody illustrated by Denslow:

I saw a man tugging at his Boot-Straps.
"It is futile," I said,
"You can never lift yourself that way."
"You lie!" he cried,
And tugged on.[13]

2. The chatter of a death-demon from a tree-top
   August, 1895 (1.3:93; unpaginated)

THE CHATTER OF A DEATH-DEMON FROM A TREE-TOP.

BLOOD--BLOOD AND TORN GRASS--
HAD MARKED THE RISE OF HIS AGONY--
THIS LONE HUNTER.
THE GREY-GREEN WOODS IMPASSIVE
HAD WATCHED THE THRESHING OF HIS LIMBS.

A CANOE WITH FLASHING PADDLE,
A GIRL WITH SOFT, SEARCHING EYES,
A CALL: "JOHN!"
* * * * * * * * *
COME, ARISE, HUNTER!

LIFT YOUR GREY FACE!
CAN YOU NOT HEAR?

THE CHATTER OF A DEATH-DEMON FROM A TREE
TOP.

First appearance. Katz #94; 100, 206-207. VA #87; 56, 263-264. Stallman, 163-164. Dickason notes that the line, "Lift your grey face!" is omitted in *War Is Kind* (282n.).

3. Each small gleam was a voice
September, 1895 (1.4:124; unpaginated)

A LANTERN SONG. [title in all caps]

EACH SMALL GLEAM WAS A VOICE
--A LANTERN VOICE--
IN LITTLE SONGS OF CARMINE, VIOLET, GREEN, GOLD.
A CHORUS OF COLORS CAME OVER THE WATER,
THE WONDROUS LEAF-SHADOWS NO LONGER WAV-
ERED,
NO PINES CROONED ON THE HILLS,
THE BLUE NIGHT WAS ELSEWHERE A SILENCE
WHEN THE CHORUS OF COLORS CAME OVER THE
WATER,
LITTLE SONGS OF CARMINE, VIOLET, GREEN, GOLD.

SMALL GLOWING PEBBLES
THROWN ON THE DARK PLANE OF EVENING
SING GOOD BALLADS OF GOD
AND ETERNITY, WITH SOUL'S REST.
LITTLE PRIESTS, LITTLE HOLY FATHERS,
NONE CAN DOUBT THE TRUTH OF YOUR HYMNING
WHEN THE MARVELOUS CHORUS COMES OVER THE
WATER,
SONGS OF CARMINE, VIOLET, GREEN, GOLD.

First appearance. Katz #101; 107, 208-209. VA #94; 60, 266-267. Stallman, 169.

4. A slant of sun on dull brown walls
December, 1895 (2.1:8; unpaginated)

A SLANT OF SUN ON DULL BROWN WALLS
A FORGOTTEN SKY OF BASHFUL BLUE.

TOWARD GOD A MIGHTY HYMN
A SONG OF CLASHES AND CRIES,
RUMBLING WHEELS, HOOF-BEATS, BELLS,
WELCOMES, FAREWELLS, LOVE-CALLS, FINAL MOANS,
VOICES OF JOY, IDIOCY, WARNING, DESPAIR,
THE UNKNOWN APPEALS OF BRUTES,
THE CHANTING OF VIOLETS, (VIOLETS)
THE SCREAMS OF CUT TREES,
THE SENSELESS BABBLE OF HENS AND WISE MEN--
A CLUTTERED INCOHERENCY THAT SAYS AT THE
STARS:
"O, GOD SAVE US!"

First appearance. Katz #89; 201-202. Katz gives page 9 instead of page 8. VA #82; 53, 259. Above variant not noted. Stallman, 215.[14]

5. "I have heard the sunset song of the
birches
January, 1896 (2.2:62; unpaginated)

"I HAVE HEARD THE SUNSET SONG OF THE BIRCHES
"A WHITE MELODY IN THE SILENCE.
"I HAVE SEEN A QUARREL OF THE PINES.
"AT NIGHTFALL,
"THE LITTLE GRASSES HAVE RUSHED BY ME
"WITH THE WIND-MEN.
"THESE THINGS HAVE I LIVED," QUOTH THE MANIAC
"POSSESSING ONLY EYES AND EARS.
"BUT, YOU--
"YOU DON GREEN SPECTACLES BEFORE YOU LOOK AT
ROSES."

Second appearance. (First appearance in Hubbard's "*The Time Has Come*, . . .") Katz #82; 88, 198-199. VA #75; 49, 255-256. Stallman, 183.

6. "What says the sea, little shell?
February, 1896 (2.3:94-95; unpaginated)

"What says the sea, little shell?
"What says the sea?
"Long has our brother been silent to
us,

"Kept his message for the ships,
"Awkward ships, stupid ships."

"The sea bids you mourn, oh, pines,
"Sing low in the moonlight.
"He sends tale of the land of doom,
"Of place where endless falls
"A rain of women's tears.
"And men in grey robes--
"Men in grey robes--
"Chant the unknown pain."

"What says the sea, little shell?
"What says the sea?
"Long has our brother been silent to
  us,
"Kept his message for the ships,
"Puny ships, silly ships."

"The sea bids you teach, oh, pines,
"Sing low in the moonlight,
"Teach the gold of patience,
"Cry gospel of gentle hands,
"Cry a brotherhood of hearts,
"The sea bids you teach, oh, pines."

"And where is the reward, little shell?
"What says the sea?
"Long has our brother been silent to
  us,
"Kept his message for the ships,
"Puny ships, silly ships."

"No word says the sea, oh, pines,
"No word says the sea.
"Long will your brother be silent to
  you,
"Keep his message for the ships,
"Oh, puny pines, silly pines."

First appearance. Katz #77; 82-83, 193-194. VA #70; 46, 251-252. Stallman, 230. In his *Letters*, Stallman gives the first line as "What says the little sea-shell" (126n.).

7. To the maiden
   April, 1896 (2.5:152; unpaginated)

TO THE MAIDEN
THE SEA WAS BLUE MEADOW
ALIVE WITH LITTLE FROTH-PEOPLE
SINGING.

TO THE SAILOR, WRECKED,
THE SEA WAS DEAD GREY WALLS
SUPERLATIVE IN VACANCY
UPON WHICH NEVERTHELESS AT FATEFUL TIME,
WAS WRITTEN
THE GRIM HATRED OF NATURE.

First appearance. Katz #78; 84, 195. VA #71; 47, 252. Stallman, 226.

8. Fast rode the knight
June, 1896 (3.1:20; unpaginated)

FAST RODE THE KNIGHT
WITH SPURS, HOT AND REEKING
EVER WAVING AN EAGER SWORD.
"TO SAVE MY LADY!"
FAST RODE THE KNIGHT
AND LEAPED FROM SADDLE TO WAR.
MEN OF STEEL FLICKERED AND GLEAMED
LIKE RIOT OF SILVER LIGHTS
AND THE GOLD OF THE GOOD KNIGHTS [sic] BANNER
STILL WAVED ON A CASTLE WALL.
* * * * * * * *

A HORSE
BLOWING, STAGGERING, BLOODY THING
FORGOTTEN AT FOOT OF CASTLE WALL.
A HORSE
DEAD AT FOOT OF CASTLE WALL.

Second appearance. (First appearance in Hubbard's *A Souvenir and a Medley*.) Katz #83; 89, 199. VA #76; 49, 256. Dickason notes that the line, "And the gold of the good knights [sic] banner" was transposed to, "And the gold of the knight's good banner" in *War Is Kind* (282n.).

9. Two or three angels
March, 1897 (4.4:118)

Two or three angels

Came near to the earth.
They saw a fat church.
Little black streams of people
Came and went in continually
And the angels were puzzled
To know why the people went thus,
And why they stayed so long within.

Katz #32; 34, 178. VA #32; 19, 245. Stallman, 227. This is not actually a contribution, as Hubbard prefaces this excerpt on the previous page with, "Stephen Crane, who told us this two years ago:".[15]

10. The impact of a dollar upon the heart
February, 1898 (6.3:back cover)

SOME THINGS.

THE IMPACT OF A DOLLAR UPON THE HEART
SMILES WARM AND LIGHT
SWEEPING FROM THE HEARTH ROSILY UPON
THE WHITE TABLE
WITH THE HANGING COOL VELVET SHADOWS
MOVING SOFTLY UPON THE DOOR.
THE IMPACT OF A MILLION DOLLARS
IS A CRASH OF FLUNKEYS
AND YAWNING EMBLEMS OF PERSIA
CHEEKED AGAINST OAK, FRANCE AND A SABRE.
THE OUTCRY OF OLD BEAUTY
SIMPERED AT BY PIMPLED MERCHANTS
TO SUBMISSION BEFORE WINE AND CHATTER.
SILLY RICH PEASANTS STAMP THE CARPETS
OF MEN,
DEAD MEN WHO DREAMED FRAGRANCE AND
LIGHT
INTO THEIR WOOF, THEIR LIVES.
THE PELT OF AN HONEST BEAR
UNDER THE FEET OF A CRYPTIC SLAVE
WHO SPEAKS ALWAYS OF BAUBLES
FORGETTING PLACE, MULTITUDE, WORK AND
STATE,
CHAMPING AND MOUTHING OF HATS,
MAKING RATFUL SQUEAK OF HATS,
HATS.

First appearance. Katz #95; 101, 207-208. VA #88; 57, 264-265. "Whored by pimping" was changed to "Simpered at by pimpled" by Hubbard (VA, 265.) Stallman, 183-184. This was reprinted in the October 1899 (9.5) issue of the *Philistine,* pages 149-150. It was Hubbard's favorite Crane poem. The following parody appeared in April, 1898 (6.5), pp. 146-147:

Some More Things, by E.M. to S.C.:

The imprint of a finger upon the purse
Smiles grim and hard--
Sweeping from the necessities of life obstinately
Upon the cold greenbacks;
While the grim, growling, cadaverous shadows
Move stealthily nearer the door!
The impact of a million dollars
Is a crash of cardiac muscularity
(For no heart could endure it!)
Is a glittering emblem of prosperity
Backed up by nothing substantial;
Is oft the bribe of old reprobates
Simpering at beauty.
The impact of a thousand dollar hope
On the cerebrum of an aspiring | |
Pen-holder
Produces the warp and woof of a
Temporary aberration of the intellect,
On the cover of
An honest folio:
Forgetting place, multitude, critics and victims.
Meanwhile continues the champing and
Mouthing of cats after rats.
One thing to devour another--
Cats after rats in this world,
Cats after
R-a-t-s!

11. You tell me this is God?

April, 1898 (6.5:back cover)

LINES.

YOU TELL ME THIS IS GOD?
I TELL YOU IT [THIS] IS A PRINTED LIST,
A BURNING CANDLE AND AN ASS.

First appearance. Katz #85; 91, 200. VA #78; 50, 257. Stallman, 233. These lines are the postscript to a poem which Hubbard did not print in the *Philistine.* That poem, published as No. IV in *War Is Kind* (*Letter*, 297-298), and given below, apparently did "over-balance" Hubbard's discretion:

What?
You define me God with these trinkets?
Can my misery meal on an ordered walking
Of surpliced numbskulls?
And a fanfare of lights?
Or even upon the measured pulpiting
Of the familiar and true?
Is this God?
Where, then, is hell?
Show me some bastard mushroom
Sprung from a pollution of blood.
It is better.

Where is God?

12. On the desert
May, 1898 (6.6:166-167)

Lines.

On the desert
A silence from the moon's deepest val-
ley.
Fire-rays fall athwart the robes
Of hooded men, squat and dumb.
Before them, a woman
Moves to the blowing of shrill whistles

And distant thunder of drums,
While mystic things, sinuous, dull with terr-
ible color
Sleepily fondle her body,
Or move at her will, swishing stealthily over
the sand.
The snakes whisper softly;
The whispering, whispering snakes
Dreaming and swaying and staring, | |
But always whispering, softly whispering.
The wind streams from the lone reaches
Of Arabia, solemn with night,
And the wild fire makes shimmer of blood
Over the robes of the hooded men,
Squat and dumb.
Bands of moving bronze, emerald, yellow,
Circle the throat and the arms of her,
And over the sands serpents move warily
Slow, menacing and submissive,
Swinging to the whistles and drums,
The whispering, whispering snakes,
Dreaming and swaying and staring
But always whispering, softly whispering.
The dignity of the accursed;
The glory of slavery, despair, death,
Is in the dance of the whispering snakes.

First appearance. Katz #86; 92, 200-201. VA #79; 51, 257-258. Stallman, 202.

13. When a people reach the top of a hill
June, 1898 (7.1:9-10)

LINES.

When a people reach the top of a hill
Then does God lean toward them,
Shortens tongues and lengthens arms.
A vision of their dead comes to the
weak.
The moon shall not be too old
Before the new battalions rise,

Blue battalions.
The moon shall not be too old
When the children of change shall fall
Before the new battalions,
The blue battalions.

Mistakes and virtues will be trampled deep.
A church and a thief shall fall together.
A sword will come at the bidding of the eyeless.| |
The God-led, turning only to beckon,
Swinging a creed like a censer
At the head of the new battalions,
Blue battalions.
March the tools of nature's impulse,
Men born of wrong, men born of right,
Men of the new battalions,
The blue battalions.

The clang of swords in thy wisdom,
The wounded make gestures like thy Son's,
The feet of mad horses is one part--
Aye, another is the hand of a mother on the
brow of a youth.
Then, swift as they charge thro a shadow,
The men of the new battalions,
Blue battalions.
God lead them high, God lead them far,
God lead them far, God lead them high,
These new battalions,
The blue battalions.

First appearance. Katz #74; 76-77, 188-191. VA #125; 82, 276-278. Cited in Williams, 87; listed erroneously as being in Vol. 3, with this error repeated by Stallman, 161.

14. Rumbling, buzzing, turning, whirling Wheels,
December, 1898 (8.1:front cover)

Rumbling, buzzing, turning, whirling Wheels,
Dizzy Wheels!
Wheels!

First appearance. Katz #75; 78, 191. VA #129; 85, 279. Stallman, 231. Cited in Williams, 131. "It is quite possible that EH might have undertaken to write and publish this as Crane's as a means of advertising his association with the poet. But the similarity of this poem to 'A grey and boiling street' has warranted its inclusion in the canon" (Katz, liv).

15. I stood upon a high place
March, 1899 (8.4:back cover)

I stood upon a High Place,
And saw, below, many Devils
Running, leaping,
And carousing in Sin.
One looked up, grinning,
And said, "Comrade! Brother!"

Katz #9; 11, 172-173. VA #9; 7, 242-243. Stallman, 187-188. In the accompanying illustration by W. W. Denslow, Crane is depicted as the "comrade."

What conclusions may be made about the Crane poems which made their way into the *Philistine* during a span of almost four years? Starting with the three selected for reprint by Hubbard, it is significant that all three are from *The Black Riders*, which was first printed in April or May, 1895, in an edition limited to fifty copies and printed in green ink (Thompson, 49). This volume of poems held a special place in Crane's estimation: writing to an editor of *Leslie's Weekly* (circa November, 1895), he acknowledged his gratitude for the reception of *The Red Badge of Courage*, but admitted,

> I am much fonder of my little book of poems, "The Black Riders." The reason, perhaps, is that it was a more ambitious effort. My aim was to comprehend in it the thoughts I have had about life in general, while "The Red Badge" is a mere episode in life, an amplification. (*Letters*, 79)

The first of these poems which Hubbard admired ("I saw a man pursuing the horizon") is an illustration, *ad absurdum*, of the effects of illusion, and the other two ("Two or three angels" and "I stood upon a High Place") are concerned with sanctimony and its attendant illusions. All have the Crane penchant for ironic distancing: the realist looks at the dreamer pursuing "the horizon"; the angels look down at "little black streams" entering a "fat," white church (how masterfully Crane allows the reader to supply the juxtaposition of colors); and the "saint" looks down from a "High Place." All have a "punch line" of sorts, a touch of perverse humor, which obviously Hubbard finds most congenial, another instance of his compatibility with the young Crane.

Among the remaining verses (all but two are from *War Is Kind*, these two being "When a people reach the top of a hill" and "Rumbling, buzzing, turning, whirling Wheels," from *Uncollected Poems*) the topics of warfare, religion and nature predominate, and are, of course, the great topics of the Crane canon. Pathetic fallacies are common in the verses of nature, which appear from August, 1895, through April, 1896: the "impassive" woods "watched" the death of the "lone hunter" ("The chatter of a death-demon from a tree-top"); the pebbles "sing good ballads of God" ("Each small gleam was a voice"); the violets chant and the cut trees scream ("A slant of sun on dull brown walls"); the pines "quarrel" ("I have heard the sunset song of the birches"); the sea lectures to the pines ("What says the sea, little shell"); and, to the maiden safe on shore, the sea is "alive with little froth-people singing" ("To the maiden").

Probably one reason why Hubbard was moved to feature "The impact of a dollar upon the heart" twice in the pages of his magazine was because of his own fluttering upon the bars of the gilded cage, his having renounced the life of a soap baron for the life of literature (at least during the early years of the *Philistine);* certainly he believed that he was dreaming "fragrance and light" (a debt to Arnold's "sweetness and light"?) into his own life, in contradistinction to the nouveaux riches who babble only of "baubles."[16]

Then appear, in April, May, and June, 1898, the three most somber and provocative of Crane's contributions. "You tell me this is God?", as noted earlier, was the postscript to a longer poem, and Hubbard wisely decided that the postscript said better in three lines what Crane had been belaboring to express in thirteen. This poem (called "Lines") is printed brazenly on the back cover of the April issue, and it is difficult to imagine a more shocking statement regarding religion appearing in any popular American periodical of the 1890s or any other period.

"On the desert" and "When a people reach the top of a hill" must have been among those Crane contributions which drew "mystified" notices, and they are arguably the finest poems to appear in the *Philistine.* The first is an erotic celebration of "whispering, whispering snakes" which fondle a woman's body in the presence of "hooded men, squat and dumb." The description is dream-like, hypnotizingly cadenced and alliterated, with brilliant phrases, such as "over the sands serpents move warily / Slow, menacing and submissive"--the oxymoronic coupling of these last adjectives is dazzlingly perfect.

The second echoes the futility and horror of warfare sounded in "Fast rode the knight," with its horse "blowing, staggering, bloody thing / Forgotten at foot of castle wall." This apocalyptic poem, which Hoffman asserts is Crane's most significant (162), combines the topics of warfare and religion in three highly-structured stanzas. The opening lines, "When a people reach the top of a hill / Then does God lean toward them, / Shortens tongues and lengthens arms" are vivid and Biblical, and announce the time of the fall of the "children of change" before the "new battalions, / The blue battalions." When "mistakes and virtues," a "church and a thief" are indistinguishable, then shall the "God-led . . . Swinging a creed like a censer," march at the head of the blue battalions. Then shall the "clang of swords" be "wisdom," and the wounded suffer Christ-like, before the blue battalions are led "high" and "far" by God. This is Crane's retort to his clergymen father and grandfathers, his "black mass" construal of the days of revelation; instead of the triumphant vision of the day of reckoning which all devout Christians look forward to, it is yet another nightmare of "feet of mad horses" and final caresses of "the hand of a mother on the brow of a youth," another damning equation of God and his worship with a "printed list, / A burning candle and an ass."

Crane's Prose in the Philistine

In addition to the above poems, seven prose works appeared in the *Philistine,* as listed below in the order of their appearance:

1. A Great Mistake
   March, 1896 (2.4:106-109)

First appearance. Williams, 99. Stallman, 178. This is this issue's lead contribution, following a poem by Eugene R. White.

2. A Prologue
   July, 1896 (3.2:39; unpaginated)

A PROLOGUE.

A GLOOMY STAGE. SLENDER CURTAINS AT A WINDOW, CENTRE. BEFORE THE WINDOW, A TABLE, AND UPON THE TABLE, A LARGE BOOK, OPENED. A MOONBEAM, NO WIDER THAN A SWORD-BLADE, PIERCES THE CURTAINS AND FALLS UPON THE BOOK.

A MOMENT OF SILENCE.

FROM WITHOUT, THEN--AN ADJACENT ROOM IN INTENTION--COME SOUNDS OF CELEBRATION, OF RIOTOUS DRINKING AND LAUGHTER. FINALLY, A SWIFT QUARREL. THE DIN AND CRASH OF A FIGHT.
A LITTLE STILLNESS. THEN A WOMAN'S SCREAM.
"AH, MY SON, MY SON."

A MOMENT OF SILENCE.
CURTAIN.

Second appearance. (First appeared in *Roycroft Quarterly*, May, 1896.) Williams, 115-116. Stallman, 206.

3. An Ominous Baby
   October, 1896 (3.5:133-137)

Williams, 112. Stallman, 201. Reprinted from the *Arena*, May, 1894 (Holton, 64).

4. The Men in the Storm
   January, 1897 (4.2:37-48)

Williams, 109. Stallman, 196. "There is no doubt that Stephen Crane's sketch in the *Philistine* . . . is one of the most powerful pictures he has ever drawn of the tragedies of life among the poor of New York" (*Commercial Advertiser*, 11 Jan. 1898. [n.p.]). (Stallman, 263) This is also a reprint from the *Arena* (October, 1894).

5. An Old Man Goes A-Wooing
   July, 1899 (9.2:44-50)

Williams, 112. "A bastardized text, as is the title" (Stallman, 201).[17]

6. A Fishing Village
   August, 1899 (9.3:71-77)

Williams, 95. Stallman, 172. This and the previous story, two of Crane's "Irish Notes," were printed in the United States only in the *Philistine* (*Letters*, 145n). Only two of the four "Irish Notes have been traced as having appeared anywhere but in the *Philistine* in 1899" (*Letters*, 148n).

7. At the Pit Door
   September, 1900 (11.4:97-104)

First appearance. Williams, 84. Stallman, 158. In a letter to Hubbard (17 Oct. 1900), Cora Crane asked "from whom" he got "the little sketch," and reminded him, "Of course all these things belong to my late husbands [sic] estate until all obligations are settled and then to myself" (Sorrentino, 236).

Of the six short stories to appear in the *Philistine,* two of them are "baby sketches" ("A Great Mistake" and "An Ominous Baby"), two are "social injustice" sketches ("The Men in the Storm" and the similar "At the Pit Door") and two are "Irish notes" ("An Old Man Goes A-Wooing" and "A Fishing Village"). "A Great Mistake" is, according to Katz, an episode from the childhood of Maggie's brother Tommy. It describes his fascination with the treasures displayed on a fruit stand kept by an Italian. The "babe" was a "simple worshipper at this golden shrine," and gazed longingly at the "massed [the version cited by Holton has "horrid"] joys of the world" (2.4:107; Holton, 64). After painstakingly nearing the stand, while the vendor is reading a newspaper and then apparently napping, the babe steals a "round bulb," only to be caught in the act: "And it was written that the Italian should at this moment open his eyes" (109). Howling, the vendor "whirled him fiercely and took from the little fingers a lemon" (109). This ironic ending, with the babe clutching bitter fruit instead of an orange, would be a representative formative experience in the embitterment of a slum-dwelling child such as Maggie's brother, and the title is deliberately vague as to exactly who is making the mistake.

"An Ominous Baby" also reads like an episode excised from *Maggie*. It describes a "tattered child" whose clothes were "soiled and showed the marks of many conflicts, like the chain-shirt of a warrior" (3.5:133). This description recalls the opening of *Maggie*, in which the scrapping boys are described in mock-heroic language. This child "from the poor district," who is "wandering in a strange country," espies a treasure of another sort--a tiny fire engine. (Fire engines, both toy and real, appear in Crane's "The Monster.") This toy belongs to a "pretty child in fine clothes," who is no match for the "wanderer": the outcome of their encounter is easily guessed by the reader. After the inevitable act of plunder the "small barbarian" admired his "booty," and when his victim showed signs of pursuit "the little vandal turned and vanished down a dark side street as into a swallowing cavern" (137).

The impressionability of young boys, and the need for careful and indulgent nurturance during their formative years, are themes dear to Hubbard. One of his most popular pieces in the *Philistine* (December, 1901; 14.1:22-24) was devoted to these topics, and was published as an editorial column in the *New York American* (19 Mar. 1912). He writes that "grimy, ragged, tousled boys in the street often attract me strangely. A boy is a man in the cocoon--you do not know what it is going to become--his life is big with possibilities" (22). He concludes with the caution, "Be patient with the boys--you are dealing with Soul-stuff--Destiny waits just around the corner" (24). Hubbard reprinted two excerpts from this piece as epigrammatic fillers in a later issue of the *Philistine* (April, 1903; 16.5:158).

Moreover, Hubbard's older brother died in childhood, as did Tommy Johnson in *Maggie*, and he considered his sentimental short story "How I Found My Brother" (July, 1907; 25.2:33-49), frequently published by the Roycrofters in booklet form, one of his most satisfying literary accomplishments.

"The Men in the Storm," perhaps the finest of Crane's short stories to appear in the *Philistine,* is a haunting description of homeless men thronging before a New York City soup kitchen entrance during a snow storm. One of the more striking images in this twelve-page story is that of the prosperous proprietor of a shop across the street from the massed men, another example of distancing which is so prevalent in Crane's verses. He stood

> in an attitude of magnificent reflection . . . and looked down at the snow-encrusted mob. From below, there was denoted a supreme complacence in him. It seemed that the sight operated inversely and enabled him to more clearly regard his own delightful environment (4.2:45). [The version cited by Holton reads "his own environment, delightful relatively." (Holton, 67)]

The remaining three stories are less memorable; like the first three discussed above, they are concerned with males who are both physically and spiritually impoverished. "An Old Man Goes A-Wooing" is about old Mickey, a "melankoly fisherman," who is dragged out of the village inn by the "giantess" Nora when he falls asleep. In "A Fishing Village" the still melancholy Mickey is literally and figuratively at dock's end, fishing "hopelessly," while disparaging the load of mackerel in the younger men's dinghy. Finally, "At the Pit Door" is reminiscent of Crane's early New York City sketches, such as "An Experiment in Misery."

In regard to Crane's other fiction, perhaps the finest book review to appear in the *Philistine* is T. W. Higginson's review of *The Red Badge of Courage.* "A Bit of War Photography" is the lead article in the July 1896 (3.2:33-38) issue. Thomas Wentworth Higginson was a Bostonian famed as a Unitarian clergyman, soldier (who led the first Negro regiment in the Civil War), editor, and writer. He is perhaps best known for his correspondence with Emily Dickinson and for editing (with Mabel Loomis Todd) her *Poems* (1860).

His review is intelligent and adulatory. After noting that it is natural for a reaction to set in after the initial applause won by Crane's novel, he adds that this reaction "has already taken, in some quarters, a form quite unjust and unfair" (33). He goes on to compare Crane's ability to bring out "the daily life of war" with Tolstoy's; quoting Emerson, he says of Crane's sentences, "Cut these and they bleed" (34). Yet it is this very "Tolstoy quality--the real tumult and tatters of the thing itself" (34), which is, paradoxically, being called a defect (35). He praises Crane for having "that marvelous intuitive quality which for want of a better name we call genius" (35), and defends him against the charge that the book does not "dwell studiously on the higher aspects of the war" (36):

> Let the picture only be well drawn, and the moral will take care of itself; never fear. The book is not a patriotic tract, but a delineation; a cross section of the daily existence of the raw enlisted-man. In other respects it is reticent, because it is truthful. (36)

In the final analysis, he claims, the test of a book is in the way it holds the reader, and he reports that every time he takes up *The Red Badge of Courage* he reads it over and over, just as he does with Tolstoy's *Cossacks* (37). Even Crane's "slipshod grammar" is defended by this Boston Brahmin editor, as "part of the breathless life and action" (38). His prophetic reservations have to do only with Crane's future, and he quotes Goethe's dictum that "as soon as a man has done one good thing, the world conspires against him to keep him from doing another" (38). Higginson worries that Crane, having done "onc good thing, not to say two," may not be equal to the public admiration for him, and he earnestly hopes that Crane will be able to withstand the temptation "to test his newly-found English reputation" by expatriation, "an experiment by which Bret Harte has been visibly dwarfed and Henry James hopelessly diluted" (38).

After Crane's death, Hubbard wrote a six-page paean to his memory in the September 1900 (11.4:123-128) number. In his opinion, Crane had two written claims to immortality. *The Red Badge of Courage* was the "strongest, most vivid work of the imagination ever fished from ink-pot by an American," and "The Open Boat" was the "sternest, creepiest bit of realism ever penned" (124). Hubbard believed that the reason why Crane received so much abuse from critics was the "vagueness,

& the loose, unsleeked quality of his work" (214), but he notes that Crane made "no fetich of a grammar--if the grammar gets in the way so much the worse for the grammar" (127). Comparing Crane to Chopin, Hubbard described him as an artist in his ability to

> convey the feeling by just the right word, or a word misplaced, like a lady's dress in disarray, or a hat askew. This daring quality marks everything he wrote. The recognition that language is fluid, and at best only an expedient, flavors all his work. (126-127)

This essay is arguably Hubbard's best attempt at literary analysis, and with Crane's death Hubbard lost a kindred spirit and the *Philistine* lost its most famous contributor.

Notes

[1] Stallman utilizes one-sided sources such as Claude Bragdon's *Merely Players*, and the self-serving recollections, published many years after Hubbard's death, of H. P. Taber, from whom Hubbard wrested control of the *Philistine* (see Chapter II). On page 615 of his *Stephen Crane: A Critical Bibliography*, Stallman attempts to dismiss Hubbard as "an egocentric ass"; this unsubstantiated and gratuitous comment is just one example illustrating his admission that he is "not a professional bibliographer" (xiv), and that what he has produced (since, as he admits, "What gets annotated is what interests me") is an "autobibliography" (xviii). Hubbard had the misfortune of being used as a pawn in the bitter, academic contest between Stallman and Joseph Katz in Crane scholarship, with Stallman doing his utmost to ridicule Hubbard and Katz attempting to champion his importance.

[2] These comments were certainly not intended as a serious review, as they are so categorized by some Crane scholars, who then criticize Hubbard for his "silliness" (see, for example, Katz, *Poems*, xxxvii); those incapable of enjoying Hubbard's broad sense of humor occasionally go wide of the mark in their criticisms.

[3] The poem referred to in brackets can be found in the author's discussion of Crane's poetry in the *Philistine,* item number 1. Howells, who was Crane's "former mentor," had introduced Henrik Ibsen to the American reading public in 1891 (Holton, 205).

[4] Crane reported to his friend Willis Brooks Hawkins on 19 November that Hubbard was "a clever-looking duck" (*Letters*, 75).

[5] Thomas B. Mosher, for example, the contemporary publisher of the *Bibelot*, was notorious for his taking advantage of the international copyright provisions (Mott, 426).

[6] The Williams and Starrett *Bibliography* incorrectly lists it as 2.2:70 (152).

[7] Many comparable bits of satire, parody and burlesque can be found in the early *Philistine.* In the August 1896 number Hubbard has fun with Henry James. After reporting with mock astonishment that James has resolved to write a novel with an incident, he quotes from alleged "advance sheets" of this novel:

> Algernon wondered vaguely if he had done right in leaving the handkerchief where she had dropped it, on the center table. If only it had been the arm chair, now, what a different complexion it would have put upon this dilemma--if it was a dilemma--no, hardly a dilemma, rather a quandary, or even a question. And she--did she, too, brood upon the handkerchief? Did she justify herself in dropping it, in the way she did? He arose, wearily. "I dunno," he said, defiantly, yet hopelessly, and sat down. (3.3:93)

[8] It is important to remember, when considering the charge that Hubbard exploited Crane's fame, that he sent his invitation to Crane on 5 November, several weeks before the English publication of *The Red Badge of Courage*, although Hubbard was familiar with the book and praised it as a "strong work thoroughly well sustained" (*Letters*, 68).

[9] *The Members of the Society*, 1895, contained the letters of invitation and acceptance. *'The time has come,' the walrus said, 'to talk of many things,'* 1895, was a souvenir of the dinner, and *A Souvenir and a Medley: Seven Poems and a Sketch by Stephen Crane. With Divers and Sundry Communications from Certain Eminent Wits,* was prepared as the first of the three issues of the *Roycroft Quarterly*, May, 1896 (Stallman, *Bibliography*, 242, 244). The seven poems published (as "chapter" V) are "The chatter of a death-demon from a tree-top," "A lantern song," "A slant of sun on dull brown walls," "I have heard the sunset song of the birches," "What says the sea, little shell?" "To the maiden," and "Fast rode the knight." These are items number 2 through 8 as listed in the author's text below. In addition, "I saw a man pursuing the horizon" (item number 1) appears on the copyright page, and the prose pieces "A Great Mistake" and "A Prologue" (see text below) are "chapters" VI and VII, respectively. There are 48 pages total.

[10] Cady and Wells err in stating that no Crane poem appeared between January and June of 1896--"What says the sea" appears in February and "To the maiden" appears in April.

[11] See footnote number 9 for more on the first issue. The second issue (August, 1896) was a 40-page reprint of George Bernard Shaw's "On Going to Church," and the third issue

(November, 1896) was titled, "Foreign Ideas in the Catholic Church in America," by the Rev. Father George Zurcher, pastor of St. Joseph's Church, Buffalo. Each issue cost twenty-five cents, and while there was an audience for the first two issues, perhaps only the parishioners of St. Joseph's Church would have paid for a theological polemic. The *Roycroft Quarterly* is a singular example of a failed commercial venture on Hubbard's part.

[12] See, for example, Crane's letter of 19 Feb. 1895, sent from New Orleans to Corwin Knapp Linson, which is an exuberant admixture of fractured German and French, with a Latin tag thrown in for good measure (Cady, 8).

[13] Another Denslow illustration, titled "Lines to Pegasus and Stephen Crane," appears on the back cover of the July 1898 (7.2) issue. Crane is depicted riding a winged hobbyhorse, with a quill in one hand and the reins in the other. It is an eerily apt illustration, as this latter-day Bellerophon is similarly doomed (to an early death); it also brings to mind the boy in D. H. Lawrence's story "The Rocking-Horse Winner" of thirty years later, for Crane was similarly abusing his talent for money.

Denslow, who became famous in 1900 with his illustrations of L[yman] Frank Baum's *Wonderful Wizard of Oz*, produced many popular illustrations for the back covers of the *Philistine.* As Felix Shay notes, two of these, "What's the Use?" depicting a skull with a laurel wreath propped up on a tome (March, 1899; 8.4:bap; reprinted in the April, June, and July issues), and "Every Knock is a Boost," depicting a clergyman sledgehammering one end of a seesaw with a grinning Hubbard on the other (February, 1906; 22.3), were still being pirated and sold by the "post card emporiums" twenty years later (149). The "What's the Use?" illustration is accompanied by an advertisement for twenty numbered and signed "Omar" steel etchings for $10 each, and regular proofs for $2 each. (Any doubt that the *Rubaiyat of Omar Khayyaam* is the inspiration for this phrase is dissipated by the use of "Omar.") It is interesting to note that the phrase "What's the use" was a favorite one of both George Hurstwood (Theodore Dreiser's *Sister Carrie*) and Ralph Marvell (Edith Wharton's *The Custom of the Country*), published in 1900 (though not publicly available until 1912) and 1913, respectively. (This coincidence is mentioned by Elizabeth Hardwick in "Mrs. Wharton in New

York," *New York Review*, 21 Jan. 1988, 32.)

[14] This Christmas issue is extraordinary. For one thing, it has red covers, one of the few issues of the *Philistine* to deviate from brown covers. Additionally, all of the eight front pages (unpaginated) are devoted to poetry. Pages 1 through 6 contain Kipling's "The Dipsy Chanty" (the unauthorized appearance of which prompted Kipling to sue Hubbard), and a poem by Gelett Burgess, "In Jenson Type," appears on page 7. Crane's poem appears on page 8, with the embossed imprint of "In Jenson Type" very obvious. (All of these pages are thin, brown, butcher-type paper.) This issue also occasioned the printing of a poster which included "The Philistine" and the names of Rudyard Kipling, Francis Wilson, Philip Becker Goetz, Stephen Crane, Elbert Hubbard, William McIntosh, H. P. Taber, Eugene R. White, and Gelett Burgess. This poster was reprinted for the Roycrofters-At-Large Association (East Aurora, N.Y.) in 1984, and the caption states only, "Reprinted from an Original Roycroft Poster, circa 1896." Although the poster does not specify a particular number of the *Philistine,* only the December 1895 number has these nine authors as contributors. (The front cover of this issue lists all the contributors except for Wilson.)

[15] The following paragraph in "Side Talks" (June, 1897; 5.1:32) is relevant:

> We get our religious nutriment mostly from the atmosphere, like the trees. It is a process of induction, mainly, and that, if Mr. Stephen Crane really wants to know, is why men go into church and stay so long there. The closet would suffice for their devotions otherwise.

[16] Most bibliographers mention that the reprint occurs in context with Ali Baba, whom they identify simply as Anson A. Blackman, an East Aurora handyman. What they do not seem to realize is that the rustic "Ali Baba" serves Hubbard as a vicarious mouthpiece, and that the reprint appears at the conclusion of a light-hearted discussion of hats.

[17] Stallman here again reveals his impatience with Hubbard. That Hubbard has made editorial changes is obvious, but whether the opprobrious term "bastardized" is merited bears discussion; in any case his summary judgment is of no help to either Crane or Hubbard scholarship. What is more to the

point is to realize that Hubbard, like other American editors of his time (as well as President Theodore Roosevelt a few years later), was experimenting with orthographical reforms, and this story happened to receive such "reform." In the November 1897 number, Hubbard had announced his recent election as an honorary member of the American Philological Society, and decided to show his "gratitude" to his sponsors by spelling "though," "through," and "catalogue" as "tho," "thro," and "catalog" (5.6:191). He wondered, however, why the Society employed a double adjectival ending ("-ic" and "-al") and did not spell it "Filologic." His orthographic experiments can be seen in the numbers of the *Philistine* from June, 1898 (7.1), through July, 1900 (11.2). There is a humorous "fonetik" parody of Hamlet's great soliloquy in the December 1898 issue, following a discussion of "New English," which starts, "Tew spel, or knot tew spel; dhat iz dhe kweshtin" (27).

Hubbard was thus simply being consistent when, to take just the first paragraph of Crane's story, he used the following spellings: "melankoly"; "thru" (twice); "smokt"; "talkt"; and "passt." As for his change in the title, perhaps Hubbard felt that "a-wooing" was more in harmony with Crane's use of dialect in the story. There may not be a convincing defense for this title change, and it is understandably disconcerting to a Crane scholar to see any of Crane's works altered, but it is important to remember that all material submitted to the *Philistine* (including Hubbard's own, of course) for a period of two years was subject to such orthographic "bastardization."

Chapter IV

Other Contributors

Although the *Philistine* is essentially the creation of one man, Hubbard published the work of approximately 200 contributors other than Stephen Crane, and he did so throughout the 20-year span of the magazine's publication. A few careless readers of the *Philistine,* even if not hostile to Hubbard, have assumed that Hubbard is always to be taken literally, and thus have misread the lead article in the January 1899 (8.2:33-39) issue. In the first paragraph of "A Manifesto!" (which is signed "The Pastor,"only one of many clues that he is being facetious), Hubbard promises, beginning with the next number of the magazine, "to write every article and paragraf in it, including advertisements and testimonials of Roycroft Books" (33). If readers miss the humorous tip-off in the last four words, even a cursory examination of subsequent issues (see the index of contributors, Appendix B) would reveal to them that his editorial conduct belies this "New Year's resolution." In fact, some 175 signed contributions, prose and poetry, including four Stephen Crane items, appear after this issue (out of a total of nearly 400 pieces). "A Manifesto" makes evident Hubbard's exasperation with a number of people associated with the *Philistine,* but it was certainly not intended to be taken literally. Its conclusion should leave no doubt regarding Hubbard's tone:

> And so from working for the good of all, I intend hereafter to practice Individualism, and write the whole Magazine myself, just for my own amusement.
>
> All those proposing to cancel subscriptions must pay up dues to date. (39)

A number of the more significant contributors to the *Philistine* will be discussed here, and poetry and prose contributions will be examined in turn.

Poetry Contributions

If subscribers fond of poetry did not care for Crane's experimental lines, they had a great variety of other poetic reading matter to choose from; of the 502 signed and anonymous contributions in the *Philistine* (including Hubbard's), more than half of them (282) are poems, many of them nonsense verses popular at the time (of the style continued and perfected by Ogden Nash), or otherwise inconsequential. Three examples of the former, from a volume picked at random, are given below:

Ingratitude

I think it ill becomes a Man--
(Though he be sorely swat)
Because his House has blown away,
To grumble at his Lot.

S. B. Ireland (December, 1901; 14.1:1)

Trouble

When I awaken in the morn
I'm sad, I must confess,
To think that ere I can go out
I must get up and dress.

Anon. (March, 1902; 14:4)

Distrust
Doggerel License, No. 6,169

I hate to use a Folding-Bed,
 Because I have been told
That many Sleeping Lambkins have
 Been gathered in the Fold.

Anon. (April, 1902; 14.5)

Gelett Burgess, the most famous practitioner of nonsense verse of his time, is represented by two items. The three-stanza "In Jenson Type" (December, 1895; 2.1:7) mocks the use of ornate typography by imitators of William Morris, and concludes,

Go, foolish rhyme, and dress your woes
In this prevailing garb of those
 Who call all well that fits the gauge
 Set by the mediaeval sage--
You too, may conquer, I suppose,
 In Jenson type.

The other piece provides evidence that Burgess was best when he limited himself to nonsense verse. "Karma" (November, 1896; 3.6:161) is an overwrought piece about a murderer having to "*again begin/ The long, long round of weary strife*!"

As for examples of other inconsequential poems (though not intended as such), it is not difficult to find, again from one volume selected at random, two samples:

The Twilight Hour

Softly over the tired world,
 Longing for rest and quiet night,
Twilight shadows their veils unfurled
 'Broidered with dreams and fancies light.

Peace, so dear to all worldly ken--
 Peace, from the tender God above
Brooded over the hearts of men
 Whisp'ring the calm of perfect love.

Still and silent the green hills lay;
 Stirred neither leaf, nor twig nor flower;

Rosy yet from the sun's last ray;
   Lulled to rest by the twilight hour.

Then a bird's song rose, true and clear,
   Trilling the thought it fain would tell--
Hush, ye children of men and hear,
   "God's in his world and all is well."

Eleanore S. Inslee (December, 1900; 12.1:8-9)

Too Wise

For those who hold a righteous rage,
   And blame the sinner sore:
It does not do to grow too wise,
   And see what went before--
One cannot comfortably hate
   The sinner any more.

For those who love to teach the world,
   And show mankind the way,
Who learn to preach acceptably,
   And find their preachments pay:
It does not do to grow too wise--
   There's so much less to say!

Charlotte Perkins Gilman (May, 1901; 12.6:188)[1]

These verses, and others like them, seem to be samples of those that Hubbard said would be found in "yer granny's scrapbook," as he had remarked to Stephen Crane; what is more, Inslee and Gilman each has the tripartite name that Hubbard noted (in discussing Bliss Carman) was apparently required for poetic "success." In fairness to Hubbard (and his readers), however, one must keep in mind the type of contemporary poetry that was most popular; and while it is tempting to belittle the quality of many of the poems he published, it is necessary to emphasize that the *Philistine* was a popular periodical founded in 1895, not Harriet Monroe's *Poetry*, which would not appear until 1912. Even the contemporary *Chap-Book*, a publication with avowedly literary aims and a well-deserved critical reputation, published "a good bit" of banal poetry (Schlereth, 53).

Indeed, by 1912 Hubbard had lost interest in poetry. Perhaps the tragic life of Stephen Crane embittered him regarding the efficacy of poetry and the sanity of poets. He also recognized that poetry was no longer a popular genre, and that the publication of poetry in the *Philistine* no longer increased readership; the need for Monroe's specialized publication was signal proof that poetry was no longer widely enjoyed. In a letter to the poet and playwright Sadakichi Hartmann encouraging him to try his hand at writing advertisements (16 Aug. 1912), Hubbard observed that "poetry is strictly on the bum" and that poets are "going over to the Bull Moose of the Publicity Bureaus; in other words, writing advertisements. . . . Poetry usually advertises nothing but a man's own futilities" (Hamilton, "Hartmann, Hubbard, and East Aurora," 3). This transition from the allure of literature to that of advertising is poignantly dramatized a decade later by Eugene O'Neill in *Strange Interlude*, in a scene where the ambitious, young Sam Evans writes ad copy in the study of Professor Leeds, his deceased father-in-law.

Carman and another Canadian poet of note (and cousin), Sir Charles G. D. Roberts (whose initials invited, and received, irreverent inventions from Hubbard and other editors of little magazines), are each represented in the *Philistine* by one poem. As James Doyle points out, many Canadian writers turned to American alternatives to mass circulation periodicals for their literary experiments. Doyle, while essentially disdainful of Hubbard, classing him with the (in his opinion) "irresponsible amateurs" who dominated the genre of little magazines after 1897 (182), at least gives him his due for having provided experimental writers such as Carman and Roberts a periodical outlet and free publicity (however slanted) in the pages of the *Philistine.* He also agrees that Hubbard was justified in complaining about the mutual "backscratching of the Canadians."[2] (Doyle cites issue 6.1:124 instead of the correct 6.4:124 in quoting Hubbard on this topic.)

Carman, who was Herbert Stone's co-editor for the first issues of the *Chap-Book*, and that magazine's most frequent contributor (Schlereth, 37), receives much ribbing in the *Philistine,* and his lighthearted "In Philistia" appeared in February, 1897 (4.3:65-66). This paean to the comely residents of "Philistia" (East Aurora, that is) contains twelve four-line stanzas in iambic tetrameter. The last four stanzas give the flavor of the whole:

They never heard of William Blake,
  Nor saw a Botticelli;
Yet one is, "Yours till death, Louise,"
  And one, "Your loving Nelly."

They never tease me for my views,
  Nor tax me with my grammar;
Nor test me on the latest news,
  Until I have to stammer.

They never talk about their "moods,"
  They never know they have them;
The world is good enough for them,
  And that is why I love them.

They never puzzle me with Greek,
  Nor drive me mad with Ibsen;
Yet over forms as fair as Eve's
  They wear the gowns of Gibson.

Roberts is represented by "Carpe Diem (An Old Song Resung)," which appeared in October, 1896 (3.5:143-44). His final stanza is as uninteresting as it is unoriginal:

Soon, too soon, the tale is told;
  Soon, too soon, the dumb dismay.
Full of life as it will hold
  Let us fill the fleeting day,
For to-morrow we grow old.

That Hubbard did not publish other, more representative, work by these two Canadians is undoubtedly due to their reputation as symbolists; Richard Hovey, who promoted European symbolism in the *Chap-Book*, considered Carman and Roberts two of the *Chap-Book* romantics who belonged to the new school of symbolism (Schlereth, 100). The progressive Hubbard had no patience with anything smacking of French symbolism or decadence.

There are, of course, the above samples notwithstanding, weightier poetic contributions to the *Philistine* scattered throughout its forty-one volumes. One is by the Catholic poet and essayist Louise Imogen Guiney (1861-1920), one of the most distinguished women represented by verse in the *Philistine*.

These are the first nine lines of her "To a Friend in Time of Trouble" (April, 1896; 2.5:137), which is indebted to Shakespeare:

> Believe the word our gentle augur spake:
> Sweet are the uses of adversity.
> Sweet ever, and in naught so sweet as this:
> That tho' the heavens be barred, if we but hold
> An equal, tranquil, well-illumined mind,
> Such greatness in us, laborless, must earn
> Great answers; cheer from all created things,
> And interchange of love by natural right
> With the high few: a kinship not of clan.

Another is in the form of the classic Italian sonnet, by the man who almost spoiled Crane's testimonial dinner by threatening to walk out because of its rambunctious atmosphere:

A Sonnet of Despair

> My captain calls to me to join the fray,
>   Fame holds her fillet ready for my brow,
>   Love stands with aching, open arms, and Thou,
> O God, to whom I impotently pray,
> Art ever ready to receive me--yea,
>   Dost yearn for my poor prisoned soul--then how
>   Becomes it that I linger in this slough
> Of idle, unclean days, till I grow gray?
>
> Bound am I to a corpse, face unto face,
>   Of old iniquities, and dead desire,
> Which, fair and young, of old did I embrace.
>   Now chains of habit, forged in Passion's fire,
> Hold me forever in this durance base:
>   Struggling to rise, I wallow in the mire.
>
> Claude Fayette Bragdon (November, 1895; 1.6:169)

Given the tenor of this poem, perhaps it is no surprise that Bragdon was not able to enjoy himself at Crane's riotous roast. Bragdon was not, however, humorless. In his reminiscent article "The Purple Cow Period" he recalls the illustrated whimsies, that appeared in the *Chap-Book* after Gelett Burgess printed "The Purple Cow" in the first number. He observes that the "Purple Cow Period" of American letters was contemporary with the "*Yellow Book* Period" in England, and that the "most characteristic literary products" of the 1890s were "inspired far more by the play-spirit than those of today [1929] (475)." The "dinkey magazines," as they were called, were "'young,' devouringly egocentric and self-assertive and either good-naturedly or bitterly cynical of one another. They constituted a sort of metaphysical Fleet Street, extending from coast to coast" (475). Noting that they "were always out for one another's scalp in those days, even when friendly Indians," he remembers writing a variation of a *Chap-Book* nonsense verse in the *Philistine* together with a burlesque Burgess drawing (475). This appears in the December 1895 (2.1:opp. 40) number as follows:

> When I draw pictures for *The Shark*
> I do not have to think,
> I let my fingers chase my pen
> And my pen chase the ink.

This was reprinted (with "*The Lark*" replacing "*The Shark*") in the December 1896 (4.1:opp. 16) number.

The next example of a well-crafted poem is in free verse:

Life's Voyage: A Mood

> Dark and tumultuous seas
> Have quenched the lurid sun,
> Vapors, flame riven, writhingly ascend,
> And night comes winging on
> 'Cross sullen waves,
> While Death upon the bowsprit waiting sits.
>
> Bereft of hope,
> Life's running sands low spent,
> No rudder steers--nor beacon's flame
> Tells us the course to sail.
> Alone, alone, breathed on by awful fears,
> Groping amidst life's way for light, we drift.
>
> William B. Faville (May, 1896; 2.6:194)

Finally, this quatrain is another example of poetry with literary merit that can be found in the pages of the *Philistine:*

Presentiment

From drowned Harriet the crystals dripped,
  And fled in fierce revengeful haste away,--
And Shelley shuddered, knowing that they slipped
  To keep a wild sea-tryst with him one day.

Julia Ditto Young (November, 1897; 5.6:161)[3]

Prose Contributions

Several writers well-known at the turn of the century are represented in the pages of the *Philistine.* One is George Ade (1866-1944), an American humorist and playwright who first achieved fame with his columns for the *Chicago Record.* A collection of these columns was published in 1899 as *Fables in Slang*, and one of these fables appears in December, 1899 (10.1:7-9). "The Fable of the Experimental Parents Who Tinkered with the Two Boys" tells about Joseph and Clarence. Joseph was smothered with parental supervision, went to Harvard, ran away with a girl who waited on tables at his boarding house, and ended up in charge of a cloak room at a dairy lunch. Realizing that their experiment with Joseph was a failure, the parents went to the other extreme by deciding to give Clarence no supervision, and he ended up "working the shells" with a circus. Spoiled Harvard undergraduates and hapless parents groping for "new" child-rearing techniques were two of Hubbard's favorite targets.

For several years there was a Roycroft School of Life for Boys, with Alice Hubbard as principal, where the boys worked "at the books in the forenoon," and all of the afternoon was devoted to "useful, pleasurable work out of doors" (January, 1912; 34.2:bap). (He advertised the school in the front pages of the December 1912 [36.1] issue this way: "Half a day at the books, and half a day at useful work--that's the plan at The Roycroft School for Boys.") A year later Hubbard recounted the arrival of a lawyer's son at the school: "The lad had never done a useful thing in his life. He had been mamma's and papa's boy and joy." Hubbard informed the doting father that "out-of-door work was what his boy needed," adding that if there is any better education than "mixing with life and getting on good terms with everything that grows out in the sunshine, runs, creeps, crawls, flies or swims, I do not know it" (January, 1913; 36.2:47-49).

In addition to his progressivism regarding alternative education (he has been described as a disciple of John Dewey, and visited his experimental school at the University of Chicago in 1901 [Champney, 189]), Hubbard prided himself on his ability to "rehabilitate" less than ideal workers. In his autobiographical sketch for *Cosmopolitan Magazine*, he claims the Roycrofters have "boys who have been expelled from school, blind people, deaf people, old people, jail-birds and mental defectives, and have managed to set them all at useful work" (313). He claimed responsibility for largely doing away with "hoodlumism" in the village of East Aurora, and wanted to be remembered as someone who had "something to do with stopping the mad desire on the part of the young people to get out of the country and flock to the cities" (309).

Another well-known (and notorious) contributor was Edward Carpenter (1844-1929), an English poet and writer. His socialist views caused him to leave the clergy, and he earned his living as a lecturer, farmer, and sandal-maker. A disciple of Walt Whitman, he was an apologist for homosexual love. His first contribution in the *Philistine* is "China, 1900 A.D." (February, 1901; 12.3:65-69), which is a Whitman-like panorama of China, "an outline of the nation which the Western nations would fain remodel on their own lines" (69). Here is the opening section:

> In the interior of China,
> Along low lying plains and great river valleys,
> and by lakesides, and far away up into hilly and
> even mountainous regions,
> Behold! an immense population, rooted in the
> land, rooted in the clan and the family,
> The most productive and stable on the whole
> Earth.

The second contribution (May, 1901; 12.6:181-188) is "Life and Art," an essay preaching a liberating expression of self, and the mastery of the art of life: "The Art of Life is to know that Life is Art, that it is Expression" (181). This essay was obviously fresh in Hubbard's mind when he wrote his autobiographical sketch for *Cosmopolitan Magazine* (January 1902), where he states, "Art is the expression of man's joy in his work. . . . Life is expression. Life is a movement outward, an unfolding, a development" (319-320).

Walter Blackburn Harte contributed twice to the first issues of the *Philistine* before his bitter departure from East Aurora. The first, the richly ironic "An Interview with the Devil" (July, 1895; 1.2:53-59), reports the devil's despair over the futility of competing with the nefarious power of the steampresses of journalism (55); he has decided to abdicate forever, for he explains that it is

> worse than useless for him to labor painfully to cultivate a deep and stirring delight in original sin in one promising little urchin . . . when the great and omniscient newspaper press can at any given moment set a whole nation, or even the whole civilized world, crawling upon all fours, nosing and wallowing in filth. (58)

Harte, noting that the devil was always an abandoned pessimist, archly attributes his despair over the outcome of the "great modern passion for literacy" to disappointed ambition and malevolence. For while it is true that the Sunday newspapers are surfeited with "suffocating triviality and vulgarity" of Sabbatical literature, the Monday morning issues contain "long and beautiful abstracts of sermons of soporific platitude, and charmingly convincing illogic" (58). In the second essay, "Shakespeare's Borrowings" (May, 1896; 2.6:184-187), Harte argues that "the world of readers gains when great genius takes its own where it finds it" (184). Noting that the critics would probably "howl" if any contemporary author should admit to the extent of borrowings that Shakespeare did, he maintains that Shakespeare, unlike many contemporary writers, possessed imaginative gifts that are sorely needed among the writers of the day (186). He concludes that Shakespeare, if alive during the present "gory era," would be at the forefront of the "new movement for freedom in literature, and he would steal right and left from Science!" (187)

The most famous prose writer represented in the *Philistine* is Tolstoy. Nearly three dozen references to him appear between 1895 and 1915, and it is evident that Hubbard derived much inspiration, and corroboration of his views on education and religion, from the works of Tolstoy.

In the November 1906 number Hubbard printed a short piece by Tolstoy titled "What Your Child Should Know" (23.6:161-163) in which he argues that each child should learn that "all he uses does not fall from heaven ready-made, but is produced by other people's labor" (161). Children should

> do all they can for themselves: carry out their own slops, fill their own jugs, wash up, arrange their rooms, clean their boots and clothes, lay the table, etc. Believe me that, unimportant as these things may seem, they are a hundred times more important than a knowledge of French, or of history. (162)

Hubbard's homage is most evident in his devoting the first half of the May 1901 (12.6:161-177) issue of the *Philistine* to a printing of Tolstoy's essay "Church and State." Tolstoy opens the essay by marveling at those who "anathematize, persecute and kill whom they can of the dissentients" (161). After reflecting upon this melancholy phenomenon, and the existence of hundreds of sects, "all anathematizing, persecuting and killing each other" (162), he reached the conclusion that "all religion is a human fraud" (162). Discussing the extent and origin of this fraud, he states that "of all the godless ideas and words there is none more godless than that of a Church. There is no idea which has produced more evil, none more inimical to Christ's teaching than the idea of a Church" (165). Summarizing the history of the Church, and noting that the Christian teaching always falls into two parts, the teaching of dogmas, and the teaching of moral behavior (174), he concludes by defining religion as "the meaning we give to our lives," and revelation as that which "helps a man to understand the meaning of life" (177).

One of the Hubbard citations in the supplementary volumes of *Poole's Index to Periodical Literature* is an article "Tolstoi" which appeared in a 1902 number of *Cosmopolitan* (34:442-450). Prefacing this article is an editor's note:

> There are not many who do not recognize in Elbert Hubbard one of the most delightful writers of his time. Original in thought, new in his way of seeing things, quaint in his way of putting things, he has been gradually developing into something more valuable to the world--a man with the power of seeing TRUTH. . . . [H]e, for a long time, had as a motto--apparently--"Art for Art's

> Sake." Gradually he has come to adopt what he describes as Tolstoy's guiding principle: "Art for Humanity's Sake." THE COSMOPOLITAN is fortunate in being able to number Mr. Hubbard among those who will regularly contribute to its pages for 1903. (442)

(Hubbard apparently received $25 for each of these contributions [HRHRC, Box Uniden.-J, Folder C-D].)

Another important influence on Hubbard, mentioned as often in the *Philistine* as Tolstoy, is John Ruskin. Hubbard printed a dozen epigrammatic thoughts of Ruskin's on the covers and end pages of the *Philistine,* including the following: "Of all attainable liberties, then, be sure to first strive to be useful" (April, 1903; 16.5); "There is no wealth but life" (July, 1903; 17.2); and, "The finer the nature, the more flaws it will show through the nature of it" (May, 1905; 20.6). In a brilliant epigram of his own, Hubbard stated, "If Turner had been 'clear,' Ruskin might still be Assistant Professor" (May, 1896; 2.6, 179).

Hubbard was, like Turner and Emerson, a superb epigrammatist, and hundreds of his epigrams can still be found in thesauri of popular quotations. Nearly all of these appeared first in issues of the *Philistine,* and were then published by the Roycrofters in various collections. These collections include *The Motto Book* (1909, 1914), *One Thousand and One Epigrams* (1911), *The Roycroft Dictionary* (1914), and the posthumously published *Elbert Hubbard's Scrap Book* (1923), and its companion volume, *The Note Book of Elbert Hubbard* (1927). The latter two publications, widely distributed (a million combined copies, according to Champney [5]) by Wm. H. Wise & Co., can still be found in second-hand book stores.

Reading some of these epigrams creates an occasional sense of deja vu, and an appreciation for Hubbard's subtle influence on American English. For example, the *Oxford Dictionary of Quotations* (2nd ed., 1962) includes this familiar quote taken from Hubbard's *One Thousand and One Epigrams* (1911): "Life is just one damned thing after another." ("Life is just one damn thing after another" appears in the December 1909 [30.1:34] *Philistine.*) Another thesaurus (*The Great Quotations*) starts off with this quote from an unspecified issue of the *Philistine:* "This will never be a civilized country until we expend more money for books than we do for chewing gum." Two compendia of quotations, *The Home Book of Quotations, Classical and Modern*, and the *International Thesaurus of Quotations*, each contain nearly 100 of Hubbard's epigrams. Other compendia of quotations listing epigrams by Hubbard include *Magill's Quotations in Context* and Eric Partridge's *A Book of Essential Quotations*. Even H. L. Mencken, eighteen years after Hubbard's death, felt obligated to include some of Hubbard's epigrams in his *A New Dictionary of Quotations*. Writing to Hubbard's son, Elbert Hubbard II, on 27 July 1933, Mencken reassured him that "all quotations from your father will be credited to the 'Book of Epigrams'" (HRHRC, Box Misc. M-Z, Folder M-P).

In addition to the epigrams from Ruskin mentioned earlier, Hubbard printed four Ruskin pieces, three of them allegedly letters to himself. The first appears as the lead contribution in the January 1896 (2.2:41-50) *Philistine,* and is titled "A Protest and a Prayer." In a letter from London (1 Dec. 1896) signed "Clavigera," "Ruskin" begins by noting that he has remitted four shillings for membership in the Society of the Philistines. Aside from the fact that Ruskin had all but put down his pen seven years earlier, the implausibility of Ruskin's wanting to join Hubbard's colony is a clue to the reader to suspect the authenticity of the letter. This suspicion is confirmed a few paragraphs later when "Clavigera" asks Hubbard to give five pounds to the East Aurora Orphan Asylum for each missive of his which appears in the *Philistine* (43). This piece is one of Hubbard's inspired works of "kabojolism," a Hubbard neologism meaning the opposite of plagiarism, the attribution of one's own ideas or writings to a famous writer (in the sense of, "If he did not write that, he should have"), a practice which either amused his readers who realized that this was Hubbard's odd manner of acknowledging his indebtedness to authors, or infuriated readers who believed that Hubbard was seeking self-aggrandizement (and pecuniary gain) through fraudulent means.

Perhaps the most famous of his "kabojolisms" is his paraphrase of a paragraph from Emerson's journals:

> If a man can write a better book, or preach a better sermon, or make a better mousetrap than his neighbor, the world will beat a path to his door, though he build his house in the woods.

In the June 1912 (35.1:29-30) issue Hubbard, explaining jocularly that there were a good many things the great Emerson might have said "and would have said if he had happened to think of them" (29), admits that the above was a "mousetrap that caught a lot of literary mice intent on orphic cheese" (29). In fact, some scholars lost much time trying to find this "kabojolism" in the works of Emerson. This is the apparent source, from one of his Journals:

> If a man has good corn, or wood, or boards, or pigs to sell, or can make better chairs or knives, crucibles or church organs, than anybody else, you will find a broad, hard-beaten road to his house, though it be in the woods. (1855; Bigelow, "Requiem for 'Mousetrap,'" 53)

Both statements have dubious validity, of course; as Hubbard says, no matter how good your mousetraps are, no one will beat a path to your door nowadays unless you "advertise them widely and extensively and arrange a free lunch at the mousetrap-factory, with automobiles to meet all visitors at the railroad-station" (30). Though critics are understandably offended by such a literary prank, it must be admitted that Hubbard's version is more felicitously written and more memorable than Emerson's. Hubbard has an essay on "kabojolism" in the September 1902 (15.4:97-110) issue.

The second Ruskin essay, the lead contribution to the June 1896 (3.1:1-16) issue, is also a letter signed "Clavigera," and was supposedly sent (6 Apr. 1896) from Cumberland. However, a search through Ruskin's *Fors Clavigera* reveals that a large part of this essay was written by Ruskin twenty-five years earlier, and can be found in "Letter V" in the Frank F. Lovell edition (1886) of *Fors Clavigera*. Titled "Some Things America Needs," and dated 1 May 1871 from Denmark Hall, the essay contains Ruskin's description of the three material and three immaterial things essential to life, and is excerpted below:

> There are three Material things, not only useful, but essential to Life. No one knows how to live till he has got them.
>
> These are, Pure Air, Water and Earth.
>
> There are three Immaterial things, not only useful, but essential to Life. No one knows how to live till he has got them also.

These are, Admiration, Hope and Love. (1)

Hubbard reprinted one sentence from this essay ("We will try to make some small piece of ground beautiful, peaceful, and fruitful" [15]) on the back cover of the July 1900 (11.2) *Philistine.* Hubbard clearly admired the forcefulness of Ruskin's epigrammatic style.

The author at first suspected the authenticity of the entire essay, as its jocular and colloquial introduction sounds much more like Hubbard than Ruskin:

> What you call a Discerning Person has told me that THE PHILISTINE is read by all the really thoughtful people in America. This surely is not a large class, as I hear you print only twenty thousand copies a month. Now I do not exactly admire your brown paper cover, but I do like your wholesome spirit, and although you have a touch of Yankee flippancy, yet I will help you all I can in clearing the ground, that we may sow a crop worth harvesting. . . . (1-2)

In addition, a line such as the following gives further cause for questioning the essay's authorship: "Meantime, your wife in the house has also got a goblin to weave and wash for her; and she is lying on the sofa, revelling in Stephen Crane's lines" (10). The absence of any correspondence from Ruskin among the Hubbard manuscripts at the Harry Ransom Humanities Research Collection, The University of Texas at Austin, can be interpreted as the final piece of evidence regarding the extent of Hubbard's "kabojolism" in the contributions he attributed to Ruskin.

The third piece attributed to Ruskin appears in the July 1897 (5.2:52-55) *Philistine.* Hubbard introduces it by claiming, "My dear old friend 'Fors Clavigera' sends me the following." What follows, in fact, is a specious, satirical review of a *Belzebub* [sic] *Muzzled*, by "Gamlin Geezefield" (52), perhaps a veiled attack on Hamlin Garland, a frequent contributor to the *Chap-Book* who received several negative notices in the *Philistine.* (For example, Hubbard claimed that Garland "evolved a system of literary ethics from the slaughter stalls of Chicago" [December, 1899; 10.1,4].) "Ruskin" begins by complaining that "various newspapers in The States keep standing an item to the effect that I am losing my mind" (52). Continuing, he explains that since no modern American periodicals (except for, of course, the *Philistine)* contain any sense, he has turned to American novels, with equal disappointment. (A second book pilloried is *Two Flats and a Store Front*, by a Madelaine Mouseley [53].)

Finally, an excerpt identified as being from "Letter No. XLV" appears in the May 1900 (10.6:190-191) *Philistine.* This excerpt, with slight differences in punctuation, is in fact taken from Ruskin's letter from Lucca, Italy, dated 2 Aug. 1874, which appears as "Letter XLV" in the John Wiley & Sons edition (1886) of *Fors Clavigera* (vol. 4, p. 129). A portion of this excerpt (observing the punctuation used in the Wiley edition) is as follows:

> And all this monarchy and glory, all this power and love, all this land and its people, you pitifullest, foulest of Iscariots, sopped to choking with the best of the feast from Christ's own fingers, you have deliberately sold to the highest bidder;--Christ, and His Poor, and His Paradise together; and instead of sinning only, like poor natural Adam, gathering of the fruit of the Tree of Knowledge, you, who don't want to gather it, *touch* it with a vengeance,--cut it down, and sell the timber.[4]

Only two women have multiple prose contributions in the *Philistine.* One of them is Marilla Marks Ricker (died 1920), who was a lawyer, author, and humanitarian known as the "prisoners' friend." Her father, a New Hampshire farmer and cousin of Brigham Young, raised her as a free thinker, suffragist, and Whig. She was the author of three "free thought" books and a disciple of Thomas Paine and Col. Robert G. Ingersoll. She was admitted to the bar of the superior court of Washington, D.C., in 1882, opened the New Hampshire bar to women in 1890, and was admitted to practice before the U.S. Supreme Court in 1891. In 1910 she was a candidate for governor of New Hampshire.

"A Square Deal" (September, 1907; 25.4:97-115) begins by attacking Theodore Roosevelt for calling Paine a "filthy, little atheist" (97), and then extols Paine's contributions to the United States. She concludes that without him, "there would not have been liberty enough in this land to allow the publication of THE PHILISTINE Magazine" (115). Hubbard must have raised the issue of Roosevelt's calling Paine "filthy" with the President himself, for Roosevelt replies (22 Jan. 1907) from the White House that, according to an anecdote, Paine stayed in bed a week, "not even getting out to perform the operations of nature. If this did not warrant the adjective I have used in describing him, I do not see what conduct would" (HRHRC, Box Recip. K-Z, Folder O-R).

She praises Ingersoll in two articles, one in August, 1908 (27.3:66-80), and the other in February, 1909 (28.3:65-78). The severity of her treatments of John Calvin (January, 1911; 32.2:33-44) and Jonathan Edwards (September, 1911; 33.4:97-110) can be readily surmised. Finally, in "Howe and Why" (December, 1912; 36.1:1-5), she berates an article in the July 1912 issue of *Ed Howe's Monthly* for Howe's remarks concerning the "suffragette business" (1). Howe had argued, "You can't change Nature, and Nature is against the suffragette" (2), and termed Susan B. Anthony the "most disagreeable" woman he ever knew (3).

The front pages of the January 1913 (36.2) issue advertise a Roycrofters publication of *The Four Gospels*, which is a collection of Ricker's articles on Ingersoll, Paine, Calvin, and Edwards. (It is noteworthy that she uses "Gospels" and Alice Hubbard uses the title "An American Bible" for a book published the same year.) She is described as a taxpayer who has protested her taxes for forty years, "on the grounds that taxation without representation is tyranny." (Article XIX of the U.S. Constitution was not ratified until 1920.)

The other woman with multiple contributions is Ouida (Marie Louise de la Ramee). Her first is "A Word About Art" (August, 1895; 1.3:74-78), in which she asks how it is possible to have great art without faith, arguing that "belief of some sort is the lifeblood of art" (74). She argues that the artificiality and cynicism of modern life militate against greatness in art: "Sadness and sarcasm make a great Lucretius and as a great [sic] Juvenal; and scorn makes a strong Aristophanes; but they do not make a Praxiteles . . ." (75). "The Gold That Glitters" (April, 1896; 2.5:138-141) is a fable warning against the fruits of greed, and "The Captives" (August, 1896; 3.3:73-76) makes a comparison between the enslavement of Apollo toiling at a corn-mill and "the genius of a man, which, being born of a god, yet is bound as a slave to the grind-stone" (76).

A contributor of both poetry and prose was the journalist Eugene R. White (1872-1906), of Buffalo. Eight poems appear in the *Philistine,* five of them lead pieces. The following appeared in September, 1896 (3.4:97):

> Poor mintage of a life,--these deeds rough
> pressed,
> Not worth an obol for old Charon's toll;
> Though molten in my heart, cast by my soul,
> Fate's was the die that made them manifest.

Of particular interest, however, is his sole prose contribution, "Where Is Literature At?" (July, 1895; 1.2:33-38). This essay is a response to Max Simon Nordau's *Degeneration*, an immensely controversial work of the 1890s. White admits the truth of Nordau's charges that the literature of the decade is "self conscious" and marked in general by "a hopeless lack of unity" (34), but counters that there "must be a certain self consciousness nowadays if anything is to be done" (35). Furthermore, far from denoting decay, the "present diversity in literature" is a step towards universality, due to "a declaration of individual independence in literature, built upon the lack of single leaders and the abolition of a great literary center" (36). Dismissing *Degeneration* as, on the whole, worthless (34), White declares that it is a "Gargantuan task to get at the heart of this multiple age" (38), and that Nordau is not equal to the task.

Another frequent contributor to the *Philistine* was Michael Monahan (1865-1933), whom Hubbard enjoyed ribbing. In the April 1896 (2.5:163) issue Hubbard writes, "I warn the public against a book called *Youth: A Poem of Soul and Sense* . . . It is dedicated to 'The True and the Chaste,' which evidently was an attempt to flatter me. But I'm not for sale." He calls him the "Poet Laureate of Albany" (April, 1898; 6.5:145) and reports that when Monahan arrived in East Aurora one week, the potatoes were ready to hoe, so he stayed only one day (September, 1899; 9.4:127). Monahan contributed two poems and eight essays, from May, 1898, to October, 1901.

According to the *National Cyclopedia of American Biography*, Monahan, who came to the United States from Ireland when he was a boy, was secretary to the mayor of Albany from 1896 to 1900, when he joined Hubbard's "socialistic colony" and assisted in the editorship of the *Philistine*. In 1903 he went to New York City and founded the *Papyrus*, a literary magazine which became the *Phoenix* in 1914, with Monahan remaining as its editor, chief contributor, and publisher. A follower of the

American critic James Gibbons Huneker, after 1916 he became an independent writer, whose work is "characterized by moderate realism and reflected his veneration for style." Among the periodicals he wrote for are the *New York Weekly Review*, *Independent*, *Freeman*, *Forum*, *Double Dealer* and *Catholic World*.

Most of his contributions to the *Philistine* are lighthearted, except when his topics are Ireland and Kipling. "Hibernia Nova" (May, 1898; 6.6:167-174) is an essay on the rising estimation of the Irish and the prospects of independence for Ireland. Kipling is the subject of both his poem "To Villon" (September, 1899; 9.4:106-108) and his essay "The Kipling Blue Pill" (October, 1901; 13.5:129-136). The poem consists of eight stanzas and asks,

> . . . Favored of Hermes, were you still
> With us upon this earthy site,
> Could you, Sir, by your ancient skill,
> Rifle a Kipling Copyright?

Other stanzas conclude with the following variations: "Ruddy Kipling Trust"; "Evil Stuff"; "Kipling Pool"; "Kipling Syndicate"; "Kipling Pile"; and, "Kipling Bulge." The essay is even more virulent and graphic; Monahan notes with considerable satisfaction that the "dear American public has gagged at last on the blood-boltered [sic] gospel of Ruddy Kipling" (129). While conceding that he "has not in point of power a single rival in the English world today" (131), he calls him the "laureate of loot and lust, of carnage and crime, of the strong against the weak" (133). He attributes his vogue in the United States to "the rampant Anglomania which has vitiated our national sentiment during the past decade, & for which our bloody bungling in the Philippines has but lately furnished a curative" (132). At last the American public is "taking its blue pill in a spirit of hearty repentance" (136).[5]

He is a biting and clever critic of American cultural life, as revealed in his "Culturian Observations" (April, 1899; 8.5:141-147) and "The McClure Continuous: A Vaudeville" (December, 1899; 10.1:1-6), which mocks the proposal of the S. S. McClure Company to establish a literary lyceum, "or Continuous Authors' Show" (1). Perhaps his best essay in this vein is "Loquacious Literarians" (June, 1900; 11.1:18-21), in which he reports that "cacoethus loquendi has broken out among our best litterateurs," whose common cry is, "On to the Lyceum!" (18) For example, William Dean Howells is "adventuring a hazard of late fortunes" (18), even though Uncle Billy Bushnell (a town character) of East Aurora is the better elocutionist. (Howells's *A Hazard of New Fortunes* had just been published.) Next is "Major" (James B.) Pond, the lecture circuit impresario, who, having written his reminiscences of great lecturers in the *Ladies' Home Journal*, "has logically started out as a great lecturer himself" (19). After him in importance is Edwin Markham, who has prepared "an ingenious lecture entitled, 'How I Wrote the Man With the Hoe'," although Monahan speculates that many of the "afflicted" are "rather more concerned to learn why he did it, and what redress remains for his readers" (19). He notes that William Jennings Bryan has written about the Markham poem for the Sunday papers, and, "as a critic, he reveals as many wheels as he possesses in his capacity of currency reformer" (20).

There are, according to the tongue-in-cheek Monahan, still "other stars in this firmament" (20). Mr. Bolton Hall, having received an inheritance, has renounced the "dangerous delights of pornografic literature, and is now lecturing on the Single Tax" (20). The "alleged" humorist Col. John Kendrick Bangs is also among their number. Bliss Carman and Charles G. D. Roberts recite their verses and, "what is extraordinary in this age, live by them" (21). These poets are supposedly in great demand at young ladies' seminaries, where "the passions are of a lofty, unrealized character, answering to the cold raptures of their hyperborean verse" (21).

Monahan, despite the rupture between him and Hubbard, had a soft place in his heart for East Aurora, as evidenced by his comments in "The Gospel of Content" (November, 1900; 11.6:bap [13-17]). In an address he gave at the Roycroft Chapel on September 25, 1900, he told the audience, "I like to feel that I 'belong' myself, in spirit at least" (14), and envies those who are building "in this weary world a little Gospel of Content" (15):

> In the midst of a material civilization that subordinates the true nobility of life, of a head-long race for wealth that grinds the faces of the poor, you are favored to set here, in an idyllic frame, the picture of an antique simplicity.

> I have myself been the object of a vastly flattering attention . . . because some faint ray of the light of East Aurora was reflected upon me.
>
> Let this light of East Aurora shine ever the brighter! (16-17)

The most frequent contributor (after Crane) to the *Philistine* is William McIntosh, the "Great Original Philistine" (3.5:147), who contributed twenty-one verses and essays from June, 1895 (1.1:1-4) to September, 1903 (17.4:97-102). Seven of his essays were lead contributions.[6] McIntosh was the managing editor of the *Buffalo News*, which, according to Hubbard, had a larger circulation than any daily "between New York and Chicago" (3.5:147).

His two verse contributions are moralistic. The first, "Stigmata" (June, 1895; 1.1:30), is given complete:

"Behold the miracle!" he cried--
The sombre priest who stood beside
A figure on whose snowy breast
The outlines of a cross expressed
In ruddy life-drops ebbed and flowed;
"Behold th' imprimatur of God!"

A kneeling woman raised her eyes;
Lo! At the sight, in swift surprise,
Ere awe-struck lips a prayer could speak
Love's stigma glowed on brow and cheek;
And one in reverence bent his head--
"Behold the miracle?" he said.

The other is an attack on the amorality expressed in the work which profoundly influenced the "decadent" 'nineties, Omar Khayyam's *Rubaiyat*. It appears in September, 1895 (1.4:125-126, opposite Crane's "A Lantern Song"), and contains eight stanzas. The cleverest part of it is the title:

THE RUBAIYAT OF O'MARA KHAYVAN.

Erin (Iran?) Year of the Hegira 94--via
Brooklyn.

Two stanzas which represent what McIntosh fears will happen if the philosophy of life expressed in Fitzgerald's famous translation is widely adopted are given below:

Wake! for the bearded goat devours the door!
And now the family pig forbears to snore,
And from his trough sets up the Persian's cry--
"Eat! drink! To-morrow we shall be no more!"

And is this all? Shall skies no longer shine,
Or stars lure on to themes that seem divine?
Ah, Maker of the Tents! is this thy hope--
To feed and grovel and to die like swine?[7]

Yet, in his essay "The Fruit of Good Living" (May, 1898; 6.6:175-180) McIntosh insists that "the fruit of good living is still one of the kindly fruits of the earth which we may duly enjoy" (180), and attacks the forces of Puritanism and the age-long antipathy of philosophers to luxury (175). He notes that theories of social economy are deficient, that it may be necessary to "look beyond production for the ultimate good. Work that distributes may have its function also" (178). He thanks "Providence" for implanting the instincts which prompt people to invest "their surplus energies in art and feasting & love-making," for these activities "disturb the congestion of accumulated treasures and give the poor man a chance" (178). He contrasts the poet to the philosopher, claiming that the latter is blinded by his study of "the how of things" to the duality in life, which manifests itself to the poet: "the message that the poet hears is that a force underlies even the corrupting influences of wealth and indulgent living" (179).

Turning to his other prose contributions, his first essay is "Philistines Ancient and Modern" (June, 1895; 1.1:1-4). (Hubbard speculated in jest that McIntosh will "live in history because he wrote the leading article in the first number of the *Philistine* Magazine" [3.5:147].) This article, in praise of Philistines and Philistinism, is central to an understanding of the choice of the periodical's title.[8] McIntosh states that "Tradition has been unkind to Philistinism . . . The Serpent in the Garden is the earliest embodiment of the genius of protest" (2). He holds that it is the Philistines who are the regenerators of society, much in the same vein as the thought expressed in Emerson's witticism, "The barbarians who broke up the Roman Empire did not come a day too soon," which is the cover motto of the April 1900 (10.5) issue of the *Philistine.*[9] He claims that Shakespeare ("a despised player and holder of horses") was a Philistine, and that Thackeray, Dickens, Hugo,

Tolstoy, and Ibsen, the "imaginative authors who most strongly sway mankind today," those who lifted the "mask from aristocracy and exposed its sordid servility," are also Philistines (3). In short, those "who protest, who exalt purpose and measure achievement thereby," are defined as Philistines (3). They are revolutionaries in the world's "perpetual crusade" who "see evolution in all, and hold naught that is finite to be final" (3). While revering tradition, Philistines despise "commonplace in purple" (3).

In the same June issue, Mark S. Hubbell greeted the new magazine in the name of "all who have hated shams, [and] in the name of all brave knights whose lances have shivered against the dead walls of human stupidity, ignorance, malice and convention" ("Philistinism in General," 12). He denounces Richard Watson Gilder, John Brisben Walker, Edward W. Bok and others of "the Mutual Admiration Society" for reading the "lucubrations of the contributors to the dreary masses of illustrated inanities they edit" (15).

In his subsequent essays McIntosh often rails against the materialism rampant in society. In "A Free Lunch League" (July, 1895; 1.2:46-51) he berates those "literary people" who sponge off others, and urges them to "crystallize their scattered atoms of protest in an Anti Free Lunch League" (49). He protests that Philistines believe that there is something "finer than feeding in courtesy," and that they object to materialism, "even when it swamps only the things of this world" (49). In "Our Masters" (February, 1897; 4.3:73-79) he adds that it "needs no Philistine to discover the wreck of splendid powers of brain and will in the mastery of money-getting over the mind" (75), and in "Commonplace in Purple" (June, 1897; 5.1:15-19; the title is the phrase which concluded his first essay) he denounces the "perfect cameo art of Tennyson" and says that "it is the aristocracy of Business that rules England" (17). Looking closer to home, he notes that there was a time when "the cleavage of American society was intellectual . . . when Americans discussed great problems of government," but that was before luxury became, as was in England, "enthroned commonplace" (18). In "At Christmas" (December, 1898; 8.1:1-5), he remarks sadly that even "our confessions of faith are narrowed by material definitions"; in a discussion of the custom of giving gifts at Christmas, he concludes, "We do so love and fear the things measurable by our five senses that even things spiritual must come under their domination" (4).

McIntosh had faith in the socially redeeming powers of journalism. In his otherwise pessimistic "Commonplace In Purple" he claims that "the press of the New World" is the "least commonplace of all expressions of modern life," and thus "offers a promise of something better than the dry-rot of a purely commercial society" (5.1:19). And in "The Ex-Cathedra Habit" (April, 1899; 8.5:130-134), while admitting that newspapers "make war or peace for circulation nowadays," he nevertheless supports the adoption of the "ex-cathedra attitude" by many newspapers. He argues that it is safer for newspapers to adopt such an attitude than for the clergy to do so, for newspapers permit letters to the editor, while "no man openly disputes" the interpretations of the "pulpit oracle" (131).

He seems to have less optimism for the quality of popular literature. In "The Literary Sweat Shop" (October, 1896; 3.5:129-132) he faults authors for trying to feed the maws of "monumental" metropolitan newspapers (131). He explains that the successive groups of writers, "the paragraphers, the short story builders, the dialect poets, the feulletonists [sic], the humorists of the [Danbury] Bailey and [Bill] Nye school, met the same fate": engulfment in the literary sweat shop (131). These authors failed to realize that the big city paper "counts its pages by the ream," that the "glory of bigness is the destruction of individuality in literary work" (132). "Tonnage" in American literature has led to the little magazines, he theorizes: "The bibelot is born of the surfeit of the big newspaper" (132). He bravely hopes that the product of the literary sweat shop will take "its rank with the other things commercially dear to the money changers and despised of all Philistines" (132). While he praises "the recognition of healthy life that we find in some of the new literature," such as the work of Anthony Hope, Maarten Maartens and Hall Caine ("A Matter of Background," 1.4:118-122), he is depressed by the ascendancy of "The How of Science," which holds that literature "need be original no longer" and results in the "pathology" of authors such as Emile Zola ("The Evolution of the How," 4.5:129-133).

In perhaps his most lighthearted essay, "Headwaters of Castaly," (June, 1900; 11.1:13-18), he discourses upon the rising flood of verses which are inundating newspaper offices. He wonders why there should now be a "special eruption of verse in the most practical nation on earth" (13), and states that these "modern despoilers of white paper have been up in the Greek hills in the past year or so, but they do not appear to have run across any Muses" (14). He allows that in England it takes special skill for the Laureate or Mr. Kipling "(if the official rhymster falls short)" to "unmask Russian diplomacy and set forth the Boer Policy in verse" (15), but compares the verse that newspapers receive to the "headwaters of Castaly--jugged and extra dry as the precious draught may be" (16). He concludes that it is high time for a "singer with a truer gauge of the universal undertone" to arise (17).

His social views are somewhat self-contradictory. On the one hand, two of his contributions are devoted to the evils of poverty. In the first, "The Kind That Paul Forgot" (December, 1895; 2.1:9-13), he sarcastically attacks the emotionalism of charity. Explaining that God "created evil as part of the system," he urges us to organize, to put all impulse "in cold storage" so that the "millenium of organized charity will come" (11-12). His next contribution, "The Filling of the Joneses" (March, 1896; 2.4:114-119) is a melodramatic illustration of organized charity in action. The impoverished head of a household is a mechanic who can work only "until over-production or under-distribution or something else turned everything upside down" (116). When he comes home to his starving children after another day of fruitless search for employment, he finds a package left by a visiting committee. It is a copy of Smith's "Psyche," on loan for his spiritual sustenance. His four-year-old Kit says plaintively, "Papa, I fought it was somefing good to eat" (118). On the other hand, McIntosh, like Hubbard, is no muckraker. As he says in "A Matter of Background" (September, 1895; 1.4:118-122),

> The new realism for which Philistines contend is no expose of the evils of modern society, no uncovering of a witch's pot. It holds all these manifestations in perspective, but substitutes none of them for a general view of life and human destiny. . . (121).

Another contributor to the *Philistine* was William Marion Reedy (1862-1920), the distinguished editor of the *St. Louis Mirror* who made it "one of the leading artistic, literary-critical journals" in the United States (*National Cyclopedia of*

American Biography). As Max Putzel notes in his biography of Reedy, he was a partisan of Edgar Lee Masters, Theodore Dreiser, and other literary dissenters, he helped establish the reputations of Nathaniel Hawthorne and Emily Dickinson, and helped to introduce to American readers Walter Pater, Thomas Hardy, William Butler Yeats, George Bernard Shaw, and the French symbolists (6-7).

Reedy admired Hubbard, and the admiration was mutual; as early as April, 1896, Hubbard praised him as one of "the strongest writers this glorious Republic contains" (2.5:162). And in June, 1905, after announcing the Roycroft publication of *The Law of Love*, Reedy's first printed book, Hubbard goes on to praise him and his work (21.1:10-14). In a collection of essays bearing his name, *The Feather Duster or, Is He Sincere?* (Roycrofters, 1912), Reedy notes that he has been pestered for eighteen years by people wanting to know what he thinks of Elbert Hubbard. His response is that he has "never met any one who had a particle of proof that the founder of the Roycroft Shop was not on the level with himself and others" (11). He describes East Aurora as a "sort of realized Erehwon [sic], a Yankee Tir an Og" (12). And as for his "disciples," the people who "follow Hubbard do not stay half-baked. They come out of it. He makes lovers of books out of people who never knew books before. His biographies of great men and women [*Little Journeys*], filtered through himself, are the beginnings of humanism for hundreds of thousands of people" (14).

As often happens in studies of Hubbard's contemporaries, Hubbard's existence is ignored or slighted. (Even those kindly disposed toward Hubbard occasionally reveal their ignorance regarding his life. For example, Jay Martin states in his *Harvests of Change: American Literature 1865-1914* that "as late as 1917, Elbert Hubbard . . . could title a book *The Romance of Business* [245]." Hubbard could do no so such thing, however, as he had died two years earlier.) Max Putzel, in his *The Man in the "Mirror": William Marion Reedy and His Magazine*, mentions Hubbard only three times. Henry F. May (*The End of American Innocence: A Study of the First Years of Our Time 1912-1917*) acknowledges that Hubbard was a close friend of Reedy, but dismisses him as a "weird combination of William Morris arts and crafts, 1890s aestheticism, progressive uplift, rags-to-riches inspiration, and village eccentricity" (32).

Attempts to slight the Reedy-Hubbard relationship notwithstanding, Reedy's friendship with Hubbard spanned nearly fifteen years, and there survive 39 pieces of correspondence from Reedy to Hubbard and his son, Elbert Hubbard II, at the Harry Ransom Humanities Research Center, The University of Texas at Austin. (The apparent animosity that appears in references to Reedy in the *Philistine* is bogus; the running feud that Reedy and Hubbard participated in was designed for publicity and entertainment.) In order to write Hubbard out of the picture, someone like Putzel needs, of course, to demean Hubbard. He takes exception (without providing supporting evidence), for example, to the inclusion of Hubbard by Frank Luther Mott (whose authority in these matters is extremely redoubtable) in a quadrumvirate of distinguished editors which includes Reedy, W. C. Brann [editor of the *Iconoclast*], and H. L. Mencken (preface, page x).

He also makes the unsupported (and unsupportable) claim that by 1900 the *Philistine* had lost "what little savor" it had ever had and with it much of its following (169). An inspection of *N. W. Ayer & Son's American Newspaper Annual* (1895 to 1915) reveals steady circulation figures (exceeding 100,000) until Hubbard's death, when the *Philistine* was discontinued. Moreover, Hubbard gained an even larger following in the last six years of his life as a result of the editorial columns he wrote for the Hearst syndicate's *New York American*. He was so increasingly popular, in fact, that starting in 1915, a few months before his death, his columns appeared daily. (The author has located 607 of these columns, from January 8, 1909, to May 15, 1915.) Balch reports that he earned $30,000 annually for these columns (268), though it would be more accurate to say that Hubbard was apparently being paid $100 per column, so that only if he had continued living would he have earned such a princely annual salary. (There is extensive correspondence to Hubbard from Morrill Goddard of the *New York American* at the Harry Ransom Humanities Research Center, The University of Texas at Austin.)

Reedy's first article in the *Philistine*, "Knocking and Knockers," appears in the June 1901 (13.1:1-5) number. Reedy's point is that the call of "our genial Fra Elbertus" to avoid knocking must not be carried to extremes, that one "must knock the Evil every time it puts up its head" (1). (The motto on the December 1906 [24.1] cover, for example, is,

"Opportunity knocks once at each man's door, but if you, yourself, happen to be knocking when she calls you 'll never hear her.") Moreover, he points out, Hubbard himself is a knocker, particularly against war and imperial expansion. Without knockers the world would not progress, and Reedy cites the "glorious knockers" against slavery, William Lloyd Garrison, Wendell Phillips, and Abraham Lincoln (2). In literature, Shelley, Wordsworth, Browning, and Poe were "knockers against the petrifying effect of formalism in poetry" (3). In short, whoever disparages the knocker "sets himself against progress," for the knocker is "necessary to prod us on" (3).

The second contribution, "Letters About Love," appears in May, 1904 (18.6:167-171). This is a denunciation of the publication of the Kempton-Wace letters, which are full of "rotten pseudo-science" regarding love: "When I find a man insisting that men shall be bred as cattle are bred, 'for points,' I am convinced that he has only a cattle-like apprehension of what love means" (169). Love does not have to be explained to be enjoyed, and for those readers who wish to find worthwhile literature on love Reedy recommends Shakespeare, Mrs. Browning, "Bobby Burns, with plenty of sex in it, too," the "'Letters of a Portuguese Nun,'" Wilfrid Scawen Blunt's "Love Sonnets of Proteus," and Ernest M'Gaffey's "Sonnets to a Wife" (170).

His third contribution (21.1:2-10) is a paean to the famous American actor Joseph Jefferson (1829-1905), evoked by seeing a recent performance of "Rip Van Winkle." Reedy acknowledges that while this play, "the only American play that has lived," has the charm of the Washington Irving tale in it, the play succeeds only because of Jefferson's personality (6). All of Jefferson's roles have the qualities of winsomeness and artlessness common to "Rip." Jefferson makes everyone feel better, less conceited, and more tolerant of others (9).

"'Frisco the Fallen" appeared in July, 1906 (23.2:55-64), three months after the earthquake and fire that devastated San Francisco. Reedy gives a sweeping account of the city's history and emphasizes its literary and intellectual importance. San Francisco was "a little of Paris, of Rome, of Florence, of Pekin" (61), and he recounts the accomplishments of Henry George, Edwin Markham, Gelett Burgess, Ambrose Bierce, Joaquin Miller, Robert Louis Stevenson, and William Randolph

Hearst. Reedy predicts that 'Frisco will again be a great city, and will "realize the dreams not only of those who have vowed their dreams shall not be defeated, but the unfulfilled ambition of those lovers of the city who went down in the ruin" (64).

The final piece by Reedy in the *Philistine* appears in the end pages of March, 1907. He denounces Captain Richmond P. Hobson for prophesying war with Japan over the denial of admission of Japanese children to the public schools of San Francisco. Though there is no occasion for war, too many "flibbertigibbits in Congress and out" are inclined to agree with Hobson. Although Hobson, in view of the insufficient Asiatic squadron and the unprotected Hawaiian Islands and the Philippines, argues for greater army and navy appropriations, Reedy counters that Japan is "extremely short" of money, and given America's "unlimited credit" the probability of war is scant.

Hobson's militarism was criticized by Hubbard as early as March, 1899 (8.4:103-104). Hubbard resented the self-serving manner in which Hobson (and Roosevelt) had tried to exploit his participation in the Spanish-American War, and Hubbard belittled his (and the nation's) accomplishment:

> Spain is an old, weak, little knock kneed country, and we deserve no special credit for pinching her ear. . . . [A] becoming modesty would have been in order for all who took part in the scrap. (103-104)

Hubbard devotes an essay to him and his dangerous desire to "sink two billion, five hundred million dollars in a navy" in the February 1904 (18.3:65-70) *Philistine.* Hobson, whose "business is death and destruction," must be stopped from attempting to "saddle upon the toilers of America the biggest and most costly implement of death this tired, blood-stained earth has ever seen" (65). Displaying great prescience a decade before World War I, Hubbard warns that if the Americans have a navy that "outclasses any one navy of Europe, there will be a combination of European Powers, and they will evolve a navy that will outclass ours" (67).

The final significant essayist in the *Philistine* to be discussed is Benjamin De Casseres (1873-1945), a newspaperman, poet and biographer. His books include *The Shadow-Eater* (1915), *Black Suns* (1936), and *Don Marquis* (1938). Hubbard must have been attracted to his radical individualism and flamboyance, although there is also some evidence that Hubbard felt sorry for him and bought some of his work out of charity. In an amusing letter to Alice Hubbard, De Casseres asks whether the "Big Boss" has got back from a tour yet, and touts his enclosed contribution as a sensation created for the "Fillstein." Finally coming to the point, he adds, "What's more important, I need $15. . . . Look under the mattress" (HRHRC, Box Misc. Uniden.-L, Folder C-E). Apparently De Casseres was habitually broke. In a letter to Hubbard dated 8 Jan. 1910, he describes his enclosed essay as looking "like a good twenty-five dollars' worth to me, and when one of my books gets published I shall dedicate it to you--sure." He closes with, "Meanwhile, let me hack this essay with you . . . for twenty-five bones. As Ever or Never" (HRHRC, Box Recip. Uniden.-J, Folder C-D).

There is also evidence that De Casseres served as a ghost writer for Hubbard, writing some of the essays in the *Philistine* anonymously. In a letter to the *Saturday Review* (16 Mar. 1940) regarding Frederick Lewis Allen's review of David Arnold Balch's biography of Hubbard, he claims that from 1903 to 1915 he wrote "essays, paragraphs and epigrams for Hubbard's *Philistine* and *Fra*." Additionally, of the 13 essays printed by Hubbard in the book called *Olympians*, ten were allegedly written by De Casseres, "to the last comma." He ends by saying that after negotiations with Elbert Hubbard II, his own work was reassigned to him, "as the Copyright Office in Washington will attest." He repeated this information in a letter to the *New York Times Book Review* (5 May 1940).

Additional evidence supporting the charge that Hubbard used the work of staff writers during his last years comes from an unpublished manuscript by Sadakichi Hartmann:

> His method of success was easy. Six or seven writers on his staff were assigned to the same detail, which, when finished, would be submitted to Fra Elbertus. He would combine the stories, select the best parts of each, and give the final gleaning his wonderful twist. I don't read Hubbard any more for I never know what is his, nor what originally belonged to me. (Hamilton, "Hartmann, Hubbard, and East Aurora," 4)

Unfortunately, it is not clear from this excerpt whether this process (assuming Hartmann's description is factual) was used only for advertising copy and for articles in the *Fra*, or whether it was also applied to material appearing in the *Philistine.*

Of the four contributions by De Casseres, the first three are lead articles and the last is the sole non-Hubbard piece in the September 1908 (27.4) issue. The first, "Ralph Waldo Emerson" (December, 1904; 20.1:1-10), is a glowing tribute to "The Viking of Concord" (6), one of Hubbard's individualist heroes. De Casseres groups Emerson with Socrates, Jesus, and Marcus Aurelius, calling him "an incorporate influence, a disembodied world-power" (10). The second, "Enter Walt Whitman" (November, 1907; 25.6:161-172), compares Whitman and Emerson: "In Emerson the heroic life found a tongue; in Whitman the heroic life found a body. Whitman was greater than Emerson or Nietzsche or Ibsen" (164). He was the "universal man, the law-giving anarch" (164), whose composition of *Leaves of Grass* was "one long majestic gesture, which translated a knowable universe into an unknowable fourth dimension that must forevermore claim our amaze" (172).

The third contribution by De Casseres, "Is New York Civilized?" (May, 1908; 26.6:161-166), is refreshingly amusing. Most of the essay is a scathing attack on the city "where Noise is a god and Ugliness is a creed," where people "live so fast . . . that they set fire to their clothes" (162). If civilization means "experiencing the best of everything" (165), then no city in the world "approaches New York in barbaric splendor," where each soul is "a mere measuring utensil" (164). His final sentence is, "In closing, let me say that I live in New York, but for the life of me I can't tell why" (166).

His most flamboyant essay is the last, "Hate Everlasting" (September, 1908; 27.4:115-119). The opening paragraph is arresting:

> Philosophic and poetical gentility have prated for thousands of years of the creative and transforming power of love. I wish to say something of the creative and transfiguring power of hate . . . (115).

De Casseres contends that universal love "would insure universal catalepsy," and that "the conditions of individuality" are repulsion, hatred and opposition (116). It is hate that creates, not love, and "Eternal insurrection, challenge, hatred and battle are the conditions of the survival of everything" (116). Hate is not only ethical, but "a barometer of mental and spiritual life" (118). Most importantly, all great literature is "rooted somewhere in an ideal hatred" (118), for the "revealer" is able to move the world because "the lever of intellectual perspective rests on the fulcrum of aversion" (119). Classifying Hubbard as a hater in good standing, he concludes,

> The "Prometheus" of Aeschylus, the "Timon" of Shakespeare, the "Zarathustra" of Nietzsche, the "Ghosts" of Ibsen--THE PHILISTINE Magazine--are the fruits of a sublime rage, a perfect frenzy of contempt, hatred and militant spite. (119)

Notes

[1] Ethelbert Nevin wrote (4 Jan. 1901) for Hubbard's permission to use "The Twilight Hour" in a musical setting (HRHRC, Box Recip. K-Z, Folder M-N). Gilman (1860-1935), great-granddaughter of the preacher and author Lyman Beecher, was a feminist, reformer, and writer, who edited the *Forerunner*.

[2] In addition to his frequent allusions to these two Canadians, Hubbard often alludes to Canada throughout the run of the *Philistine.* Extended treatments include a description of the Dukhobors and his suggestion that they be coerced to give up their clannishness and "mix with the outside world" (June, 1903; 17.1:4-14), an account of the prospering province of Manitoba (July, 1905; 21.2:51-63), and a description of train travel from Toronto to Vancouver, with a closing plea for Free Trade between the United States and Canada (December, 1910; 32.1:15ff.) President Taft wrote Hubbard (6 Feb. 1911) thanking him for his telegram approving a Canadian reciprocity agreement (HRHRC, Box Recip. K-Z, Folder S-T). Legislation enabling free trade between the two countries was finally drafted for United States congressional ratification in 1987.

[3] Julia Ditto Young prepared the invaluable "Index and Concordance" to the first twenty volumes of the *Philistine.* This extremely reliable work, which took Young six months to complete, was published by the Roycrofters in 1905, together with a list of all Roycroft publications to date. It can be found at the beginning of the microfilmed *Philistine* (#05422, APS III, Reels 589-590). The author has compiled a selective index for volumes 21 through 41 (see Appendix A).

[4] Hubbard printed two books by Ruskin, *Sesame and Lilies* (1897), and *King of the Golden River* (1900), and published "little journeys" to the homes of Ruskin and Turner (*Ruskin-Turner*) in 1896. The title of Hubbard's biography of John Brown, *Time and Chance* (1899), is undoubtedly indebted to Ruskin's *Time and Tide.*

[5] Hubbard reprinted Kipling's "The Last Chanty" (from the *Pall Mall Magazine* of June, 1893) in the December 1895 (2.1) issue of the *Philistine* as "The Dipsy Chanty" and as a book in 1898. By altering the title of this verse, he gave Kipling an opening for a legal suit. Kipling, as reported in a "Note" in

the *Literary Digest* (1 July 1899), although the verse was not protected by copyright, contended that Hubbard had no right to change the title, even though, as he admits, the expression "Dipsy Chanty" occurs in the verse. Even though Kipling must have acknowledged that Hubbard's revised title was as at least as good as the original, and despite the fact that the verse first appeared in a magazine in England, so that it was not copyrighted in the United States, Kipling apparently hoped to win his case on the technicality of Hubbard's unauthorized revision of the title. Hubbard was not Kipling's only target, however; as the "Note" concludes, "Mr. Kipling has twenty-three suits in process, against as many different publishers and booksellers throughout the United States" (12).

[6] R. W. Stallman, in his *Stephen Crane: A Critical Bibliography*, follows H. P. Taber in misspelling his name MacIntosh, and also accepts Taber's claim that "MacIntosh" was the actual writer of Hubbard's "A Message to Garcia" (299, 311). His name is spelled MackIntosh by Tom Daly, who presented Taber's side of the Roycroft rebellion in a column in the *Philadelphia Evening Ledger* a year after Hubbard's death. (See Chapter III for more details.)

[7] This is not the only parody of the *Rubaiyat* to appear in the *Philistine.* "Doggerel License No. 1672 A," modeled after tetrastich number seven, appears in the May 1903 (16.6) issue:

> So fill the Cup--for Life and Love are Young,
> Let R. E. Morse be in the Corner flung;
> The Bee of Time has but a little Sweet
> To gather,--and the Bee is on the Bung. (161)

(Morse would seem to be a clergyman or a temperance leader.) This effort is answered in the July (17.2) issue, together with evidence that Hubbard wrote these verses himself:

> A rogue in El Paso, Texas, by the name of
> Jessup, amends my beautiful Omar quatrain in the
> May PHILISTINE, like this:
> We drained the Cup when Life and Love were
> Young,
> And now our Conscience by R. E. Morse is Stung;
> The Bee of Time our little Sweet
> Has gathered, and we are in the Corner Flung. (64)

[8] A few years earlier George Santayana had contributed an

essay to the *Harvard Monthly* (May, 1892) titled "What Is a Philistine?" Then a junior member of Harvard's philosophy department, Santayana gives a humorous historical account of the Philistines, and recounts what Heinrich Heine and Matthew Arnold had written about modern Philistines. He argues that the Philistines' "one essential trait" is conventionality. Though no proof exists that Hubbard read this essay, his residence in Boston early in 1893 (as a student at the Emerson College of Oratory) and his enrollment at Harvard as a special student in the fall term of 1893 (he withdrew on December 11), lend considerable plausibility to this hypothesis, and it is intriguing to conjecture whether he got his inspiration for his magazine's title from Santayana's essay. (Hamilton's biography, *As Bees in Honey Drown*, provides the most complete record of Hubbard's trips to Boston, Hingham, and Concord, Massachusetts, trips made largely so that he could be with Alice Moore.)

[9] In his essay on Emerson's influence on Hubbard ("Elbert Hubbard, *The Philistine*, and the Legacy of Emerson"), Edward R. Stephenson considers Hubbard one of Emerson's disciples, one who shared Emerson's genius for coining epigrams.

Chapter V

Hubbard's Contributions

In addition to his approximately 90 signed essays (including those signed as "Fra Elbertus" and "The Pastor"), Hubbard's writings constitute the bulk of most of the *Philistine* numbers, usually appearing under the title "Heart to Heart Talks with Philistines by the Pastor of his Flock," or variants thereof. Everything interested Hubbard, and he had unbounded energy and curiosity. He read widely and quickly, memorized easily (if not always accurately), and apparently never suffered writer's block; he often wrote a month's copy on train trips between lecture engagements. In attempting to write about his writings in the *Philistine*, one is reminded of a line from Howard Nemerov's poem "Life Cycle of Common Man": "If you merely printed all his commas the result would be a very large volume." Much of what he wrote for the *Philistine* is topical and ephemeral, necessarily so for any successful periodical. But there is much of enduring interest, and in discussing his contributions in this chapter, it is appropriate to take note of the homily which has been read by more people than anything ever written by an American, to summarize his pioneering efforts in advertising, and to explore his influential, freethinking essays on the themes of religion and pacifism.

"A Message to Garcia"

The most famous piece ever to appear in the *Philistine* or in any other American publication was "A Message to Garcia." Based on an exploit in Cuba during the Spanish-American War, it made Hubbard internationally famous and doubled the magazine's circulation. The tale is based on a newspaper story about Lt. Andrew Summers Rowan (1857-1943), who was given a mission by the United States war department to contact the Cuban insurgents protesting Spanish rule. Rowan completed his mission against great odds and reported the results of his interview with General Calixto Garcia Iniguez to the U.S. government. It was printed in the March 1899 (8.4:109-116) issue as part of "Heart to Heart Talks with Grown-Ups by the Pastor of His Flock," and by 1913, Hubbard estimated, he had earned $250,000 from this slender story, and 40,000,000 copies had been printed (Beisner, 109). By 1938 Hubbard's son placed the total, world-wide reprint figure at 80,000,000 copies, and the Roycrofters were still printing 150,000 copies annually (Beisner, 109).

The focus of this homily is not the daring exploits of the young Rowan, but Rowan's reputation for competence, dependability, and self-initiative, qualities which many subordinates lack. When President McKinley gave the letter to Rowan and instructed him to deliver it to Garcia, Rowan accepted the letter and the mission without asking foolish questions. He did not, for example, waste McKinley's time by asking, "Where is he at?" and it is Rowan's ability to carry out a job with a minimum of supervision that so electrified Hubbard, who was the employer of hundreds of Roycrofters:

> By the Eternal! there is a man whose form should be cast in deathless bronze & the statue placed in every college of the land. It is not book-learning young men need, nor instruction about this or that, but a stiffening of the vertebra [sic] which will cause them to be loyal to a trust, to act promptly, concentrate their energies: do the thing--"Carry a message to Garcia!" (110)

Shortly after the story's appearance, George H. Daniels, the general passenger agent of the New York Central Railroad, ordered 100,000 reprints. The flabbergasted Hubbard, realizing that he could not accommodate an order of such magnitude, gave Daniels permission to reprint them on his own, and Daniels printed 2,000,000 copies (Beisner, 108). Orders for reprints by the millions came from churches, schools, businesses, armies, and governments. Wanamaker's department store in New York ordered 200,000 copies, and Macy's Jesse Straus gave a copy to each of his employees. Over two hundred newspapers and magazines reprinted the "Message," and two movies were made on Rowan's exploits (Beisner, 109). Every member of the U.S. Marine Corps and the Boy Scouts of America was given a copy. It was translated into nearly 20 foreign languages. Prince Hilakoff, Director of the Imperial Russian Railways, happened to be visiting the United States as a guest of the New York Central during the "carry the message to Garcia" mania; when he saw the essay he ordered it translated into Russian and distributed to every Russian railroad employee (Zanger, 100). The czar's officers carried the "Message" into battle against the Japanese in 1904, and when the Japanese found that their prisoners carried Hubbard's essay, they in turn had it translated and "outdid the Russians by giving copies to enlisted men as well" (Beisner, 109).

Vail's article on the "Message," subtitled "A Bibliographical Puzzle," presents a thorough history of its reprints. His studiousness is so exacting, however, that he does not recognize a "translation" from the Japanese, supposedly by Yone Kichikaschi, of the "Message" which appears in the December 1906 (24.1:i-vii, end pages) *Philistine* as the parody it is. Vail is, at least, amused by the "surprising and delightful metamorphoses" he discovers in the "translation" (75). Regular readers of the *Philistine* would have caught the silly play on the name of Yone Noguchi (done somewhat in the manner of Sid Caesar "speaking" Japanese), sometime protege of Joaquin Miller. (For information regarding their relationship see the author's "The Liberal Stances of Joaquin Miller," *Rendezvous,* 19, No. 1 [Fall 1983], 86-94.) This ludicrous name is undoubtedly inspired by the name of fellow Roycrofter Sadakichi Hartmann. (Moreover, "Kichikaschi" is identified as being from the University of Tokyo, where Noguchi taught following his return to Japan.) Because readers were aware of Noguchi's awkward English constructions in his verse, the supposed translation of the lively and slangy "Message" from Japanese to English prompted a highly entertaining exercise. A comparison of the first sentence and its "translation" follows:

> In all this Cuban business there is one man stands out on the horizon of my memory like Mars at perihelion.
>
> In all this Cuban commercial enterprise there is one honorable gentlemen [sic] stands out on the horizon of my memory like Mars at the time she is nearest earth.

Vail shows that the phrase "message to Garcia" remained a popular phrase for at least 30 years after its first appearance by citing a cartoon in the *New York Evening Post* of 11 Dec. 1929. Two men-about-town have the following exchange:

> What can you do on that old motorcycle, Sonny?
> Eighty-five.
> Could you take a message to Garcia?
> Where does the dame live?

It survives even to this day. The actor Harrison Ford haplessly conflates the ancient epigram about killing the bearer of bad tidings with Hubbard's phrase when he acknowledges that his failure to be more witty is not the fault of his interviewer: "No fault of the messenger to Garcia" (*Playboy* April 1988: 144).

The "Message" brought Hubbard not only fame but also his only honorary degree, from Tufts College (now University). At its forty-third commencement in May, 1899, Tufts presented him with a Master of Arts degree. The citation is as follows:

> Elbertus Hubbard, qui artificius operisque hominum novam dignatatem atque honorem dedit, in libris edendis alliisque rebus fabricandis excellens, dignus quiverus et antiqui artium magister appeletur.---ARTIUN MAGISTER

Professor Louis Townsley, of Gallaudet University, translates this as follows:

> Elbert Hubbard, who gave new worth and honor to man's arts and literary works, (who was) distinguished in publishing books and in making various things, who is truly worthy of being called a master of arts in the ancient way--ARTIUM MAGISTER.

Tufts University's historian and archivist, Russell E. Miller, states that Hubbard was probably at the conferral, and that there is no record that he made any remarks at the time or made any financial contribution to Tufts (letter to the author, 2 Aug. 1985).

Hubbard was not overwhelmed by this recognition from Tufts; his granddaughter Mary Roelofs Stott wrote that he "apparently" enjoyed the ceremony (22), but as Hubbard remarked in his autobiographical sketch for *Cosmopolitan* (January 1902), "since I did not earn the degree, it really does not count" (317). (Stott adds that receiving the honorary degree eased his "rankling" over his expulsion from Harvard, and when his daughter Miriam went to the University of Michigan, he was "very proud" of her [22].) Ever the protester, some years later he takes to task an issue of the Alumni Society's "Bulletin," which he sarcastically expects to contain something about academics instead of news about smokers and football, and he belittles the supposed liberality of the denominational (Universalist-Unitarian) college (June, 1911; 33.1:11-15). (It is surprising he does not mention that the circus impresario Phineas T. Barnum donated the stuffed elephant Jumbo to a campus science building, providing the unhappy name "Jumbos" for the football team. Hubbard's corpulent personal secretary was nicknamed "Jumbo.") In the same vein, he also protests a food strike at Syracuse University led by a student who was there just to enjoy college life (June, 1912; 35.1:27- 28).

Though he may not have made any financial contributions to Tufts or any other well-endowed colleges, he did make donations to the Tuskegee Institute. In a letter dated 13 Nov. 1913, Booker T. Washington thanks him for a donation made the previous year and hopes he can "send something now" (HRHRC, Box Recip. K-Z, Folder U-W). Hubbard had published "A Little Journey to Tuskegee" in the July 1904 (19.2:41-60) issue of the *Philistine,* which contained glowing accolades for the accomplishments of the Tuskegee Institute and its founder. "A Message to Garcia" was printed in the Tuskegee student newspaper, and Washington had sent copies of it to George H. Daniels, of the New York Central Railroad.

Freeman Champney calls the "Message" a "showpiece" of the "onward and upward literature" of the turn of the century (89; quoted in Zanger, 99), and R. W. G. Vail describes the "Message" as the "gospel of the new order of things" (71).

Jules Zanger argues, however, that to consider it only in this light, as do also Henry Steele Commager and James Hart, is to misunderstand the essay; he maintains that the "Message," which was probably the most widely disseminated piece of writing in the history of American printing (with the exception of the Bible), is a "significant and revealing document in American social and cultural history and especially in the history of class relations" (99).[1] The thrust of Zanger's argument is that this message, which he says must be read in light of the climate created by the Pullman strike of 1894, was written not as a "morale-building document" preaching the possibilities provided by the American economic system to diligent workers, but rather as an "ultimatum, threatening violent reprisal for any further disaffection from that system" (102).

Such an interpretation of the "Message" is understandable, but Zanger is confusing Hubbard with robber barons. In the "Message" Hubbard is simply venting his spleen over the perennial problem of hiring good help. When he proposes a hypothetical task of asking a clerk to prepare a memorandum covering the life of Correggio (one of the subjects of Hubbard's *Little Journeys*), he presents an amusing list of ten exasperating questions to be expected from the unsatisfactory employee, including "Who was he?" and "What do you want to know for?" (111-12) Hubbard's exasperated attitude toward slack employees stems not so much from an attempt to produce propaganda for the managerial class as from personal experience, from directing (through his wife's supervision while he was away on frequent speaking tours) a conglomerate of up to 500 employees at his community of Roycrofters in East Aurora. As always happens with the establishment of such communities, the Roycrofters attracted their share of malcontents, misfits and moochers, and Hubbard occasionally had to resort to a figurative kick with "a thick-soled No. 9 boot" (114). He complains, if with exaggeration,

> Nothing is said about the employer who grows old before his time in a vain attempt to get frowsy ne'er-do-well's to do intelligent work; and his long patient striving with "help" that does nothing but loaf when his back is turned. (113)

Having been both an employee and an employer, he knows

"there is something to be said on both sides"; moreover, all employers are not "rapacious and high-handed, any more than all poor men are virtuous" (115). It is less in anger than in sorrow that Hubbard decries "incapacity for independent action" among employees, for it is this incapacity and other failings which "put pure Socialism so far into the future" (112). His "heart goes out" to the man who works diligently whether the "boss" is present or not, and that is why he declares that civilization is "one long anxious search" for those who can quietly and efficiently "carry a message to Garcia" (116).

Hubbard as Advertising Pioneer

Hubbard's flair for advertising in the *Philistine* begins, quite literally, with the turn of the century. With the January 1900 (10.2) issue he initiates fifteen successful years of brilliant advertising copy in his magazine. The front pages contain an ad for Heinz and more examples of Hubbard's distinctive humor used in ads for *Philistine* subscribers. For example, in one of these ads an offer for a combined subscription to both the magazine and the *Little Journeys* for one dollar is pronounced to be "a Missionary Move, and in the interests of the Higher Criticism." It is in the back pages of this issue, however, that he begins his advertising innovations in earnest. Facing the last page of text (64) is a well-disguised, full-page ad for Postum Cereal Coffee. In large type at the top of the page, printed in red, is this arresting "grabber": "A message to ye who monger words & break down gray matter," surely a unique lead for copy advertising coffee, or anything else, for that matter. But only in the third paragraph of the text does the name of the product appear.

Next appears an ad in which Hubbard, anticipating the ire of his *Philistine* subscribers who had previously paid one dollar for "only" a subscription to the magazine, urges all Life Members of the American Academy of Immortals to please

> keep perfectly cool on reading the offer . . . You are slated to receive the *Little Journeys* without charge, as they are a part of the perquisites to which your station

> entitles you.

In other words, his subscribers would now get twelve issues of the magazine and twelve issues of the biographies, twenty-four booklets, for the grand total of one dollar, which works out to less than five cents a copy. The biographies carried less advertising, and were costlier to produce, so it is plain that the revenues from the ads in the *Philistine* were of critical importance.

And yet, on the page facing this subscription deal of the century is a facetious half-page ad. Hubbard would never eliminate the use of an occasional humorous advertisement, probably realizing that the revenues lost thereby were more than recouped by his readers' careful reading and enjoyment of the advertising pages, and, hence, by the rates he could then justifiably command from advertisers. He also would never compromise the integrity of the back cover, regardless of the price he could have commanded for advertising there. An inspection of other popular magazines of the time reveals the singularity and wisdom of this practice: the *Philistine* always retained a more "literary" or distinguished appearance.

The bogus ad in question is for "Ball Bearing Bluffs," which come in

> fifty-seven varieties, in sizes suitable for either ladies or gentlemen. These bluffs are all mounted on our patent noiseless castors, and can be operated effectively, even by a novice. Do not forget that the value of a bluff depends upon getting it into line quickly. For catalog, address
>
> JENKINSON, STOGIE & CO.,
> East Aurora, N. Y.

This ad not only subtly doubles the impact of the Heinz ad which appears in the opening pages (by its allusion to the "fifty-seven varieties"), but gives the readers a chuckle and impetus to pore over the remaining ads. Hubbard clearly knows what he is doing.

Hubbard has been called the "father" of modern advertising (Bragdon, 477), and is credited with being the first (approximately 1910) to produce signed essay advertisements, an art which he carried to perfection. As Walter Davenport and James C. Derieux note in their entertaining *Ladies, Gentlemen and Editors* (1960), Hubbard was "years ahead of Madison

Avenue's fly-casting ad writers in the southpaw approach to the reader's attention--the association of ideas pitch" (133). To Hubbard, advertising was simply literature with a purpose (Bigelow, *Elbert Hubbard: Pioneer Advertising Man*, 12).

Hubbard truly believed this, and he considered advertising an extremely creative and responsible endeavor which could have at least as much influence on ushering in material and cultural progress as reformers, preachers, and politicians. It is this attitude, and not a base appeal to profits, as alleged by Hubbard's harshest critics, which can explain how Hubbard could host summer conventions at East Aurora of both socialists and advertisers. In an appeal (June, 1909; 29.1:fap) to "summer advertisers" for the *Fra,* which will be the "Magazine on the Spot" at East Aurora, Hubbard announces that there will be five conventions of the "Intellectually Elect" during the summer of 1909, and invites "High-Grade" advertisements from those wishing to appeal to these conventioneers with "Class." The five conventions are as follows: Convention of Advertisers, June 1-6; Socialistic Convention, June 20-30; Roycroft Convention, July 1-10; Free Thought Convention, August 1-10; and, Woman Suffrage Convention, August 20-30.

One example of his "associated idea" advertisements, chosen at random, will suffice. In the end pages of the November 1906 (23.6:i-vii) issue of the *Philistine* is a lengthy advertisement for Macy's, but the reader does not learn what is being advertised until the fourth page. This is the opening sentence: "George Washington did his shopping by mail." Intrigued, and not knowing for sure if he is reading a supplemental essay or an advertisement, the reader learns that Washington ordered his clothing and household supplies from London because London was then the world's financial metropolis and the center of fashion. Times have changed, however, and now New York City is the home of fashion, and since the merchants of the country do their buying in New York, "why should not the housekeepers?" (i) Hubbard then continues for the next two pages discussing the importance of trust in the merchandiser, the evils of buying on credit, and the need for women to control their own finances. Finally, on the fourth page, Hubbard invites those readers who do not live in New York City to order from Macy's, promising them, "YOU CAN HAVE YOUR MONEYBACK [sic] WITHOUT QUIBBLE OR

QUESTION" (iv). The remainder of the advertisement expounds on the virtues of R. H. Macy & Co. Hubbard has entertained and edified his readers, campaigned for more fiscal autonomy for women shoppers, and done a masterful job of encouraging them to use the mails to do business with Macy's. Such an advertisement, though quaint in its leisurely progression, is a refreshing change from most modern print advertisements, which rely largely on provocative art work to arrest and sustain the reader's attention for, at most, a few seconds.

Hubbard's superb ad copy also boosted readership of the *Philistine,* and enabled him to command lucrative advertising rates.[2] At the end of 1900, for example, appears a notice to advertisers from the bursar of East Aurora, announcing that the circulation of the *Philistine* is now 92,000, and that of the *Little Journeys* is 36,000, with a steady, monthly increase of several thousand for the former and five hundred for the latter (12.1). Then come the pertinent details of cost:

> The price for advertising space now in either periodical is ninety dollars a page, net. Half page and quarter page at same rate. No discount on time contracts. All matter is prepared and arranged by our own Tachydidaxical Expert--a man who thinks he understands.

He did indeed. At a rate of $22.50 for a quarter page ad in the *Philistine,* for example, with its circulation of 92,000, an advertiser could be assured that his product would be favorably noticed at a cost of less than three-hundredths of a cent ($0.0002445) per subscriber. At the same time, even if only ten of the sixteen front and back pages were given over to paying ads, Hubbard was taking in $900, plus subscription revenues of at least $3,680 (92,000 X $0.04), for a monthly income from the *Philistine* of $4,580, or $54,960 for the year 1901. A year and a half later (May, 1902; 14.6:fap), the advertisement rate for the *Philistine* increases to $100 per page (for a circulation of 110,000). Circulation figures and advertising fees continued to increase, making the *Philistine* the most successful of all the "little magazines."

Hubbard and Religion

In "Why I Am a Philistine," one of his first signed essays in the magazine (February, 1896; 2.3:74-86), Hubbard uses a letter received from a "Retired Clergyman" as a springboard for launching into an attack (tempered by his predilection for humor) on the "Chosen People" and a defense of his assuming the appellation of "Philistine."[3] Usually, Hubbard begins, he does not respond (in his magazine) to the anonymous epistles he receives from the "Great Obscure," with "life being short and the waste basket wide" (74). However, in gratitude for this gentleman's having retired, thus making the world "his debtor," he will make an exception.

Hubbard states that the gist of this retired clergyman's "scholarly argument" is that

> The Society of the Philistines is endeavoring to make free-thought universal and paganism popular. He stoutly avers that the ancient Philistines were the enemies of Jehovah, that they worshipped strange gods and that they were the sworn foes of the Chosen People. (74)

The clergyman adds that the only reason he has read the *Philistine* is that his daughter, an "unmarried lady of thirty-two," had purchased (no doubt surreptitiously) several copies. A most amusing anecdote regarding the *Philistine* as "forbidden fruit" was told to Freeman Champney by a friend who grew up in a small Pennsylvania town. Unable to obtain copies in town, he had to travel to the county seat, where a fruit-stand man "smuggled in a supply of each issue beneath a bunch of bananas, and did a brisk undercover business while they lasted" (82). The friend's mother burned as many of these copies as she was able to find.

After commiserating over the plight of the clergyman's daughter, Hubbard begins his attack. He praises the ancient Philistines as being the strongest, most intelligent and most virtuous of any of the neighboring tribes; it is, in fact, because of their superior qualities that the country of Palestine received its name (75-76). In contrast, the ignoble "mob" of Israelites, claiming to be the "Chosen People," "stampeded the herds of the Philistines, scattered their flocks, [and] destroyed their gardens" (79). Only after they were unable to defeat the outnumbered Philistines did they settle down and, "following the good example of the Philistines made themselves homes" (79). Hubbard asserts that the "sterling qualities in the Jew are derived from his Philistine ancestry," noting that Solomon, David, and Jesus were descended from Philistines (80). Even waiving the matter of the "maternal transmission of excellence," he rests his case on the fact that Solomon married over four hundred Philistine women; quoting Sir Walter Besant, "a newly married woman always tells her husband everything she knows," Hubbard concludes that Solomon's "transcendent wisdom was derived from Philistine sources" (81). For corroboration of his apologia for the Philistines, he directs his readers to the Second Book of Samuel, a book, he notes with a characteristic ironic twist (undoubtedly with the "Retired Clergyman" and his ilk in mind), which "no respectable girl should allow her mother to read." Another book of the Bible falling into the same category is the Song of Solomon, and it is significant that the first and second productions of the Roycroft press (both in 1896) were the paganish, poetic, and philosophical books of the Bible, *The Song of Songs* and *The Journal of Koholeth: Being a Reprint of the Book of Ecclesiastes*.

Turning to a discussion of one the most illustrious of the "Chosen People," Hubbard alludes to a few of the more reprehensible deeds committed by David, "a literary man of acknowledged merit," and calls him "an all 'round rogue":

> With forty-one distinct crimes to David's charge, the killing of nine hundred thousand men and two hundred thousand women and children, the houghing [sic] of thousands of horses, all of which is set down in infallible Holy Writ, his record is very bluggy [sic]. In fact, his whole life's pathway is streaked with infamy. (83)

In contradistinction to David's Jehovah, who, if half of what "His Chosen People" say about him is true, "surely wasn't very nice," the pagan god Dagon was "eminently respectable," and Hubbard cannot find "a single stain on his record" (83). Thus, his sympathies are with the Philistines (84). In literature the modern Philistine seeks to express his personality in his own way and brooks no "hindrance from the tipstaffs of letters" (85).

Although some biographers try to play down Hubbard's

extreme strictures regarding religious beliefs and practices, the sentiments he expressed in the essay "Why I Am a Philistine" are only a tame preview of those expressed in essays to come, and a close reading of the *Philistine* reveals that Hubbard was a courageous freethinker. Champney accepts the assessment of Mary Hubbard Heath, Hubbard's sister, that Hubbard's life was a "search to find God," and then repeats this dissemblance born of sisterly benevolence at least twice (114, 115, 143). Familial attempts to downplay Hubbard's irreligion resurfaced in 1975 in a biographical sketch (*Elbert Hubbard, Rebel with Reverence*) by another family member, this time his granddaughter, Mary Roelofs Stott.

Heath recalls in her biography (*The Elbert Hubbard I Knew*) that the church was "the center" of their social life when they were growing up, and that Hubbard (who owed his given names "Elbert" and "Green" to two Baptist ministers) acted for a short time as a vestryman in the Episcopal Church of East Aurora (where he had moved his family in 1884) (130, 132); she admits, however, that "some fundamental honesty in his nature made him resist conversion . . . and he respectfully refused salvation" (130). Heath also recounts parodies of sermons that the young Hubbard wrote for the amusement of his sisters. One appeared in the *Buffalo Sunday Morning Times* (no date given, but probably 1881), and takes as its text a nursery rhyme:

> The Greek expression "Hi diddle diddle" has been the cause of much disputation. . . . The Evangelical Alliance spent four days discussing the expression, and came to the conclusion (and I sustain them in it) that it is synonymous with the classic expression "I should relax my countenance" or more probably "Oh, tickle me with a straw" (with a glass at one end). (170-171)

Another, brilliantly done, appeared in the *Morris* [Illinois] *Herald* in 1881, taking as its inspired text the story of Jack and Jill:

> [M]y beloved hearers, what did Jack and Jill do? "*They went.*" Listen while I read it again, and dwell on the precious words, and roll them as a sweet morsel upon my tongue. "Jack and Jill went." . . . [N]o dalliance, no wavering, no procrastination, no hesitation, but firm determination, perfect faith! . . . What did they go for?

> A pitcher of beer? *No.* A flask of Jersey Lightning? *No.* What then? "A pail of water." Glorious temperance lesson! (167-168)

But whereas Heath would treat these parodies as youthful plays of the imagination, they in fact reveal Hubbard's antipathy toward organized religion, an attitude that would strengthen over the course of his life.

In the February 1901 (12.3) number Hubbard explains how a statement made in a recent *Philistine* has "kicked up a cloud of dust, and added generously to my list of cancellations" (90). What he had said was that "the best men are never found in churches" (90). Denigrating the Protestant churches of the United States as "social centers," which should not be classed as religious institutions at all, he cites as examples to support his point the following: Benjamin Franklin, Leo Tolstoy, Max Muller, John Burroughs, Prince Kropotkin, George Eliot, Thoreau, Walt Whitman, Lincoln, Emerson, Ruskin, William Morris, and Carlyle (91).

Earlier (February, 1899; 8.3:78) he had admitted archly that,

> Under right conditions church-going is to be commended. You must be very careful, however, and either visit the church during weekdays or at such other hours when the preacher is not there, or else attend only such houses of Worship where the clergyman is warranted dekel[sic]-edge and free from wood filler.

And a striking testament to the force of his appeal and his anticlerical reputation is contained in a letter (13 Jan. 1910) to Hubbard from Earl Grey, Governor General of Ottawa. He informs Hubbard that he is looking forward to meeting him in Ottawa in February, but that it would be "impossible for me as Governour General to associate myself with you publicly without running the risk of seriously offending the churches who regard you as worse, if possible, than the Devil himself" (HRHRC, Box Recip. Uniden.-J, Folder E-G).

Bouts of cancellations were to be expected from respectable readers when Hubbard often said outrageous things and said them so well. But, as he remarks philosophically, for every person who cancels ten subscribe, and while the *Philistine* is constantly "preaching people out thru one door, there is another door thru which others are constantly coming in" (November, 1901; 13.6:186).[4] He does not expect his readers to approve of everything he writes; he may think differently the next day, and wants the privilege of contradicting his words as often as he chooses. His main concern is that his magazine should make his readers think for themselves (186).

Because of his low opinion of institutionalized religion, it is not surprising that he frequently calls for the taxation of church property. For several years (1907 to 1911) Hubbard conducted a campaign in the pages of the *Philistine* for the taxation of church (and college) property, asserting that the amount of untaxed church property in the United States amounted to $5,000,000 (January, 1911; 32.2:55). He argued that "the churches will never do the good they are capable of doing until they throw off mendicancy," and that "the Church must meet her responsibilities, and not shift her burden of taxes upon the people who do not believe her creed" (October, 1910; 31.5:143). (This issue contains his longest essay in the *Philistine* on this topic, pages 130 through 143.) This is an astonishingly radical venture for a publication of its circulation and readership. Other than in a periodical for atheists, it is difficult to imagine today any publication with a circulation in excess of 100,000 printing even one article to this effect, let alone attempting such a reform. Those critics who charge that Hubbard was interested only in making a profit from his publications must admit that this quixotic quest could result only in additional cancellations and lost advertising revenue.

As for Hubbard's personal religious stance, he was not so much an atheist as an agnostic. (One of his "dictionary" epigrams is, "An atheist is a person who does not believe in himself," and Hubbard certainly had faith in himself.) In an advertisement (July, 1914; 39.2:bap) for the tenth annual summer convention of free thinkers, he seems to espouse a belief in monism, but eighteen years earlier, in an essay prefacing the Roycroft publication of the Book of Ecclesiastes (*The Journal of Koheleth*, 1896), he espouses agnosticism. This book is the first that Hubbard published himself (the publication of *The Song of Songs* had been directed by H. P. Taber), and his essay is extremely subjective and sympathetic to the philosophic tenor of Ecclesiastes. An indication of the importance this book held for him is its acknowledgment to Dr. Frederic W. Sanders, of Columbia University, for his assistance. Given Hubbard's antipathy toward professors, it is clear that he very much wanted to reprint Ecclesiastes, even if it meant accepting academic guidance for his preface. This is how he summarizes Koheleth's thought:

> We are unable to fully reconcile the events of life with any satisfactory theory of the government of the Universe. Let us be frank: For all we know this life is the sum of existence for us; there is no proof of a future life. . . . It is better to be absolutely honest and admit that we do not know. Speak today what you think is true and contradict it all tomorrow if necessary. (xxxvii)

This spirit of agnosticism reappears in many of his essays and epigrams for the rest of his life.

His arguments for fair taxation appear in seven issues. In the first, October, 1907 (25.5), he reports optimistically that seven state legislatures are considering measures to require all churches to pay taxes on their property (146). (In May, 1908 [26.6:186], he states that Illinois, Iowa, Wisconsin, Ohio and seven other states "are falling into line, but are being held up temporarily by our religious friends, who insist that people who do not believe in a certain type of religion should yet be taxed to support it.") What pleases him even more, undoubtedly, is that the commonwealth of Massachusetts ("think of this, in Massachusetts, mind you") was considering the taxation of college property (146). He deems the arguments against taxation put forth by churches and colleges unconvincing. Churches claim sacred exemption, but it is only the superstition that certain things are secular, and others sacred, that gives excuse to that "peculiar form of graft by which church property evades taxation" (153). (He elaborates on this idea in the March 1908 [26.4] issue, saying that it is a fallacy that "some lines of human endeavor are higher, nobler, holier than others" [120]. He also reports approvingly of a Judge Vaughn of Illinois, who ruled that parsonages should not be exempt from taxation [121].) Harvard's President Charles William Eliot put forth the "specious plea" that the traditions of New England should not be "violated," and that colleges "increased the valuation of property in their vicinity, and therefore absolutely added to the wealth of the community" (147). The same is true, retorts Hubbard, of factories, hotels, opera houses, and railroads. Moreover, the good that colleges do is conjectural; in some respects colleges may even do harm (148). Churches and colleges should "get into line and obey the great law of Equality which declares that in human service there is no high nor low degree" (148). (It is puzzling that Hubbard does not also use as an argument the U.S. Constitution principle of the separation of church and state.)

Hubbard's writings on taxation were influential. In the May 1908 (26.6) issue he tells his readers that a few days earlier he had the pleasure of hearing himself quoted in a United States Court on the subject of the right to tax church property (184). The church representatives were trying to argue that "all property vested in the name of a 'religious corporation' or that contributed to the support of a church, was church property" (185), and hence exempt from taxation. (As an example of egregious abuse of "religious corporation" tax exemptions, the December 1908 [28.1] issue reprints an advertisement from Baker University [Baldwin City, Kansas] announcing that its annuity bonds "afford an ideal opportunity for those who wish to give their property to the Church, but who wish the income from it for life" [27]. Hubbard sneers that "smuggling, riding on railroad trains without paying fare, and evasion of taxes may all be properly called Christian Virtues since many good Christians, unrebuked, openly practice them" [25].) In rebuttal, Hubbard was quoted as saying that "all property was constructively religious property," for enlightened people agree that "any business which does not contribute to the welfare and happiness of the community is immoral" (185). The judge's response was, "The Fra is not, I believe, the highest authority on ethics, but in this instance, he certainly is right" (185-186). Hubbard is pleased to announce that it is now the law in Illinois that church property is defined as only the real estate upon which a church edifice is situated, with ten feet leeway, and no more, on each side (186). His pleasure is not unalloyed, however, as he reports that the University of Chicago not only pays no taxes, but refuses to pay water rates (186). He closes with the cry, "Tax all College and Church Property!" (187).

He posed enough of a threat to clergymen throughout the United States to be frequently denounced. The Rev. M. E. W. Allmond, of the St. James Methodist Episcopalian Church in Chicago, in explaining his refusal to participate in public debates with Hubbard on the topics of Christianity and the Church, quoted from a solemn periodical called the *Inter Ocean*:

> [P]eople were advised against reading The Philistine because its atmosphere was wholly poisonous to Christian

> minds in view of the fact that the writer in that sheet is not only opposed to Christianity but talks of all sacred things in such a way as to render many of his observations wholly blasphemous. . . . It was held that in order to be a pastor of a flock as was the pose of this sheet there should be a fine spiritual insight and lofty motive, neither of which could be deduced from the journal in question. (HRHRC, Box Recip. Uniden.-J, Folder Uniden.-A)

The public debates mentioned above were one of the highlights of the lecture circuits in 1908, and took place in such places as Chickering Hall (Boston) and Carnegie Hall between Hubbard and the Reverend Dr. Charles C. Albertson, of the Rochester Central Church. Albertson wrote Hubbard on 3 August, "You suggested a series of joint-debates last winter, on the question, Is the Church Deteriorating? Have you matured your plans for *next* season? . . . Why not issue a formal challenge in *The Phil* for Sept?" (HRHRC, Box Recip. Uniden.-J, Folder Uniden.-A) Hubbard must have responded quickly, for on 8 August Albertson suggests changing the question to, "Is Christianity Declining?" (The full debate between them was printed in the January 1909 issue of Hubbard's *Fra* magazine.)

As another indication of the force of Hubbard's threat to clergymen, on November 24, 1901, the Rev. Dr. Richard Orme Flynn, pastor of the prosperous North Avenue Presbyterian Church in Atlanta, Georgia, warned his congregation against attending Hubbard's lecture the following night at the Grand Opera House. Hubbard quotes from his sermon, as printed in the next day's *Atlanta Journal*:

> Tomorrow night there will lecture in this city a man who is commanding much attention throughout the world. This man is a graceful speaker, a polished writer, and is possessed of a keen and forceful intellect. . . .
>
> But I do find on reading his publications that he has reviled our Presbyterian faith, that he has held religion up to ridicule, and that he has scorned all that we hold true and sacred. Yet this has all been done so deftly, and with such exquisite diction, that many have been led astray by the subtleties of the PHILISTINE Magazine, and the speech of its editor; especially have women, and the youth of both sexes, been inoculated with error through

> this man's oratory and writings. (February, 1902; 14.3:67)

The pastor's call for a boycott of his lecture only succeeded in publicizing it, predictably, and all 1500 tickets were sold. As Hubbard conjectures, "probably three-fourths of the people in the congregation had never heard of Fra Elbertus; and most of them, of course, immediately resolved to go to the lecture and see how bad the man was" (69). As another instance of the animosity Hubbard engendered among many clergymen, Champney gives the following excerpt from a clergyman's address to a YMCA meeting:

> When some of these little, narrow-minded, East Aurora type of vaudeville artists try to tell you that the Bible amounts to nothing and that Christ was the illegitimate child of a peasant girl, you'd better take their "Little Journeys" and chuck them into Hell through the sewer and put such men down as unprincipled asses. (82)

Not all clergymen, however, damned Hubbard and his magazine. The most famous of the exceptions is the Rev. Edward Everett Hale, pastor of the South Congregational Church in Boston, and author of *The Man Without a Country*. While a special student at Harvard, Hubbard went at least once to hear him preach, on October 1, 1893 (Hamilton, *As Bees*, 75), and several letters from Hale to Hubbard are extant (HRHRC, Box Recip. Uniden.-J, Folder H-J). In one (31 Jan. 1894) Hale observes that though some readers may not like Hubbard's theology, that is their fault and not Hubbard's. A Life Member of the Society of Philistines, he assures Hubbard that he "always enjoys the Phil" (2 Mar. 1900). In an amusing aside on the burgeoning number of American periodicals, he observes that in "this century every man thinks he has to have his own magazine." In the previous century Hale himself had published his own magazine, *Old and New* (1870-1875), before it was absorbed by *Scribner's*.

One of the indications of how "bad" a freethinker was at the beginning of the century is his or her views regarding Robert Green Ingersoll, "the Great Agnostic." Hubbard shared much more than his middle name with this fellow "graduate of the University of Hard Knocks" (November, 1904; 19.6:189), the most famous American orator. While Hubbard was still a youth selling soap, he attended a lecture by Ingersoll, who became "one of his first heroes" (Champney, 27). Their relationship can be documented from as early as 1892, and Ingersoll receives frequent, adulatory mention in the *Philistine.* For example, there are two biographical essays on him by the feminist Marilla M. Ricker, the first woman lawyer admitted to practice before the United States Supreme Court, one appearing in the August 1908 number (27.3:66-80), and the second (which was reprinted under an amplified title in the *Truth Seeker*, 20 Feb. 1909, pp. 113-114) discussing Ingersoll as a politician (February, 1909; 28.3:65-78). There is also a long and mordant account by Hubbard of Ricker's futile efforts to present the complete works of Ingersoll to the East Aurora Library (October, 1908; 27.5:129-150); the decision of the town fathers of East Aurora to decline the gift was soon repeated by the trustees of Syracuse University, who refused a set of Ingersoll's works from the *Truth Seeker*, fearing that such material was unsuitable for young minds (24 Apr. 1909, 258-259).

Hubbard, whose "Little Journey" sketch of Ingersoll (August, 1903; vol. 13, no. 2) has been cited by at least one Ingersoll biographer (Cramer, 146, 280), apparently was the initiator of their relationship, sending Ingersoll a section of a novel (*The Man*) written with his future second wife, Alice Moore, and published as a paperback under the pseudonym "Aspasia Hobbs" (i.e., Alice *H*ubbard) in 1891 by J. S. Ogilvie Co. This was Hubbard's only literary work written before he left the Larkin Co., and years later he would destroy the copies he had (Hamilton, *Roycroft Collectibles*, 11-12). It would appear that any praise for the book, such as that he had received from Ingersoll, did not outweigh his dissatisfaction with this early effort. Writing from New York on 8 Apr. 1892, Ingersoll noted that he was "much struck with the beginning of Chapter 15, page 87, in what you say about Shakespeare's education" (Wakefield, 369), referring to Shakespeare's lack of advanced formal education. He continues:

> Of course I was greatly interested in all that you have said with regard to the woman in the case. . . . I think every man of genius has a feminine mind, and every woman of genius has a masculine mind.
>
> I would like to read your whole book. . . . I will try to give my opinion on it.
>
> Thanking you, I remain . . . (370)

One wonders whether this praise about what was said about the woman properly belonged to Hubbard or to Alice Moore (Hamilton, *As Bees*, 32). Whether Hubbard sent a copy of the entire book is unknown, but he did send a copy of *One Day*, for Ingersoll expressed his thanks for its receipt (Thorne, 20).

We also know that Hubbard was a frequent guest at Ingersoll's Sunday evening receptions at his 400 Fifth Avenue residence. Orvin Larson states in his biography, *American Infidel*, that among the freethinkers who attended were Charles Watts, Samuel Putnam, J. P. Mendum, George Macdonald (editor of the *Truth Seeker*) and John Lovejoy Elliott, and among the writers were Elbert Hubbard, Horace Traubel, Edgar Fawcett and Ella Wheeler Wilcox (Larson, 230). These gatherings must have been most entertaining, for Larson adds that the luminaries from the fields of music and theater outnumbered those from other callings (230). Undoubtedly it was at these Sunday evening soirees that Hubbard absorbed freethinking ideas and received encouragement to travel the vaudeville circuit as a lecturer in the 1909-1910 season.

Ingersoll, who would challenge God to strike him dead on the lecture platform in rebuttal (Champney, 27), was famous for his inflammatory comments regarding religious "superstition," coining such aphorisms as these: "Many people think they have religion when they are merely troubled with dyspepsia"; "With soap, baptism is a good thing"; and "An honest God is the noblest work of man." He never wrote for the *Philistine,* being close to his death when Hubbard was just starting to make a name for himself, but Hubbard did reprint his "Crimes against Criminals" in February, 1903 (16.3:76-86); given in 1890 before the New York State Bar Association at Albany, this speech is described by Hubbard as one of the most eloquent addresses ever given by Ingersoll. Additionally, the back cover of the May, 1901 (12.6) issue bears this Ingersoll aphorism: "The dead carry in their clenched hands only that which they have given away." Hubbard also praised Ingersoll's famous lecture "The Gods," given in 1872 at Cooper Union, New York City, as the "shot heard 'round the world. It was the boldest, strongest, and most vivid utterance of the century" (July, 1901; 13.2:48).

Another indication of Hubbard's stature among American radicals is his being mentioned in George E. Macdonald's autobiography, *Fifty Years of Freethought*, published in 1931. In writing about "Comstockery," which was the repressive campaign and legislation spearheaded by Anthony Comstock against matter which he considered obscene, Macdonald reports that in 1913 Hubbard had appeared before the federal district court in Buffalo and, though innocent, pleaded guilty to circulating through the mails "certain prints of an obscene character," as it was "more economical to pay a fine of $100 than to put up a fight for free mails" (409). Hubbard had alluded to "Colonel Antonious [sic] Comstock" in December, 1899 (10.1:26), when he explained that he was not printing any of the "joyous Canterbury Tales" he heard from some politicians because he did not want to have an edition of his magazine confiscated.

As noted by Champney (195), one of the counts in the indictment against him referred to the following humorous, veiled allusion to birth control in the June 1911 (33.1:32) issue of the *Philistine:*

> The bride of a year entered a drugstore. The clerk approached. "Do you exchange goods?" she asked.
> "Oh, certainly! if anything you buy here is not satisfactory we will exchange it."
> "Well," was the reply; "here is one of those whirling-spray affairs I bought of you, and if you please, I want you to take it back and give me a bottle of Mellin's Food, instead."
> And outside, the storm raged piteously, and across the moor a jay-bird called to his mate, "Cuckoo, cuckoo!"

Because of his federal conviction for sending such "filthy" matter through the mails, Hubbard had to appeal to President Wilson for a pardon in order to obtain a passport, which he received just in time to book passage on the *Lusitania* (Hickey, 25). (His first appeal failed, as President Taft had deemed his application for a pardon premature.) The final paragraph in the above quotation, which Hubbard tacked onto a number of other jokes from 1911 to 1913, was a satirical variation of a coy literary device used by Elinor Glyn in her notorious *Three Weeks* to represent an erotic episode. Hubbard's reaction to this sensational novel is amusingly recounted in Champney's biography (162-164).

Recalling the first time he saw the "long-haired and broad-brimmed" speaker at the centenary Paine rally at New Rochelle in 1909, Macdonald continues that he found Hubbard "hard to classify," at least going only by his appearance: "he might turn out to be a progressive Quaker or a poet or a benevolent Pawnee Indian, and he might offer one a poem or a sermon, or a bottle of Pawnee Remedy" (330). After hearing him speak, however, he admitted that he "proved to be an entertainer of rare gifts" (330).

This rally was featured on the front page of the *Truth Seeker, A Freethought and Agnostic Newspaper* on 12 June 1909. This 16-page weekly, published in New York, was certainly among the vast number of periodicals read by Hubbard. Hubbard was only one of the speakers, but he was the last, and, presumably, the best, as the reporter intimates:

> After Prof. Wakeman's lengthy address had closed, he introduced the star from East Aurora, or more properly perhaps not a star at all, but the Aurora Borealis. To those who do not understand the reference, the next and last speaker of the day was Mr. Elbert Hubbard. His speech was likewise a long one, and jocular as well, holding the closest attention of the audience.

The condensed version of his speech which follows this introduction is more than a thousand words in length, and there are three parenthetical notes indicating that Hubbard's remarks generated laughter. A look at this example of his speechmaking provides an instructive look at his thought and rhetoric.

Hubbard opens by alluding to Maurice Maeterlinck's *Life of the Bee* (1901), making the point that just as a bee removed from its hive is lost and a bee alone can make no honey, so a man "separated from his kind is lost and undone; after a very few hours of absolute separation, reason reels and the mind totters" (*Truth Seeker*, 377). People succeed only when they work with others, and "the badge of sanity is the ability to co-operate with other people"; those who cannot cooperate end up in either criminal or insane asylums (377).

After this literary allusion to the famous Belgian quasi-mystical dramatist and novelist, who would win the Nobel prize for literature in 1911, Hubbard recounts his visit to the state hospital at Utica:

> When I got off the train a man came up to me and asked, Is this Mr. Hubbard? and he said, I was sent up from the

> hospital to meet you. . . . I said, You do not talk like an insane man to me, what is your trouble? He said religion. He said, What is yours? I said, I want to do away with all of the doctors, lawyers and preachers. Well, he said, I think you are in it for life (laughter).

After praising the "Quakeress [Elizabeth Fry] who struck from the English records the madhouse," he describes his uncertainty regarding how to speak to the 800 residents of the hospital:

> What shall I say to them? I never talked to insane people. He said, You do not need to talk insanely, give them the best you have got and you will find they have got something in common with you. I had talked about half an hour when an old lady arose and said, "I cannot, my God, I cannot stand this foolishness any longer!" and she walked out. The doctor said to me afterward this was the first sign of returning sanity (laughter). (377)

Skillfully pulling the threads of his speech together, with his audience in rapt attention, Hubbard becomes serious and reviews the contributions made to the treatment of the insane by the Quakers, and reminds his audience that Paine's mother was a Quakeress. Noting that one of the distinguishing features of the Quakers is their belief that God "speaks to women just the same as to men," he says that he loves Thomas Paine because of "the ideas of equality that he expresses, not only the equality of men, but the equality of men and women" (377). Closing, he observes that Paine "made the mistake of living too long and dying in a peaceful way. If you are going to live in history, you must not live too long" (377). From bees to an insane woman to Elizabeth Fry to Paine's mother to feminism--Hubbard had an extraordinary ability to segue from one seemingly disparate topic to another, all the while both educating and entertaining his audience.

When it came to inflammatory statements regarding religion and the church, Hubbard was in the same league with Ingersoll. We have already discussed in Chapter III his willingness to publish the controversial lines of Stephen Crane ("You tell me this is God? I tell you it is a printed list, a burning candle and an ass"), and Hubbard fully shared Crane's, as well as Ingersoll's, contempt for sanctimony and the stultifying effects of religious dogma on liberality of thought. Among the mottoes on the covers of the *Philistine* relating to religion are the following:

We are not punished for our sins, but by them (January, 1900; 10.2);

He is a sinner who nails a man because he is another (June, 1903; 17.1);

Piety is pretty fair--but not so good as performance (September, 1903; 17.4);

The slogan of the theologians--Cough! (June, 1906; 23.1);

Faith in yourself and faith in humanity is faith in God (January, 1907; 24.2);

It is better not to know quite so much, than to be a theologian and know so many things that are not so (July, 1907; 25.2);

It is just as religious to pass the medicine ball as the hat (April, 1908; 26.5);

THE FEAR OF THE LORD IS THE FINISH OF WISDOM (June, 1908; 27.1);

God looked upon His work and saw that it was good. That is where the clergy take issue with Him (February, 1909; 28.3);

What the world needs is a Greedless Christianity (April, 1910; 30.5);

To be popular, hitch your wagon to a lie. Ask Billy Sunday! (July, 1910; 31.2);

Opinion, Faith, Belief--so much dust that gathers on the abandoned Machinery of Thought (May, 1911; 32.6);

A successful clergyman is one who does nothing in Summer but teach widows to swim (December, 1912; 36.1);

POPE: The first man to throw the bull (July, 1914; 39.2);

COME LET US WARSHIP! (February, 1915; 40.3); and,

THE DEVIL: Say, Bill [William II], I am giving you yours because you insisted in calling me "God"! (June, 1915; 41.1).

After 1900, then, Hubbard becomes increasingly radical in his attitude toward the power and practices of institutionalized and politicized religion.

The practice of using a communion cup, for example, was barbaric in Hubbard's estimation. As a champion for improved hygiene, he could not understand how society could progress by banishing the common cup at the well, while continuing to allow the common cup in church rites. In the January 1912 (34.2) issue he berates the Right Reverend Bishop C. C. Grafton, of Fond du Lac, Wisconsin, for protesting recent legislation in Wisconsin banning the use of public drinking cups, observing that faith is a "wonderful thing; but science, I believe, is better for a working policy" (51). Someone had asked Wisconsin's Attorney-General whether the bill would apply to "the folks who passed the deadly church goblet," and he had replied in the affirmative (52). The Bishop, needless to say, objected, claiming that the

> good Lord would not permit the transmission of disease to any of His worshipers thru the means of their worship of Him. There has never been an authentic case of contraction of disease thru the communion-cup; tho the common drinking-cup elsewhere should be strictly forbidden. To legislate against the communion-cup would be a sacrilege. (52-53)

As a result of his protest, an amendment was attached to the bill exempting the communion-cup from the law, and Hubbard wonders just when the Dark Ages ceased to be dark.

Before moving on to Emerson's decision to leave the Unitarian Church because he could not continue administering the communion service, and to a discussion of Holy Water, the "most villainous microby mixture," Hubbard ridicules Bishop Grafton's belief that God and Nature are two different things, that

> God is in charge of Nature, and at times God steps in and renders the laws of Nature inoperative. Hence, when the worshipers drink the blood of God out of a goblet--fifty or one hundred of them--they can put their microby lips on the same identical spot and mix spit without the slightest danger to anybody concerned, because God in his goodness makes the worshipers impervious to contagion as a reward of their partaking of His blood as a tipple.

(53-54)

In short, Bishop Grafton's indifference to bodily health is "essentially the attitude of the Dark Ages" (59). His attitude is understandable, however, because the Christian religion is neither "rational, logical, scientific nor philosophic. In order to accept it you have to open your mouth and shut your eyes" (61). He concludes on a somber note, realizing that logic and reason are powerless against the superstitions of religion (62).

One of his most sustained attacks against church and clergy is his essay "Theology vs. Social Science," which appears in the March 1905 (20.4:97-117) issue. (The cover motto of this issue is, "Life consists in moulting one's illusions," and this warning is printed in red from top to bottom: "This number is printed on asbestos and is intended for neither children nor fools.") This essay attacks the role of the church and clergymen in performing marriages and denying divorces. Hubbard is not writing from disinterest, of course, as he suffered an excruciating and well-publicized divorce from his first wife, and he is passionate in arguing against any interference from the church in what should be civil matters.

He minces no words: "Theology believes that marriage is a bad thing given to bad people as reward for not being worse--read St. Paul!" (102) And if a marriage fails, the "Church still sticks to it that their marriage is a consecration," for a fact is nothing to a Churchman, who swears that wine turns to blood, although "nobody sees it, nor does the microscope reveal a single corpuscle; still, when the bell rings, the miracle takes place" (104-105). Hubbard does not single out priests of the Roman Catholic Church exclusively, for Protestantism has been "as bitter a foe to science as Catholicism" (107).

Hubbard, speaking from experience, argues that there is only one thing worse than going through with a divorce, and that is going through life "manacled hand and foot, with an iron compress on head and heart" (109). The clergy, however, cannot consent to divorce for that would be a "tacit acknowledgment that in the priestly rite there is no virtue" (110). Hubbard finds the ludicrousness of this priestly power astonishing:

> A man from Mars would surely suppose that these high-chokered, self-appointed guardians of their neighbors'

> business had invented the Sexual Impulse, duly filed caveats on it, and were now renting it out on royalty, on terms and regulations dictated by themselves in convention assembled. (110)

What is most galling of all to Hubbard is that adultery is the "only Biblical excuse for divorce," and that theologians assume that a request for divorce stems from a move "toward laxity and license," rather than from a "passion for purity" (117). Hubbard admits that it would be "quite absurd to claim that all divorces spring from right motives," but he believes that divorce is not, necessarily, "any more base than the desire to wed. Just take a little time and think that over!" (111) Until the power of the clergy to perform marriage and divorce is taken from them, divorce will continue to mean having your "soul dragged naked at the cart's tail for the amusement of the mob-- and more" (109).

Pacifism in the Philistine

Hubbard was an ardent pacifist who surely would have been sentenced to prison along with Eugene Debs for his antiwar writings if he had not died in 1915. He argued frequently and vehemently for world peace. The ideas and feelings he expressed in a lengthy essay in the March 1900 (10.4:115-123) number, in which his plea for pacifism is combined with his anticlericalism, are typical and were often repeated in subsequent numbers of the *Philistine.*[5]

He begins the essay (the bulk of the "Side Talks with Philistines by the Pastor of His Flock" in this number) by assuming that it is "perfectly safe to say that ninety-nine men out of a hundred, in civilized countries, are opposed to war" (115). Most people want to be left alone to attend to their own business, but the "demagogs, politicians and rogues intent on the Strenuous Life" say that "this life is warfare" and that they must fight (116). After this blatant allusion to Theodore Roosevelt,[6] he brings in the clergy for vituperation. These members of the so-called "Superior Class," in order to establish a reason for their being, "pretend to follow in the footsteps of

Christ--they call themselves Christians" (117). Most preachers, however, who enjoy "immunity from work," believe in war, and "wherever men go to war and bayonets glisten and gleam in the name of God, a preacher in uniform is found" (118). And since most people do not think for themselves, and are "peaceably disposed," when they see this deception backed up by so many preachers, they accept it (117). The claim that standing armies are needed for the protection of the country is, according to Hubbard, "pure fraud and pretense" (119).

Because this fraud is abetted by the clergy, who will not permit the laity to obey the Golden Rule, what shall be done about these members of the Superior Class, the only enemies of the country? It is futile to fight them, for they have the guns and the money, and would use these guns which were "taxed out of us" to kill us (121). Hubbard believes that the only remedy is education. People need to be taught not to support the preachers who cry for war. People need to refuse to enlist, to refuse to shoot on their order (122). Only when educated men refuse to "bow down to their fetich of bullets" will America ever be able to become the "Ideal Republic" (122).

He again attacks the "cross and saber" nexus in November, 1900 (11.6:161-176).[7] Under the usual catch-all heading of "Heart to Heart Talks with Philistines by the Pastor of His Flock," Hubbard states his feelings regarding the atrocities being committed during the Boxer Rebellion. He begins with an essay on religion and the developments leading up to the atrocities. Taking his cue from the work of Friedrich Max Muller, he explains that every religion began as a matter of reason and then degenerated into a superstition; that it is the history of all religions that "the ignorant, led on by the designing, use the language of hyperbole, poesy and symbolism as if they designated concrete things" (161). And when superstitious people of one nation, martially aroused by the symbolic preachings of their priests, clash with superstitious people of another nation, war is the inevitable result. In short, the Boxer Rebellion resulted because "We love our religion and our country, and so do they, and so we fight" (165).

Giving a sympathetic historical sketch of Confucianism, Taoism, and Buddhism, Hubbard blames the arrival in China of the Nestorian Christians for the developments leading up to the ninth-century imperial edict abolishing all Buddhists and

Christians in China. Hubbard, stating that while he believes in the teachings of Christ, he is not a Christian (171), gives a catalog of the evils to be found in the "Christian" United States, sounding very much like Mark Twain in one of his misanthropic essays:

> In every large city of America no unarmed man is safe at night; not a day passes but women-thugs [sic] rob men on the public streets of certain large cities in daylight; we have poverty, vice, prostitution, destitution on every hand. Half of our population live in the cities: the spirit of Christ has small place in our government, and it is notorious that our cities are governed by the worst.[8] Drunkenness exists to a degree the world has never elsewhere seen, excepting in England & Scotland. And as it was Schlitz beer that made Milwaukee famous, so likewise much of the wealth and prestige in many of our cities was secured by ministering to perverted appetites.
>
> The idea of such a country as this, where purity, honesty and truth are exceptional, sending missionaries abroad is the very acme of bigoted assumption. (172-173)

What is worse, these missionaries never "fully know or sympathize with the people they are attempting to teach," and end up making hypocritical "'rice converts,'" as Lafcadio Hearn points out in his *Out of the East* (173).[9]

Among the most apposite of Twain's essays resembling those of Hubbard's are "The United States of Lyncherdom," "To the Person Sitting in Darkness," and "The War Prayer," all of which were published in *Europe and Elsewhere* (1923). All three essays, intriguingly, were written after the appearance of Hubbard's essay, so that it cannot be argued that perhaps Hubbard was following Twain's lead. (As noted in Chapter II, Hubbard disliked Twain.) According to an editorial note in the *Complete Essays of Mark Twain* (Doubleday, 1963), "The United States of Lyncherdom" was written sometime in 1901 (673), and this is a relevant excerpt:

> Let us import American missionaries from China, and send them into the lynching field. With 1,511 of them out there [China] against an uphill birth rate of 33,000 pagans per day, it will take upward of a million years to make the conversions balance the output and bring the Christianizing of the country in sight to the naked eye;

> therefore, if we can offer our missionaries as rich a field at home at lighter expense and quite satisfactory in the matter of danger, why shouldn't they find it fair and right to come back and give us a trial? . . .
>
> We ought to be careful . . . for, *once civilized, China can never be uncivilized again.* We have not been thinking of that. (*Great Short Works of Mark Twain*, Perennial Classics, 1967, 198-199)

Both Hubbard and Twain use sarcasm to express similar sentiments regarding the absurdity of missionaries attempting to impose a "superior" American religion onto the "pagan" Chinese, but Hubbard, whose prose is only occasionally caustic, is no match for Twain, whose pen drips cyanide throughout entire essays. In the excerpt just quoted, what can be more subtly devastating than "come back and give us a trial"?

Hubbard's antipathy toward the hubris of missionaries dates to at least October 1893. In a letter (exact date not given) to Alice Moore sent from Boston, he describes a service at King's Chapel and copies verbatim a speech given by Sen Chunder Mooraurah, a Buddhist who was in the United States to speak at the world's congress of religions in support of Theosophy. Throughout the long service preceding his address,

> this Indian sat with bowed head and folded arms as quiet as marble. I never saw a mortal so calm. . . . Merciful Heaven! Do we send missionaries to this people? I never saw an American as sufficient unto himself as this man. (Hamilton, *As Bees*, 82)

Now that the Americans and other foreign invaders have killed 100 Chinese for every missionary killed, Hubbard continues, the excuse that we are in China for "the sacredness of life" is seen for the lie that it is. Little wonder that the "poor heathen," seeing no virtue in the "pig-eaters who come to force a religion on them which seems no improvement on the one they have," have organized the "Society of Sanctified Fists" (175). Hubbard understands the Boxer movement, and his sympathies are altogether with the Boxers (176); he sees nothing to redeem the American Methodist bishop who says, "We will Christianize China, even if it takes a million bayonets and costs a sea of blood" (176).

One of the most vitriolic volumes of the 20-year span of the *Philistine* is volume 40, from December, 1914, to May, 1915. In this volume Hubbard anticipates by forty years Dwight D. Eisenhower's warning regarding the "military-industrial complex" in his argument that when it comes to the madness of war, the big business of armament making needs to be reined in by citizens, so that "no longer shall individuals be allowed to thrive thru supplying murder machines to the mob" (December, 1914; 40.1:3). He notes that the "war has been going on in Europe for four months or so, with at least twelve million men taken from the ranks of useful labor" (1), and that the cost, "not counting loss of labor, is thirty million dollars a day" (2). What gives the war an aura of inconceivability is that "even the sophistic apologists are at their wits' end to explain the good of this war. And no one yet has come forward and claimed the credit of beginning it" (2). He calls for "every writer, every orator--every reader and every listener" to "think disarmament" (3), and for the cessation of manufacture of weapons by private corporations. He suggests that if "murder machines" must be made, they should be produced "under an international license, with no statesmen, or their wives, as stockholders" (3).

Hubbard did not confine his preachments about disarmament to the readers of the *Philistine.* In a letter of response to Hubbard dated 5 Jan. 1915, Woodrow Wilson adds this postscript: "May I not thank you for your letter about my position with regard to an increased armament for America?" (Buffalo Rare Book Room) In an earlier letter (29 May 1908) Wilson (then president of Princeton) had expressed his desire to be a guest at the Roycrofters Inn so that he could show his "genuine interest in what the Roycrofters have undertaken and succeeded in doing," but complained (poignantly and ominously), "It just so happens that my life is caught in a great drift of things important and unimportant and that I am hardly my own master" (HRHRC, Box Recip. K-Z, Folder U-Z). As another example of Hubbard's influence, John Brisben Walker, of *Cosmopolitan Magazine*, solicited his support (1 May 1912) for the projected World Congress for 1915: "If the assent of a dozen men like yourself can be obtained, the result will be assured" (HRHRC, Box Recip. K-Z, Folder U-Z).

In an essay in the back pages of the December issue ("East of Suez") Hubbard discusses the reaction to his "Who Lifted the Lid Off of Hell?" This essay, appearing two months before, had "something to say of one Col. Kaiser [William II] and the futility of war as a corrective of commercial jealousy" (40.1:[34]). Champney notes that in this essay Hubbard "picked his scapegoat for the horrors of this war quite a bit in advance of most of his countrymen" (194). The editor of *Vaterland,* George Sylvester Viereck, had vilified the essay by attacking Hubbard's character, calling him a superannuated "swamp-puddler and offal-infector" who was famous in the "period of Jurassic rocks" (40.1:[34]). Hubbard had attacked the character of William Hohenzollern with equal venom in the October essay, describing him as having "a shrunken soul, and a mind that reeks with egomania," and as being a "mastoid degenerate of a noble grandmother" (39.5:[161]). He asserted that the Emperor does not "represent the true Germany," but symbolizes the "lust of power, the thirst for blood," and calls for disarmament and a World Federation (39.5:[165]).[10]

The cover of the January 1915 (40.2) issue has "WAR NUMBER" printed in red along the right and bottom margins, and a crude drawing of the Kaiser as the devil printed in red in the center, over which is imprinted (in black) "HELL WAS MADE IN GERMANY"; the inside of this lurid cover reads, "Kruppism and Meinself und Gottism have got to go." A nine-stanza poem by Bartholomew F. Griffin, "The Army of Bleeding Feet," leads the issue, each page of which is bordered in black.[11] Most of the pages are filled with epigrammatic denunciations of "Bill" and the war, printed alternately in black and red. Following is a representative sampling:

> Using the festering bodies of your boys for fertilizer is n't good farming. (38)
>
> Human blood is a great material for recoloring maps. (38)
>
> Business is good in Germany--with the men who make wooden legs. (39)
>
> Lloyd George is right--Bill Kaiser is the World's road-hog. (46)
>
> The worst enemy German Industrialism ever had is BILL KAISER. (49)
>
> Those wonderful moving German kitchens are not for the feeding of women and children--they are "strictly buck." (53)
>
> Send Bill Kaiser back to the DARK AGES, which he so

> ably represents. (56)
>
> What is a scrap of paper, anyway, between enemies? (56)
>
> The Kaiser is the Mad Mullah of Europe--and most of his people follow his orders with the zeal of fatalists. (59)
>
> Kill Kruppery, and cease to make God a party to murder. (64)

The back cover of this issue continues in this vein, with the inside reading, "Is Christianity a failure? Well, ask Bill--he's a Christian," and the outside printing a pseudo-advertisement for "W. Kaiser & Co. -- Dealers in Discord -- Combustibles a Specialty -- Both Phones -- We strive to please (ourselves)."

Hubbard boarded the *Lusitania* in May, and his essay "Who Lifted the Lid Off of Hell?" is excerpted in one account of the the ship's ill-fated voyage. Its authors note that he allegedly said in an embarkation press conference that to be torpedoed

> would be a good advertisement. If they sink the ship it might be a good thing for me. I would drown with her, and that's about the only way I could succeed in my ambition to get into the Hall of Fame. (Hickey, 25)

In a letter to J. M. Shumate of St. Louis, Hubbard had explained the mission of his European trip:

> The foreign authorities have been kind to me. I will be given an opportunity to observe conditions as they are. Abroad I will represent myself and I will edit my copy. I intend to store all in my bean and in that way to elude the censor. When I get back--if I do--I will give it to the readers of the *Fra* and the *Philistine* straight. I aim to be a reporter--not a war correspondent. . . . I will return 20 June (perhaps). (Hickey, 26)

And to Ernest Cowper, a journalist on board the *Lusitania* writing for the Toronto *Jack Canuck* (Balch, 312), Hubbard told of his plan to recreate the voyage for the readers of the *Philistine:* he would cable his *Lusitania Diary* from London (Hickey, 92). When Cowper asked him if he feared German submarines, Hubbard replied that they would never torpedo the *Lusitania.* When pressed for his reasoning, Hubbard replied, "If I was going to slug you as you came round the corner, would I advertise it in the newspapers?" (Hickey, 115). Cowper was not the only passenger familiar with Hubbard's interest in Germany. As the trip neared its end, Charles Lauriat remarked to Hubbard that it would not be long before he had his interview with the Kaiser, to which Hubbard replied, "You've read my piece, [in the *Philistine*], Mr. Lauriat. Do you really think I'll be a welcome visitor in Germany?" (Hickey, 180) He never found out, and there were many *Philistine* readers who were convinced that the Kaiser had the ship sunk because Hubbard was on board (Mott, 648). With consummate irony, the pacifistic vilifier of the Kaiser's Germany was killed in an incident which promoted the participation of the United States in the War to End All Wars.

Notes

[1] Zanger states mistakenly that the essay appeared in the "back pages" of the March 1899 issue. The pagination of this issue is 97 to 128; thus, the essay (109-116) appears in the center pages. And though Zanger does not mention it, he might have helpfully pointed out that the year 1899 also saw the appearance of Edwin Markham's "The Man with the Hoe," inspired by Jean Francois Millet's painting of the same title done many years earlier. Markham's poem (which recalls Thomas Hood's equally famous "The Song of The Shirt," written in 1843), of course, protests the wrongs of labor.

[2] A somewhat overbearing advertisement from the January 1913 (36.2:bap) issue of the *Philistine,* titled "The Mind and the Mazuma," brags that readers of the magazine have both (intelligence and money), which is why "preachments [ads] that appear in this perk, pesky, pungent, pertinent publication possess push and pull unparalleled."

[3] This essay was one of many from the *Philistine* that was reprinted posthumously by the Roycrofters in *The Philosophy of Elbert Hubbard.*

[4] The number of subscribers in East Aurora, though half of the inhabitants came to be employed in one capacity or other as Roycrofters, was apparently never large. In the February 1899 (8.3) issue he reports that there were seven, but that was before he had an explosive confrontation with one of them in the grocery store after he printed a "certain reference" to the local Baptist preacher (74).

[5] Champney has a paragraph on Hubbard's "Who Lifted the Lid Off of Hell?" but does not discuss his pacifism.

[6] As president, Roosevelt was a frequent target of Hubbard's attacks on imperialism and militarism, but prior to 1901 their relationship was more amicable. When Roosevelt was governor of New York he wrote Hubbard (26 Apr. 1899) for a copy of Kipling's "Dipsy Chanty" and two days later thanked Hubbard for its receipt and acknowledged his membership on the "Great Roster" (of members of the Society of Philistines), adding that he objected to Kipling's poem "The Vampire" as being in a "decadent note very much out of place in Kipling's character" (HRHRC, Box Recip. K-Z, Folder O-R). During his last months as vice president he apparently paid a visit to the Roycrofters

in the summer of 1901 (August, 1901; 13.3:80).

[7] Hubbard would no doubt approve of the Supreme Court's recent affirmation of a lower court ruling that "the First Amendment's guarantee of free exercise of religion did not require schools to allow optional attendance of classes using books that promote *'anti-Christian' themes such as feminism and pacifism*" (*Washington Post*, 23 Feb. 1988, A4; emphasis added).

[8] Most politicians are beneath Hubbard's contempt. It is for this reason that he places so much hope in the ability of capable and conscientious businessmen to effect progress in the United States. The following assertion (in which "Business" may be read for "Railroads") summarizes his feelings in this regard:

> The United States of America is ruled by a Boss, and numerous Bosslings, who run and peek about under his huge legs to find themselves dishonorable graves. The citizens are not allowed to vote for the man they wish to vote for; they are obliged to vote, if they vote at all, as the Bosslings arrange.
>
> The United States Congress, as a body, cannot be compared for an instant in brain, brawn and intellect with the men who manage the Railroads of America. . . . (December, 1899; 10.1:22)

[9] Hubbard also displayed sensitivity to the dignity of native peoples in the July 1900 (11.2) issue, in which he castigates Senator Albert Beveridge for a speech in which the senator hoped that, "perhaps in a century," the Philippines shall have adopted "American Manners, American Customs and American Ideals" (40). (Beveridge would later write the Pulitzer Prize winning biography of John Marshall.) Hubbard observes acidly that this hope carries with it the "astounding assumption that American Manners, Customs and Ideals are desirable things to send to inhabitants of the Philippines" (40).

[10] With macabre irony, it so happens that immediately following this essay, which cost Hubbard 10,000 subscription cancellations, appears a three-page advertisement by the Alexander Hamilton Institute entitled, "A War Message to American Business," which warns that business men must adapt quickly to successfully meet [i.e., profit from] "today's emergencies" (39.5:[169]). This ad would not appear again.

11 This is the poem, awkwardly constructed and melodramatic, but effective:

O'er ruined road past draggled field,
  O'er twisted stones of shaken street,
Marches an army terrible,
  The army of the bleeding feet,--

Of skirted feet that now first leave
  Immaculate field and kitchen floor,--
Old feet that slept beside the hearth,
  Wee feet that twinkled by the door.

To strange world past the parish line
  (More strange with sound and sight today),
Recruited fast at every hedge,
  The gathering army takes its way.

Commanders? Aye, they trudge ahead,--
  Not badge but babe on every breast.
The troops? They straggle at her skirt,
  From tot to crone, in ranks ill-drest.

And uniformed,--in rusty best
  From cedarn chests and linen bags;
Ah, rough the roads and chill the winds
  To sabots split and sudden rags!

Equipment? Aye, 't is furnished well,
  This army of the old and young,--
On shoulder bent a bundle small,
  A doll from little fingers swung!

Almost complete,--it only lacks
  The battle oath and cheer and song;
Save infant fret and aged sigh,
  Now dumbly marches it along.

Past gaping window, roof and sill
  It fares to red horizon's edge,
Past blackened furrow, hearth and fane,--
  And fast it grows at every hedge!

O'er ruined road past draggled field,
  O'er twisted stones of shaken street,
Marches an army terrible,
  The army of the bleeding feet. (33-34)

Selected Bibliography

Anti-Philistine; a Monthly Magazine and Review of Belles-lettres; also a Periodical of Protest. London. Nos. 1-4, 1897.

Bilioustine: A Periodical of Knock. East Aurora [Evanston], IL. Nos. 1-2, 1901.

Buffalo and Erie County Public Library. Elbert Hubbard Papers. Rare Book Room. Buffalo, NY.

Elbert Hubbard Museum. East Aurora, NY.

Harry Hansom Humanities Research Center. Elbert Hubbard Manuscripts. University of Texas at Austin.

Hubbard, Elbert. "An Interesting Personality: Elbert Hubbard." *Cosmopolitan* Jan. 1902: 309-320.

---. *The Philistine*. East Aurora, NY: Roycrofters. May 1895-July 1915 (1.1-41.2).

New York American. Editorial page. Jan. 8, 1909 to May 15, 1915.

SECONDARY SOURCES

Biographies and Reminiscences

Allen, Frederick Lewis. "Fra Elbertus." Rev. of *Elbert Hubbard: Genius of Roycroft*, by David Arnold Balch. *Saturday Review of Literature* 24 Feb. 1940: 6.

Balch, David Arnold. *Elbert Hubbard: Genius of Roycroft*. New York: Stokes, 1940. (For reviews, see Allen, Duffus, Larrabee, and "Soap Man.")

Braunstein, Simeon. Rev. of *Art & Glory: The Story of Elbert Hubbard*, by Freeman Champney. *Stephen Crane Newsletter* 3.1 (1968): 9-10.

Carson, Gerald. "One-Man Chautauqua." Rev. of *Art & Glory: The Story of Elbert Hubbard*, by Freeman Champney. *New York Times Book Review* 8 Sept. 1968: 10-11.

Champney, Freeman. *Art & Glory: The Story of Elbert Hubbard*. New York: Crown, 1968. (For reviews, see Braunstein and Carson.)

Crumrine, Janice Gaus. "Personality Development and Social Change: A Study of the Intersection of History and Biography." Diss. SUNY at Buffalo, 1976.

Dirlam, H. Kenneth, and Ernest E. Simmons. *Sinners, This Is East Aurora: The Story of Elbert Hubbard and the Roycroft Shops*. New York: Vantage, 1964.

Duffus, R. L. "Elbert Hubbard of Roycroft: A Biography of the Various-Sided Man of Letters and Affairs Whose 'Message to Garcia' Was the 40,000,000-Copy Best-Seller of Its Day." Rev. of *Elbert Hubbard: Genius of Roycroft*, by David Arnold Balch. *New York Times Book Review* 25 Feb. 1940: 4.

Hamilton, Charles F. *As Bees in Honey Drown: Elbert Hubbard and the Roycrofters*. South Brunswick, NJ: Barnes, 1973.

Heath, Mary Hubbard. *The Elbert Hubbard I Knew: An Intimate Biography from the Heart and Pen of His Sister*. East Aurora, NY: Roycrofters, 1929.

Hopkins, John Stephen. "Elbert Hubbard and the American Business Creed." M.A. Thesis Brown U, 1970.

Hubbard, Bert [Elbert Hubbard, II]. *Impressions: Being Short Sketches and Intimacies Concerning Elbert Hubbard, The Roycroft and Things Roycroftie, Together With Some Autobiography*. 2nd ed. East Aurora, NY: Roycrofters, 1927.

James, W. Bevan. *Elbert Hubbard, Master Man*. London: C. W. Daniel, 1917.

Krutch, Joseph Wood. "Fra Elbertus." Rev. of *Elbert Hubbard of East Aurora*, by Felix Shay. *The Nation* 4 Aug. 1926: 107.

Lane, Albert. *Elbert Hubbard and His Work*. Worcester, MA: Blanchard, 1901.

Larrabee, Harold A. Rev. of *Elbert Hubbard, Genius of Roycroft*, by David Arnold Balch. *New England Quarterly* 13 (1940): 352-54.

Levulis, Stanley, and Dorothy Levulis. *The Story of Elbert Hubbard and the Roycrofters of East Aurora.* New York: Blasdell, 1971.

Markham, Edwin. "Elbert Hubbard, the Practical Idealist." Rev. of *Elbert Hubbard of East Aurora*, by Felix Shay. *Literary Digest International Book Review* 26 Aug. 1926: 543-544.

Pond, Major J[ames]. B[urton]. *Eccentricities of Genius: Memories of Famous Men and Women of the Platform and Stage.* New York: Dillingham, 1900.

Putnam, George Haven. *Memories of a Publisher, 1865-1915.* New York: Putnam's, 1915.

Shay, Felix. *Elbert Hubbard of East Aurora.* New York: Wise, 1926. (For reviews, see Krutch, Markham, and Wilson.)

"Soap Man." Rev. of *Elbert Hubbard: Genius of Roycroft*, by David Arnold Balch. *Time* 26 Feb. 1940: 89.

Stott, Mary Roelofs. *Elbert Hubbard, Rebel with Reverence: A Granddaughter's Tribute.* Watkins Glen, NY: Century House Americana, 1974.

Thorne, Bonnie Ruth Baker. "Elbert Hubbard and the Publications of the Roycroft Shop, 1893-1915." Diss. Texas Woman's U, 1975.

Weber, Brom. "Spurious Sage: A Study of the Conspiracy Between Elbert Hubbard and His Times." Diss. U of Minnesota, 1957.

Wilson, P. W. "Elbert Hubbard's Breathless And Abundant Life: Felix Shay Tells How the Sage of East Aurora 'Put Over' the Medieval Ideal of Craftsmanship." Rev. of *Elbert Hubbard of East Aurora*, by Felix Shay. *New York Times Book Review* 1 Aug. 1926: 5.

Stephen Crane and Hubbard

Baum, Joan H., ed. *Stephen Crane (1871-1900): An Exhibition of His Writings Held in the Columbia University Libraries September 17-November 30, 1956.* New York: Columbia U Libraries, [1956].

Bowers, Fredson, ed. *Stephen Crane: Poems and Literary*

Remains. By Stephen Crane. Vol. 10 of *The Works of Stephen Crane*. 10 vols. Charlottesville: UP of Virginia, 1969-75.

Braunstein, Simeon. "A Checklist of Writings By and About Stephen Crane in *The Fra*." *Stephen Crane Newsletter* 3.2 (1968): 8.

Cady, Edwin H., and Lester G. Wells, eds. *Stephen Crane's Love Letters to Nellie Crouse*. Syracuse: Syracuse UP, 1954.

Dickason, David H. "Stephen Crane and the *Philistine*." *American Literature* 15 (1943): 279-87.

Hoffman, Daniel G. *The Poetry of Stephen Crane*. New York: Columbia UP, 1957.

Holton, Milne. *Cylinder of Vision: The Fiction and Journalistic Writing of Stephen Crane*. Baton Rouge: Louisiana State UP, 1972.

Katz, Joseph. "Elbert Hubbard On Stephen Crane: Two New Letters." *Stephen Crane Newsletter* 4.4 (1970): 10-11.

"Elbert Hubbard to Lyman Chandler: A Note On Crane's Poetic." *Stephen Crane Newsletter* 3.1 (1968): 8-9.

---. "Elbert Hubbard's Watermark." *Stephen Crane Newsletter*" 4.3 (1970): 8-10.

---. "How Elbert Hubbard Met Stephen Crane." *Stephen Crane Newsletter* 2.3 (1968): 8-12.

---. "The Invited to the Philistine Banquet (Part I)." *Stephen Crane Newsletter* 4.4 (1970): 11-12.

---, ed. *The Poems of Stephen Crane: A Critical Edition*. New York: Cooper Square, 1966.

---. "'Stephen Crane Flinches.'" *Stephen Crane Newsletter* 3.1 (1968): 6-7.

"Stephen Crane to the *Chap-Book*: Two New Letters." *Stephen Crane Newsletter* 2.2 (1967): 9-10.

---. "Stephen Crane to Elbert Hubbard: A New Letter." *Stephen Crane Newsletter* 1.2 (1966): 2-3.

---. "'Stephen Crane's Struggles.'" *Stephen Crane Newsletter* 1.3 (1967): 3-5.

Monteiro, George. "Stephen Crane and John Hay: Two Notes." *Stephen Crane Newsletter* 4.4 (1970): 5-6.

"Stephen Crane and *Public Opinion*: An Annotated Checklist." *Stephen Crane Newsletter* 5.1 (1970): 5-8.

Sorrentino, Paul. "The Philistine Society's Banquet for

Stephen Crane." *American Literary Realism* 15 (1982): 232-38.
Stallman, R. W. *Stephen Crane: A Critical Bibliography.* Ames, IA: Iowa State UP, 1972.
---. *Stephen Crane, A Biography.* New York: Braziller, 1968.
Stallman, R. W., and Lillian Gilkes, eds. *Stephen Crane: Letters.* New York: New York UP, 1960.
Weatherford, Richard M. "Stephen Crane in *The Lotus* and *Chips.*" *Stephen Crane Newsletter* 4.3 (1970): 2-4.
Williams, Ames W., and Vincent Starrett. 1948. *Stephen Crane: A Bibliography.* New York: Franklin, 1970.

The Philistine

Bragdon, Claude. "The Purple Cow Period: The 'Dinkey Magazines' That Caught the Spirit of the 'Nineties." *Bookman* 69 (1929): 475-78.
Dirlam, H. Kenneth. A Message to Garcia--*Bits of History from Talks Here and There.* 2nd ed. Mansfield, OH: Richland County Historical Society, 1965.
---. *The Story of* A Message to Garcia. Mansfield, OH: n.p., 1960.
---. "That Message to Garcia." *Rotarian* Apr. 1948: 11-14.
Doyle, James. "Canadian Writers & American Little Magazines in the 1890's." *Canadian Literature* CX 177-83.
Harte, Walter Blackburn. "'Fly Leaf' vs. 'Philistine.'" *Critic* 23 May 1896: 372-373.
Hunter, Dard. "Elbert Hubbard and 'A Message to Garcia,'" *New Colophon* 1 (1948): 27-35.
Millis, Walter. Introd. *A Message to Garcia.* By Elbert Hubbard. New York: Watts, 1962.
Mott, Frank Luther. *A History of American Magazines, 1885-1905.* Vol. 4. 5 vols. Cambridge, MA: Harvard UP, 1930-68.
"Notes [on Rudyard Kipling's suit against Elbert Hubbard]." *Literary Digest* 1 July 1899: 12.

Stephenson, Edward R. "Elbert Hubbard, *The Philistine*, and the Legacy of Emerson." *The Markham Review* 10 (1981): 33-36.
Sweeney, Francis, S.J. "Elbert Hubbard and 'A Message to Garcia.'" *Critic* 33 (1975): 40-43.
Taber, Harry Persons. *Ezra and Me*. New York: Coward, 1943.
Tassin, Algernon. *The Magazine in America*. New York: Dodd, 1916.
Tosquella, Maximo. *The Truth About the Message to Garcia*. Trans. J. F. Berndes and Charles Dujol. Habana: n.p., [1955].
Vail, R. W. G. "'A Message to Garcia,' a Bibliographical Puzzle." *Bulletin of the New York Public Library* Feb. 1930: 71-78.
Zanger, Jules. "'A Message to Garcia': The Subsidized Hero." *American Studies* 20.1 (1979): 99-108.

Other

Allen, Frederick Lewis. "Elbert Hubbard." *Scribner's* Sept. 1938: 12+.
Atherton, Hazen. Letter. *Time* 11 Jan. 1932: 4+.
Beisner, Robert L. "'Commune' in East Aurora." *American Heritage* 22.2 (1971): 72+.
Bigelow, Burton. *Elbert Hubbard: Pioneer Advertising Man*. East Aurora, NY: Roycrofters, 1931.
Bishop, Morris. "Roycroft Revisited." *New Yorker* 8 Oct. 1938: 48-52.
Brady, Nancy Hubbard, ed. *1001 Epigrams--Elbert Hubbard*. Englewood Cliffs, NJ: Prentice, 1973.
Carlisle, Norman. "Elbert Hubbard: Warrior With Words." *Coronet* Apr. 1955: 44-48.
Caruthers, J. Wade. "Elbert Hubbard: A Case of Re-interpretation." *Connecticut Review* 1 (1967): 67-77.
Curti, Merle. *The Growth of American Thought*. 2nd ed. New York: Harper, 1951.
De Casseres, Benjamin. Letter. *New York Times Book Review* 5 May 1940: 18.

De Casseres, Benjamin. Letter. *Saturday Review* 16 Mar. 1940: 9.
"East Aurora's Lights." *Time* 7 Dec. 1931: 62+.
Eastman, N. Brian, Sr. "Elbert Hubbard and Education De-Luxe." *Educational Forum* Mar. 1970: 333-338.
"Elbert Hubbard's Price." *Harper's Weekly* 30 Jan. 1915: 112.
Hamilton, Charles F. "The Anti-Muckraker: Elbert Hubbard." *Public Relations Journal* Oct. 1969: 65+.
---. "Hartmann, Hubbard, and East Aurora." *Sadakichi Hartmann Newsletter* 2.1 (1971): 1-5.
---. Letters to the author. 1980-1988.
---. *Little Journeys to The Homes of Roycrofters*. East Aurora, NY: S.-G. P, 1963.
---. *Roycroft Collectibles, Including Collector Items Related to Elbert Hubbard, Founder of the Roycroft Shops*. San Diego: A. S. Barnes, 1980.
Hamilton, Virginia L. *Elbert Hubbard and the Roycrofters*. East Aurora, NY: The Elbert Hubbard Museum, 1973.
Hartt, Rollin Lynde. "Elbert Hubbard." *Critic* Nov. 1899: 1005-1008.
Hopkins, Arthur. "Letters to a Lonely Boy." *Ladies' Home Journal* Oct. 1937: 53+.
Hunter, Dard, II. *The Life Work of Dard Hunter*. vol. 1. Chillicothe, OH: Mountain House, 1981.
Jenkins, Alan. "Mentor and First Publisher." *Journal of the Illinois State Historical Society* 45 (1952): 311-15.
Knox, George. "Idealism, Vagabondage, Socialism: Charles A. Sandburg in *To-Morrow* and the *Fra*." *Huntington Library Quarterly* 38.2 (1975): 161-88.
Koch, Robert. "Elbert Hubbard's Roycrofters as Artist-Craftsmen." *Winterthur Portfolio* 3 (1967): 67-82.
Kramer, Sidney. "Stone & Kimball 1893-1897, and Herbert S. Stone and Company 1896-1905: Studies in Publishing History." Diss. U of Chicago, 1938.
McGill, Anna B. "The Roycrofters." *Catholic World* Sept. 1901: 785-794.
Martin, Jay. *Harvests of Change: American Literature 1865-1914*. Englewood Cliffs, NJ: Prentice-Hall, 1967.

the First Years of Our Time 1912-1917. New York: Knopf, 1969.

Mitgang, Herbert, ed. *The Letters of Carl Sandburg*. New York: Harcourt, 1968.

N. W. Ayer and Son's American Newspaper Annual. 1895-1915.

Patnode, Jack. *English and American Literary Relations in the 1890's: The Cosmopolitan Impressionists*. Diss. U of Minnesota, 1968.

Pattee, Fred Lewis. *The New American Literature 1890-1930*. New York: Century, 1930.

Petrocelli, Orlando R. Introd. *Notebook*. By Elbert Hubbard. New York: Petrocelli, 1980.

Pollard, Percival. *Their Day in Court*. New York: Neale, 1909.

Putzel, Max. *The Man in the Mirror: William Marion Reedy and His Magazine*. Cambridge: Harvard, 1963.

Reedy, William Marion, et al. *The Feather Duster or, Is He Sincere?* East Aurora, NY: Roycrofters, 1912.

Roycrofters-At-Large Newsletter. East Aurora, N.Y. 1971+.

Sandburg, Carl [Valdemar Blad]. "Elbert Hubbard's Idea of the Value of Human Suffering." *To-Morrow* July 1906: 59.

--- [Charles A.]. "The Genial Fra Again." *To-Morrow* June 1906: 25-26.

--- [Charles A.]. "Subjugation of Elbert Hubbard." *To-Morrow* Oct. 1905: 30-32.

Santayana, George. "What Is a Philistine?" *Harvard Monthly* May 1892: 89-99.

Schlereth, Wendy Clauson. *The Chap-Book: A Journal of American Intellectual Life in the 1890s*. Ann Arbor: UMI Research Press, 1982.

Sinclair, Upton. *The Brass Check: A Study of American Journalism*. New York: Boni, 1936.

Taber, Harry Persons. Letter ["Sage of East Aurora"]. *Saturday Review of Literature* 16 Oct. 1926: 210.

Thompson, Susan Otis. *American Book Design and William Morris*. New York: R. R. Bowker, 1977.

Walsdorf, John J. *William Morris in Private Press and Limited Editions: A Descriptive Bibliography of Books by and about William Morris 1891-1981*. Phoenix: Oryx

P, 1983

Wolfe, Richard J., and Paul McKenna. *Louis Herman Kinder and Fine Bookbinding in America: A Chapter in the History of the Roycroft Shop.* Newtown, PA: Bird and Bull, 1985.

"A Writer Who Made America Think." *Current Opinion* 74.4 (1923): 419-21.

Appendix A

Index to the *Philistine*, Vols. 21-41

Julia Ditto Young, who contributed a verse to the *Philistine*, worked for two years preparing "An Index and Concordance to that Cyclopedia of Comment *The Philistine* Magazine, Volumes I to XX" [inclusive]. Her index, which also contains a list of the Roycroft publications, was advertised in 1905 issues of the *Philistine*, and was available for one dollar. It is included at the beginning of Reel 589 of Microfilm #05422, APS III. Although its organization is slightly awkward (with the article "The" alphabetized, for example), and it suffers from being more of a concordance than a subject index, it is extremely reliable and complete. The following index is much more selective, being limited to subjects and names which receive more than a paragraph of consideration in the pages of the *Philistine*, regardless of relative importance; it was compiled more as an aid to studying the periodical than as a comprehensive index. Thus, for example, "Lubricant," and "*Lusitania*" (which carried the Hubbards to their death in 1915) happen to be adjoining entries. At the end of this appendix is a listing of the month and year which correspond to the volume and number of each issue, information regarding variants on cover numbers, and a note on the available microfilm copies.

(f = front; c = center; b = back; ap = advertising pages)

--A--

--B--

--C--

--D--

--F--

--G--

--H--

--I--

--J--

--K--

--L--

--M--

--N--

--O--

--P--

--Q--

--R--

--S--

--T--

--U--

--V--

--W--

--Y--

--Z--

Appendix B

Key to Volume and Issue Numbers

1.1-6 ······· June-Nov. 1895	17.1-6 ······ June-Nov. 1903
2.1-6 ·· Dec. 1895-May 1896	18.1-6 · Dec. 1903-May 1904
3.1-6 ······· June-Nov. 1896	19.1-6 ······ June-Nov. 1904
4.1-6 ···Dec. 1896-May 1897	20.1-6 · Dec. 1904-May 1905
5.1-6 ······· June-Nov. 1897	21.1-6 ······ June-Nov. 1905
6.1-6 ·· Dec. 1897-May 1898	22.1-6 · Dec. 1905-May 1906
7.1-6 ······· June-Nov. 1898	23.1-6 ······ June-Nov. 1906
8.1-6 ·· Dec. 1898-May 1899	24.1-6 ··Dec. 1906-May 1907
9.1-6 ······· June-Nov. 1899	25.1-6 ······ June-Nov. 1907
10.1-6 · Dec. 1899-May 1900	26.1-6 · Dec. 1907-May 1908
11.1-6 ······ June-Nov. 1900	27.1-6 ······ June-Nov. 1908
12.1-6 ··Dec. 1900-May 1901	28.1-6 · Dec. 1908-May 1909
13.1-6 ······ June-Nov. 1901	29.1-6 ······ June-Nov. 1909
14.1-6 · Dec. 1901-May 1902	30.1-6 · Dec. 1909-May 1910
15.1-6 ······ June-Nov. 1902	31.1-6 ······ June-Nov. 1910
16.1-6 · Dec. 1902-May 1903	32.1-6 ··Dec. 1910-May 1911

33.1-6 · · · · · · June-Nov. 1911
34.1-6 · Dec. 1911-May 1912
35.1-6 · · · · · · June-Nov. 1912
36.1-6 · Dec. 1912-May 1913
37.1-6 · · · · · · June-Nov. 1913
38.1-6 · Dec. 1913-May 1914
39.1-6 · · · · · · June-Nov. 1914
40.1-6 · Dec. 1914-May 1915
41.1-2 · · · · · · ·June-July 1915

The June 1915 issue is the last containing Hubbard's writings, as he went down with the *Lusitania* on 7 May 1915. The final issue is a memorial issue.

The author's copies of May, 1907, and June, 1907, have incorrectly numbered covers. The May cover retains "24.5" from the previous month's cover, and the June cover has "24.6;" these covers should have been numbered "24.6" and "25.1," respectively. The July, 1907, cover resumes the correct numbering with "25.2." Charles F. Hamilton reports that some covers of the February, 1896, number have "2.4" instead of the correct "2.3" (letter to the author, 20 Sept. 1984).

There are serious difficulties in store for scholars who are unable to work with original copies of the Philistine. Microfilm #05422 (APS III, Reels 589-590) stops with number 23.6, and some covers are missing. The microfilm with the complete set of the magazine, however, has its own deficiencies. When the Library of Congress produced its Microfilm #38294 (AP2. P54, five reels) in 1973 (most likely destroying the originals in the process), all advertisements, epigrams, literary excerpts, testimonials, and essays appearing in the end and filler pages from the six numbers of each volume were grouped together at the end of each volume, rendering this microfilm nearly useless for bibliographical study.

Also making the researcher's job more difficult is the lack of a consistent content format from issue to issue. "Heart to Heart Talks" might be missing from one issue, for example, and then constitute all of the next.

Appendix C

List of Contributors to the *Philistine*

Volumes 1 through 41

(* = poem; bc = back cover; fc = front cover)

--A--

Anonymous	1.5:137-145	Rhadamanthina Ivra
---.	3.5:bc	Lay of the New Poet*
---.	4.6:bc	Moving*
---.	6.4:bc	A Prayer*
---.	8.3:bc	I saw a man tugging*
---.	12.2:33	Weariness*
---.	12.4:111	Waste*
---.	13.1:1	Lassitude*
---.	14.4:97	Trouble*
---.	14.5:129	Distrust. Doggerel*
---.	15.1:1	Weariness*
---.	15.5:129	Hardship*
---.	16.6:161	Doggerel*
---.	17.3:65	[untitled]*
---.	18.6:161	[untitled]*
---.	19.1:1-33	Respectability
---.	19.1:34-40	Smudge, Smut, Smith
---.	20.1:11	World-Weariness*

Adams, J. Howe	3.2:50-53	Heart to Heart Talks
Ade, George	10.1:7-9	Fable of Experimental
Aesculapius	7.5:143-148	The Beecham Habit
Alexander, U. G.	4.5:129	To An Idea*
Ali Baba [sic]	9.3:65-66	Town of East Aurora*
---. [sic]	13.5:140-143	A Ballade of Egoism*
Allan, Paul	7.2:33	Enfranchisement*
Almy, Frederic	2.4:110-113	Paul Knew
Andrews, Gertrude	10.4:bc	In an occasional . . .
Ayres, Nelson	1.4:136	[poem letter]

--B--

Bacheller, Irving	8.2:40-47	The Story of a Passion
Baker, Estes	3.2:40-42	A Hot Weather Idyll
Baker, Herbert L.	1.2:51-52	The New Hahnemann
Baker, William J.	1.6:182-185	A Question of Form
---.	3.1:1	Extremes*
---.	3.3:73	Sunrise Over the City*
Bann, Fred	41.2:39-43	Hubbard's Last Talk
Bardwell, E. O.	10.3:65-66	He Just Wanted to Know
Barnard, Edward	5.1:9-10	A Ballade of Entreaty*
---.	5.3:85-86	Ballade of Frocks*
Bates, Katherine	7.2:48-52	Friendly Lifts
---.	8.2:47-49	Limited Vocabularies
Beardshear, W. M.	10.6:161-167	The Charge of a Brother
Bell, Jerome B.	29.1:fap	On Death of a Friend*
Bennett, Katherine	2.6:bc	When the Ghost Walks!*
Bennett, Katherine	4.3:72-73	Welsh Rabbit*
---.	5.3:78-81	Strategy on Southern
Bicket, Thomas	5.1:14-15	The Cynic*
Bickford, L. H.	2.3:73	Victory: Chant After*
Bigelow, Walter S.	7.2:47-48	Fin-De-Siecle Fatima*
Bigelow, Her. S.	25.3:83-85	The Village Infidel
Bles, Victor A.	5.1:10-11	The Reason
---.	7.4:107-109	On Being In Love
Blodgett, Harriet	8.2:40	Evening*
Bowdle, Stanley	29.5:129-138	Snap-Shots at Legal
---.	32.6:177-180	A Lawyer on Doctors
Boyce, Neith	2.4:119-121	Complaint of Editors
Bragdon, Claude F.	1.6:169	A Sonnet of Despair*

Brooks, Florence	6.6:161	Joy*
Brown, Kenneth	2.5:143-146	After Dark
---.	3.2:54-59	Plots and Things . . .
Brown, Milton G.	29.1:1	Two of a Kind*
Browne, Irving	4.6:170	A Jail Window*
---.	7.4:97-98	Tramp, His Dog . . .*
---.	8.3:65-66	Shakespeare's Grave*
Browning, Robert	10.3:bc	Truth within ourselves*
---.	12.3:bc	Each life's unfulfilled*
Bryan, John	2.3:91-93	Two Fables
---.	2.5:146-148	The Monk
Buckham, Harriette	5.2:38-39	A Book-Lover's Apologia*
Bunner, H. C.	2.5:142	A Song of Solomon*
Burgess, Gelett	2.1:7	In Jenson Type*
---.	3.6:161	Karma*
Butts, Newington	7.5:151-156	The Consecration
Byron [sic]	13.1:10-15	Unpublished Letter

--C--

Caldwell, Eleanor	3.1:bc	Anaemic*
Cardozo, Elizabeth	2.6:197-198	"If Love Were All"*
Carleton, Emma	10.3:65	Art and Utility*
---.	11.3:82-84	Foot-Notes
Carman, Bliss	4.3:65-66	In Philistia*
Carpenter, Edward	12.3:65-69	China, 1900 A.D.
---.	12.6:181-188	Life and Art
Carruth, Hayden	8.5:129-130	Bruno and Buffalmacco*
Champlin, Edwin R.	1.2:33	Some Little Verses*
Chandler, Lyman	17.5:129-134	In Re Right and Wrong
---.	17.6:175-183	Sartor Resartus
---.	18.4:97-109	Life in Intension
Chopin, Frederic	17.1:bc	One arrives at art . . .
Clack, Sillifred	12.3:70-71	Conductor and Pennies
Claus, Fred. W.	3.6:167	Life*
---.	5.2:33	Quatrain*
Clavigera	2.2:41-50	A Protest and a Prayer
---.	3.1:1-16	Things America Needs
Cleghorn, Sarah N.	3.4:bc	Behold the Lilies*
---.	3.6:161-167	Powers at Play
---.	9.1:1-2	Ballade of Queens*

Crane, Stephen	1.1:27	I saw a man pursuing*
---.	1.3:93	chatter of a . . .*
---.	1.4:124	A Lantern Song*
---.	2.1:8	A slant of sun*
---.	2.2:62	"I have heard . . .*
---.	2.3:94-95	"What says the sea"*
---.	2.4:106-109	A Great Mistake
---.	2.5:152	To the maiden*
---.	3.1:20	Fast rode the knight*
---.	3.2:39	A Prologue.
---.	3.5:133-137	An Ominous Baby
---.	4.2:37-48	The Men in the Storm
---.	4.4:118	Two or three angels*
---.	6.3:bc	Some Things*
---.	6.5:bc	Lines. (You tell me)*
---.	6.6:166-167	Lines. (On the desert)*
---.	7.1:9-10	When a people reach*
---.	8.1:fc	Wheels!*
---.	8.4:bc	I stood upon a High*
---.	9.2:44-50	Old Man Goes A-Wooing
---.	9.3:71-77	A Fishing Village
---.	11.4:97-104	At the Pit Door
Crane, William I.	10.4:101-115	Plea for Education of
Crawford, Jack	26.2:33-35	The Womanhood of Man
Criswell, Robert	1.6:186-187	A Plea for Inebriety
---.	1.5:146	A Journalistic Note
Crosby, Ernest	10.6:167-168	At the Stock Farm
---.	17.5:129	Brotherhood and Charity*
---.	21.1:1-2	The Hero*
---.	23.3:65-68	Whitman's "Children of"
---.	24.3:65-67	Morituri Salutamus
Culp, George P.	33.2:33	East Aurora Stein Song*
---.	37.2:33	Spring Song*
Curtis, Elizabeth	4.4:115	Waiting*
---.	5.5:bc	Bird-Flight*

--D--

Dale, Alan	30.4:98-103	The Commanding Officer
Dargan, Pegram	4.1:1-8	The Motherhood of God
Dawson, Mary	1.6:186	Happiness*

Dayton	7.2:38	A Periodical Protest*
De Casseres, Benj.	20.1:1-10	Ralph Waldo Emerson
---.	25.6:161-172	Enter Walt Whitman
---.	26.6:161-166	Is New York Civilized?
---.	27.4:115-119	Hate Everlasting
Dickens, Charles	13.2:bc	Reflect upon present
Doctor Phil.	4.2:33-36	Phil. Sermons-No. I
---.	4.3:67-69	Phil. Sermons-No. II
---.	4.4:97-101	Phil. Sermons-No. III
---.	4.6:161-163	Phil. Sermons: No. IV
---.	5.1:1-5	Phil. Sermons: No. V
---.	5.2:33-38	Phil. Sermons: No. VI
---.	5.5:129-136	Phil. Sermon-No. VII
---.	5.6:167-169	Phil. Sermon-No. VIII
---.	6.4:98-103	Phil. Sermon: No. IX
Dole, Nathan H.	4.2:48-49	"All the World's a"*
Dwight, John S.	9.2:bc	Music is to me an . . .

--E--

Easton, Honor	1.5:167-168	Nothing But Leaves
Ecclesiasticus	7.5:148-151	Mr. Kinset of England
Ehrman, Max	20.3:65-66	A Prayer*

--F--

Farrar, F. W.	3.4:97-116	In Westminster Abbey
Faville, William	2.6:194	Life's Voyage: A Mood*
Ferguson, Nathan.	41.2:33	Hubbard*
Finley, John H.	3.5:139	To Cadmus [ill. poem]
Fortune, Joanna	4.1:8-10	A Chapter
Fra Elbertus	7.5:129-131	Americanus Sum
---.	8.5:134-141	As to Advertising Books
---.	9.1:2-11	The City of Tagaste
---.	9.2:33-42	A Dream and a Prophecy
---.	9.6:161-168	The Better Part
---.	10.1:9-17	In Re Robert Burns
---.	10.4:98-101	Mental Attitude
---.	10.6:169-173	Wilted Hyacinths
---.	11.1:7-13	What Shall We Do?

Fra Elbertus	11.3:74-82	Some Sonnets
---.	11.4:104-110	Consecrated Lives
---.	12.1:1-8	About Widows
---.	12.3:71-80	Advantages
---.	12.4:97-110	Chicago Tongue
---.	12.6:177-180	About Right Thinking
---.	13.1:15-21	In Re Johannes Brahms
---.	13.5:143-148	The Kindergarten
Frank, Henry	26.2:bap	Marshall P. Wilder*
---.	29.3:65-69	Billy Sunday*
Freund, John C.	29.4:98-108	To Young Girl Out West
Froemcke, Elvira	4.2:36-37	Out of Nothing*

--G--

Gilman, Charlotte	12.6:188	Too Wise*
Goetz, Philip B.	2.1:9	Quatrains*
Goodwin, L. S.	1.5:147	"De mortuis nil nisi"*
Graham, Bill	27.1:1	Immune*
Graham, Whidden	5.1:8-9	The Greatest Man
Griffin, Barth.	40.2:33-34	Army of Bleeding Feet
Guiney, Louise I.	2.5:137	To a Friend in Trouble*

-- H --

Harte, Walter B.	1.2:53-59	An Interview with Devil
---.	2.6:184-187	Shakspeare's Borrowings
Hastings, Milo	31.6:161-165	Marrying of Cousins
Heaton, John L.	2.2:41	The Unforgetting Tide*
Heine, Heinric	11.3:bc	I have never placed
Helmer, F. F.	4.2:49-51	Flory of the Farm
Hibbard, Grace	3.2:bc	Books Received*
Higginson, T. W.	3.2:33-38	A Bit of War Photography
Hilliard, John N.	1.4:105	The Birth of the Flower*
---.	2.4:109-110	Wind of the West*
Hine, Annie Laurie	7.4:105-107	Such Is Life
Hodge, J. W., M.D.	41.2:44-54	A Friend's Tribute
Howe, Harlow	4.3:70-71	Imagination*
Hubbard, Alice	24.2:33-42	The Orator and His Work
---.	24.5:129-132	Beauty as Collateral

Hubbard, Alice	26.1:1-4	Mary Baker Eddy
---.	31.2:33-41	Commensense as Authority
Hubbard, Bert	41.2:59-64	Elbert Hubbard II
Hubbard, Elbert	1.1:5-11	English Monuments
---.	1.2:39-44	Fashion in Letters
---.	1.3:82-89	Confessional in Letters
---.	1.4:105-116	A Notable Work
---.	2.1:14-23	The Song of Songs . . .
---.	2.2:51-58	Experiment in Communism
---.	2.3:74-86	Why I Am a Philistine
---.	2.4:113-114	The Port of Ships
---.	2.6:169-183	By Rule of Three
---.	2.6:194-197	Our Syndicate Letter
---.	4.5:136-149	A Word About Job
---.	5.3:81-85	A Comparison
---.	5.6:171-181	Above the Rabble
---.	6.4:115-118	Time and Chance
---.	6.6:161-166	The Passing of Brann
---.	8.1:14-21	The Collector
---.	8.4:opp. 97	[Irving Browne obituary]
---.	9.3:67-71	In Re. Joshua Reynolds
---.	9.4:97-106	William Morris
---.	14.1:1-5	About Leonardo
---.	14.6:161-178	White Slavery in South
---.	17.6:161-165	Remember the Week-Day
---.	18.6:171-181	Success
---.	19.2:41-60	Journey to Tuskegee
---.	19.4:105-121	Golden Rule Jones
---.	19.5:137-150	As To Jealousy
---.	20.4:97-117	Theology vs. Social
---.	21.2:33-50	Psychology of Revival
---.	21.5:129-142	The Cigarettist
---.	21.6:161-179	As to Science . . .
---.	23.2:33-54	Mary Baker Eddy
---.	24.3:68-93	Trust-Busting-- Inquiry
---.	25.1:1-22	Forgotten Freak Nature
---.	25.2:33-49	How I Found My Brother
---.	25.3:65-83	In Re Muldoon
---.	26.1:cap	One Man's Opinion
---.	26.2:cap	Business and the Man
---.	27.4:97-115	A Great Betterment
---.	27.5:129-150	Tempest Village Teapot

Hubbard, Elbert	34.2:33-49	Message to Ad-Men
---.	34.6:203-224	Pundit Publisher
---.	35.1:33-(68)	The High Cost of Living
---.	35.2:bap	The Loyal Order of Moose
---.	35.3:132-160	Owl Drug Co.'s Stores
---.	35.4:fap	King of America
---.	37.2:bap	Purity and Progress . . .
---.	37.5:bap	Art of Check-Raising
---.	37.6:fap	Consomme Devoutly
---.	37.6:fap	Journey to Famous
---.	37.6:bap	Journey to Thompson's
---.	37.6:bap	Nylo Girl, The
---.	38.2:bap	Blazed Trail, Hot Ad
---.	38.4:bap	Pebeco, Tooth-Pastes
---.	38.5:129-160	Message to Uncle Sam
---.	38.6:fap	Keep Your Car
---.	38.6:cap	Pay Envelope, The
---.	39.1:fap	Kalamazoo Vegetable
---.	39.1:bap	United Drug Co. Journey
---.	39.5:bap	Who Lifted Lid Off Hell?
---.	39.6:bap	San Diego, Journey
---.	40.1:bap	East of Suez
Hubbell, Mark S.	1.1:12-16	Philistinism in General
Hueffer, Ford M.	4.1:11-13	Song of the Women*
Hurbart, Elme	9.4:97	Speculation*
Huston, Ethelyn L.	8.2:49-51	Quoth the Raven
---.	28.4:98-108	L'Excuse Accuse

--I--

Ingersoll, Robert	12.6:bc	The dead carry in their
Inslee, Eleanore	12.1:8-9	The Twilight Hour*
Ireland, S. B.	14.1:1	Ingratitude*

--J--

Jackson, J. M.	8.6:161	Weariness*
James, George W.	17.6:165-175	Ramona and Her Basket
Jeffrey, Alexander	2.5:153	Death the Doorway*
Jenks, Tudor	5.1:6-7	In a Library*

Johnson, William	17.5:158-160	Thoughts about Things
Jones, L. Smythe	8.5:147-151	Some Astral Autographs

--K--

Kendall, Preston	3.6:172-175	In Re Ophelia
---.	5.1:12-14	Negative Virtue System
Kimball, Fred L.	12.6:161	A Bird and a Tree*
Kinsell, S. Tyson	30.1:bap	The Convict*
Kipling, Rudyard	2.1:3-6	The Dipsy Chanty*
Kite, Bramley	32.6:177	By the Way*
---.	40.4:97	To Yourself*
Knapp, Adeline	3.3:82-86	Let There Be Gall Enough

--L--

Le Gallienne, R.	24.4:fap	Confessio Amantis*
---.	29.1:2	To Edgar Allan Poe*
Lewis, G. M.	4.4:108-109	The Service of the Gods*
Lucas, Arthur M.	4.6:163-167	The Death of Cleopatra*
---.	9.6:161	Temptation*
Lund, Adelaide	4.6:167-169	Found Drowned
Lydston, G. Frank	9.6:169-171	A Street Car Vignette
Lyman, O. L.	11.3:84	When Toots the Trump*

--M--

MacGrath, Harold	3.5:137	The Minor Poet*
---.	4.1:bc	The Liar*
---.	4.2:33	The Epidemic*
---.	4.5:bc	An Echo from Cuba*
---.	5.1:12	What the Dew Is*
---.	5.6:170	Ballade of Confession*
---.	6.1:bc	Despondency*
Mack, John, Jr.	3.3:bc	The Ride*
Maeterlinck, M.	10.6:bc	It may happen that I
Mahany, Rowland B.	1.1:5	The Sanity of Genius*
---.	1.2:38	Laughter of the Gods*
Marigold, Triton	7.5:132-135	The Remittance Man

Marwood, Richard	28.3:bap	When Marse Hubba'd Dies*
Mason, Walt	28.4:97	The Evangelist*
---.	29.4:97	The Era of Progress
---.	30.4:97-98	Helpful Mr. Bok
McCarthy, Myles	31.5:129	The Split-Week*
McCaskey, Hiram D.	3.3:65	Miserer*
McDougal, Henry C.	11.1:1-7	In Re. Christian Science
McIlvaine, Mabel	4.6:171	Impressions*
McIntosh, William	1.1:1-4	Philistines Ancient
---.	1.1:30	Stigmata*
---.	1.2:46-51	A Free Lunch League
---.	1.3:89-92	The Social Spotter
---.	1.4:118-122	A Matter of Background
---.	1.4:125-126	Rubaiyat O'Mara Khayvan*
---.	2.1:9-13	The Kind Paul Forgot
---.	2.4:114-119	Filling of the Joneses
---.	3.5:129-132	The Literary Sweat Shop
---.	3.6:167-171	Our Friend the Enemy
---.	4.3:73-79	Our Masters
---.	4.5:129-133	The Evolution of the How
---.	5.1:15-19	Commonplace in Purple
---.	5.3:74-77	As to Some Novels
---.	6.6:175-180	The Fruit of Good Living
---.	7.2:33-38	A Man in a Robe
---.	8.1:1-5	At Christmas
---.	8.5:130-134	The Ex-Cathedra Habit
---.	11.1:13-18	Headwaters of Castaly
---.	13.5:136-140	At the Sign of the Goat
---.	17.4:97-102	History in Perspective
Mearkle, Annie L.	3.1:21-23	As to Bores
---.	9.6:171-174	Generalizations
Millard, Frank B.	7.4:99-104	Great American Novel
Miller, Joaquin	17.2:33	In men whom men . . . *
Monahan, Michael	6.6:167-174	Hibernia Nova
---.	8.1:5-13	Heinrich Heine
---.	8.5:141-147	Culturian Observations
---.	9.2:42-44	The Paretic*
---.	9.4:106-108	To Villon*
---.	10.1:1-6	The McClure Continuous
---.	11.1:18-21	Loquacious Literarians
---.	11.6:bap	The Gospel of Content
---.	12.1:9-16	The James in Literature

Monahan, Michael	13.5:129-136	The Kipling Blue Pill
Morgan, H. T.	35.1:fap	Hail, Elbert Hubbard!
Morley, John	5.6:161-166	On Truth Speaking
Morris, William	1.3:73-74	The Dream*
---.	3.6:177	Of Heaven or Hell I have
---.	10.5:bc	Forsooth, brothers . . .
Morrow, Marco	5.6:bc	The Poet*
---.	8.1:1	Aspiration*
---.	8.2:33	Hesitation*
---.	8.4:97	Eternal Fitness of*
---.	10.6:161	The Author*
---.	11.1:1	The Butcher*
---.	13.5:129	The Critics*
Myers, Bess M.	4.2:51	In Winter Time*
---.	7.2:43-44	An Impression*

--N--

Neil, Edith	3.3:76-77	"If Love Were All"*
Nettleton, Charles	2.5:148	Thoughts*
---.	3.3:81-82	Steward. Ballad of*
---.	3.3:86-88	The Worshippers
---.	4.1:18-19	Before the Fire*
---.	4.4:101-102	Quatrains on Authors*
---.	5.1:1	Quatrains on Authors*
---.	5.3:bc	The Rubaiyat*
---.	6.4:97	Too Late*
---.	7.4:109-112	Thoughts
Nichols, Chas. E.	11.3:65	Abbreviation*
Nietzsche, F.	18.4:bc	Since man came . . .
Noguchi, Yone	3.6:171-172	Lines*
Noxon, Frank W.	2.5:149-151	Passing of Clangingharp
---.	3.2:46-49	The Purple Insurgent
---.	3.5:140-143	Clangingharp Pays Up
---.	4.6:170-171	A Dejected Impulse
---.	5.3:86-87	Moments Clangingharp

--O--

Oakman, John	4.1:bc	Denial*

Ollendorff, G. J.	4.1:13-17	The Wonderhouse
Orvis, Louis	10.4:97	Staggerdodgy: A Lilt*
Ouida	1.3:74-78	A Word About Art
---.	2.5:138-141	The Gold That Glitters
---.	3.3:73-76	The Captives
Owen, J. W.	10.2:33-34	A Woman's Cry*

--P--

Palmer, Walter L.	5.3:72-74	The Queen's Island*
Pandolfini	7.5:140-143	At Parting of the Ways
Paracelsus	20.1:bc	I go to prove my soul!
Park, Clara C.	1.4:116-117	The Manners Tart
---.	2.2:59-61	A Protestant Service
Pastor, The	4.4:102-108	A Projected Reform
---.	8.2:33-39	A Manifesto!
Peavey, Francis H.	19.4:121-131	Business and Living
Penn, William	17.2:bc	I expect to pass . . .
Pentecost, Hugh O.	11.3:65-73	Righteousness
---.	13.1:5-10	Decline of the Church
---.	22.5:129-134	Compensation
Phelps, George T.	6.2:45-46	Parade at an Unveiling
Pickard, F. W.	3.2:33	A Sea Song*
Pond, Jas. B.	9.6:174-177	As to Mark Twain
Putnam, Frank	4.1:13	Reform*
---.	22.6:161-162	Ballade of Fame*
---.	23.1:1-2	Ballade of the Man*
---.	24.4:97-98	Ballade of Cowbird*
---.	28.2:33-34	Ballade of Death*
Pyle, Walter L.	29.4:98	An Echo of the Ballet*

--R--

Raftery, John H.	18.6:161-166	Truth About Triggs
Reed, Myrtle	4.3:bc	A Valentine
Reedy, William M.	13.1:1-5	Knocking and Knockers
---.	18.6:167-171	Letters About Love
---.	21.1:2-10	Joe Jefferson, My Jo
---.	23.2:55-64	'Frisco the Fallen
---.	24.4:bap	Richmond P. Hobson

Ricker, Marilla M.	25.4:97-115	A Square Deal
---.	27.3:66-80	Robert G. Ingersoll
---.	28.3:65-78	Ingersoll--Politician
---.	32.2:33-44	John Calvin
---.	33.4:97-110	Jonathan Edwards
---.	36.1:1-5	Howe and Why
Roberts, Charles	3.5:143-144	Carpe Diem*
Rochester Ad-Men	33.5:129	The Advertiser's Ode*
Ronsard, Pierre de	3.1:23-24	To My Ladye Love*
Rooney, John J.	2.6:183	A Sonnet of Hope*
---.	3.1:16-17	The Railer*
---.	4.1:1	A Beam of Light*
---.	5.1:bc	The Sun and the Star*
---.	5.4:bc	The Rahat*
Ruskin, John	9.5:bc	For this love of beauty
---.	11.2:bc	We will try to make . . .

--S--

Sanford, Mabel W.	6.6:174-175	Salammbo*
Savage, Faith B.	3.1:17-19	Shadows
---.	5.1:19-21	A Fragment
Schmidt, Emily R.	4.3:79-80	Joy's Joy*
Scollard, Clinton	2.5:141	Moods*
Scott, Harvey	33.3:65-69	Industry's Mortal Foe
Severance, C.	31.3:65-69	The Prince of Peace
---.	32.4:97-132	Marriage and Divorce
Sharpshooter, The	25.1:22-25	The Tribe of Mudsock
Shay, Edward J.	28.1:bap	What Yo' All Goin'*
Shuford, A. R.	7.2:44-47	An Interview
Simpson, Jeremiah	9.2:33	Uncertainty*
Skinner, Charles	1.6:178-182	A Thriftless Benefit
---.	2.4:121-124	Model of a Statesman
---.	3.2:42-44	Venture in Manuscript
Smiff, Chicago	7.5:136-139	Era of Good Feeling
Stevens, G. W.	2.6:187-193	Hour with Caesar . . .
---.	3.3:65-72	An Hour with Maecenas
Stevenson, R. L.	14.2:bc	The day returns and
Stringer, Arthur	4.4:97	Captivity*
Strode, Muriel	14.1:14	Experience*
Strong, Harryet	7.2:38-43	Confession of Fictionist

Sweet, Elnathan	2.2:59	Quatrain*
Swift, Ivan	27.3:65-66	I Don't Know*
---.	35.3:bap	Woodyard Kindlings*

--T--

Tabb, John B.	5.3:65	The Debtor Christ*
Taber, H. P.	1.2:71	To the Nicest Girl*
---.	1.3:94-95	Story of Little Sister
---.	1.6:169-177	The Combined Press
---.	2.1:26-28	[on Eugene Field]
Taylor, Bert L.	37.1:1-2	Invocation*
Taylor, Edward R.	5.6:166	Now*
Taylor, Ian	3.2:44-46	Micketts of a Wybirt*
---.	25.2:49-51	Micketts of Gobeille*
Teall, Gardner C.	3.5:129	A Murmur*
Thompson, Vance	14.1:7-14	Red Corpuscles and Art
Tolstoi, Leo	6.4:104-114	Zola and Dumas
---.	12.6:161-177	Church and State
---.	23.6:161-163	Your Child Should Know
Tone, Mille	31.2:42-44	Guide to Gotham
Triggs, Oscar L.	18.4:110-117	The New Education
Tripp, Howard C.	35.1:1-2	Ode to the Squash*

--U--

Urmy, Clarence	1.5:167	Fanfarronade*

--V--

Vance, Arthur T.	8.2:51-52	English as English

--W--

W.	1.4:122-123	In Slippery Places
Walker, Belle M.	14.1:6-7	A Prose Pastelle
Walker, Ernest K.	30.1:bap	Roycrofters of East
Warren, G. F.	1.1:11-12	Ballade des Ecrivans*

Warren, G. F.	1.2:45-46	The Lord of Lauturlu*
Waterman, Nixon	11.1:22	Bits of Biography*
---.	28.1:1-2	Judas Iscariot*
Watkins, J. Cal.	9.5:129	The Doubter*
---.	12.1:1	Coincidence*
Watkins, Meta G.	31.1:1	Lochinvar--Up to Date*
Watson, Thomas E.	24.4:bap	Religious Monopoly
Wells, Carolyn	2.3:90-91	Do Posters Post?*
White, Eugene R.	1.1:1	Quatrains*
---.	1.2:33-38	Where Is Literature At?
---.	1.6:177-178	To Robert Herrick*
---.	2.1:13-14	Laird of Little Grange*
---.	2.2:50-51	A Buccaneer Chorus*
---.	2.4:105-106	A Buccaneer Toast*
---.	2.6:169	Ananke*
---.	3.4:97	Quatrain*
---.	4.6:161	Quatrain*
Wickham, Harvey L.	3.3:77-81	The Man on a Bicycle
Williams, Bob	41.1:1-3	Nifty Nightmares*
Wilson, Francis	2.1:24-26	Eugene Field: Poet
Wiltbank, W. M.	2.3:86-90	Chopin and George Sand
---.	4.4:109-115	Art for Art's Sake
Winegar, Jerusha	9.1:11	Caution*
Winn, Eleanor M.	3.6:176	The Cricket: A Fable
---.	7.4:104-105	Cycle Gossip*
Winterwood, G.	5.3:65-72	In Fly Time
Wright, Jean	1.3:79-82	For Honor
Wright, John L.	4.3:71-72	The Fullness of It

--Y--

York, Ethelline	8.6:161-170	The Frogs
Young, Julia Ditto	5.6:161	Presentiment*

Appendix D

Gallery of Back Covers of the *Philistine*

Vol. 24 No. 5, April 1907

Vol. 25 No. 3, August 1907

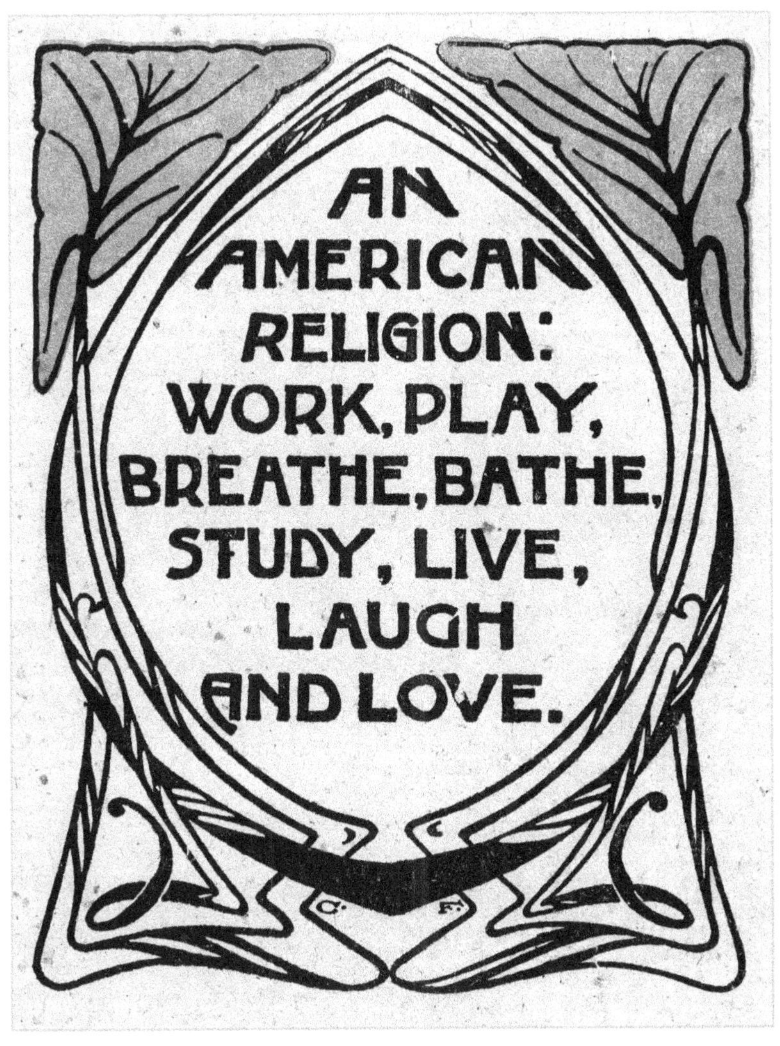

Vol. 26 No. 6, May 1908

Vol. 22 No. 3, February 1906

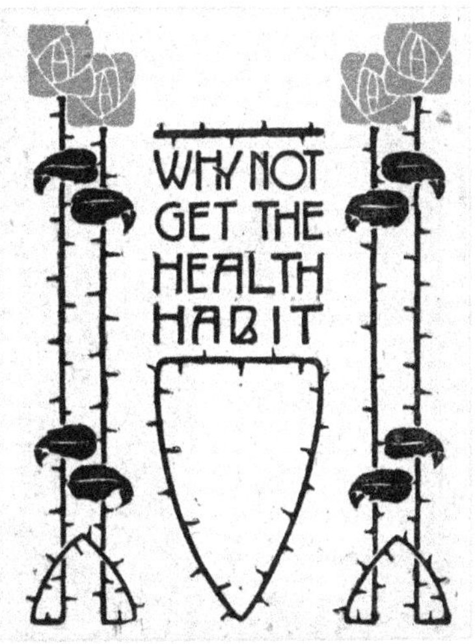

Vol. 26 No. 3, February 1908

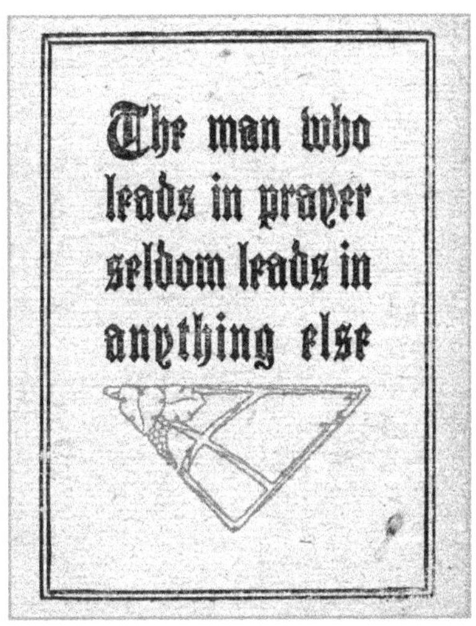

Vol. 32 No. 6, May 1911

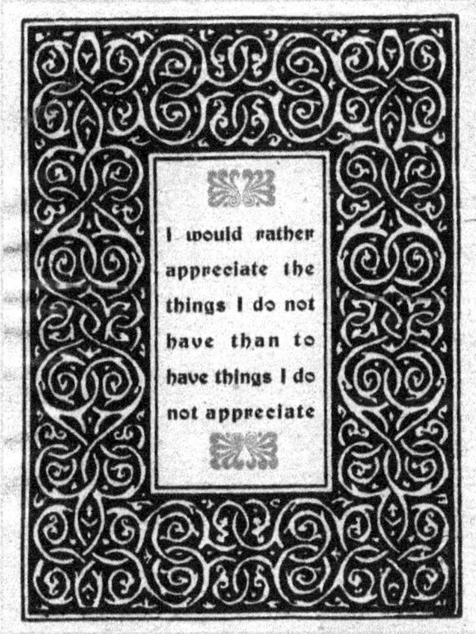

Vol. 16 No. 4, March 1903

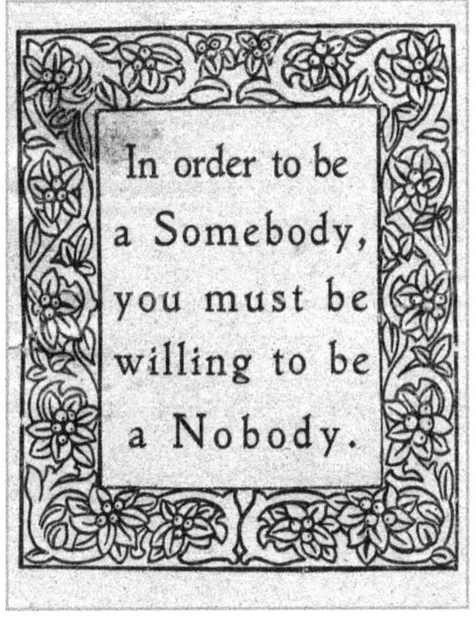

Vol. 18 No. 2, January 1904

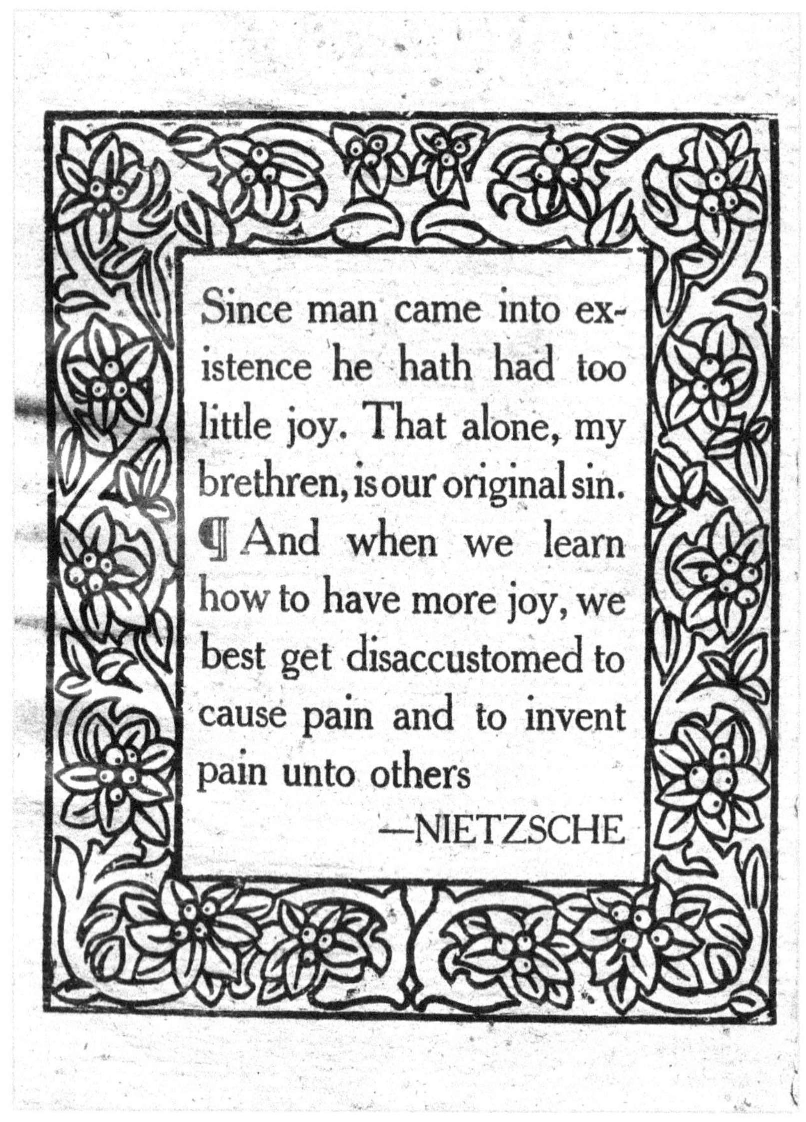

Since man came into existence he hath had too little joy. That alone, my brethren, is our original sin. ¶ And when we learn how to have more joy, we best get disaccustomed to cause pain and to invent pain unto others

—NIETZSCHE

Vol. 18 No. 4, March 1904

Vol. 23 No. 4, September 1906

Vol. 24 No. 5, May 1907

Vol. 26 No. 2, January 1908

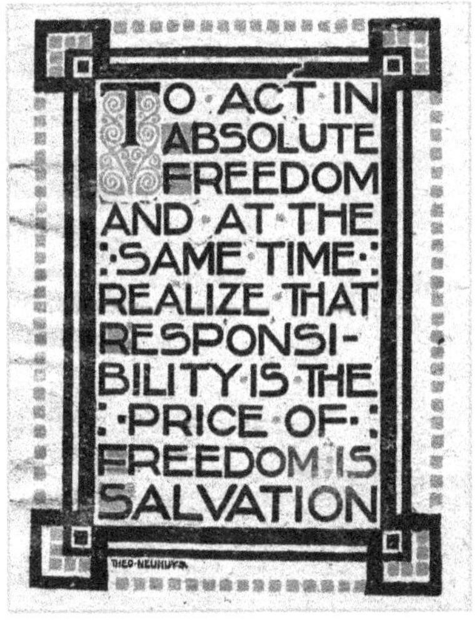

Vol. 21 No. 2, July 1905

Vol. 23 No. 6, November 1906

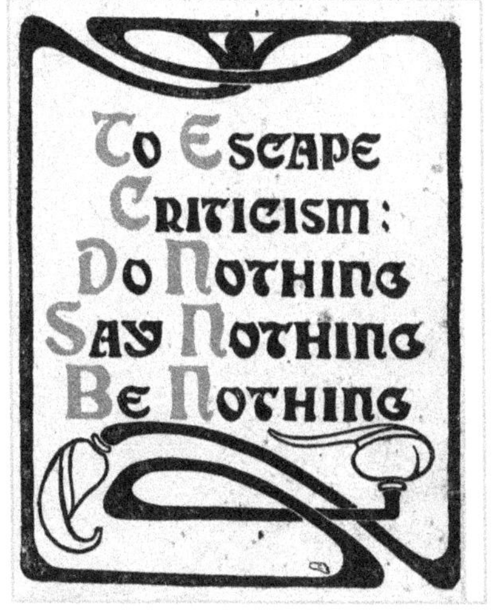

Vol. 26 No. 5, April 1908

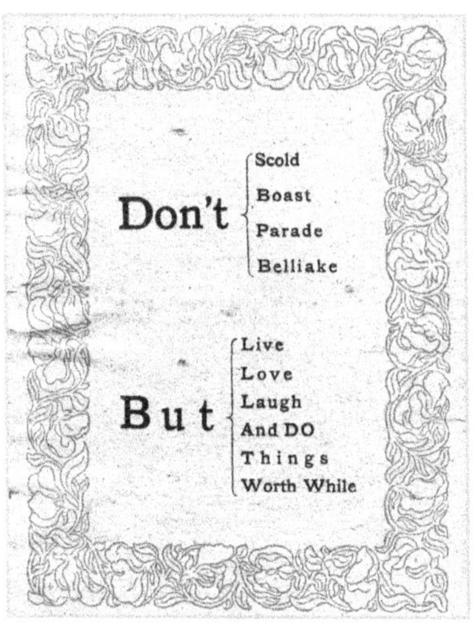

Vol. 20 No. 3, February 1905

Vol. 34 No. 3, February 1912

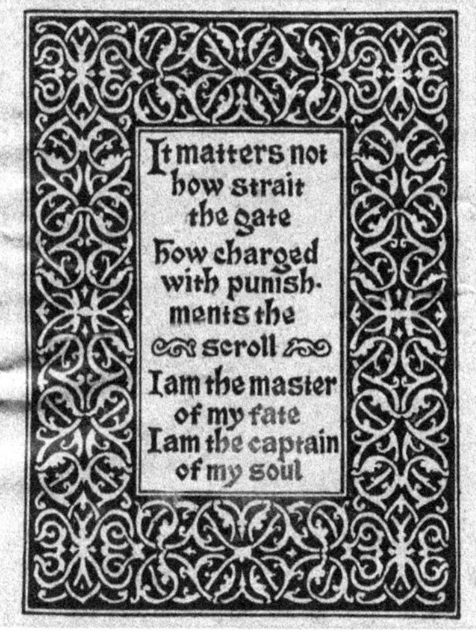

Vol. 14 No. 3, February 1902

Vol. 35 No. 4, September 1912

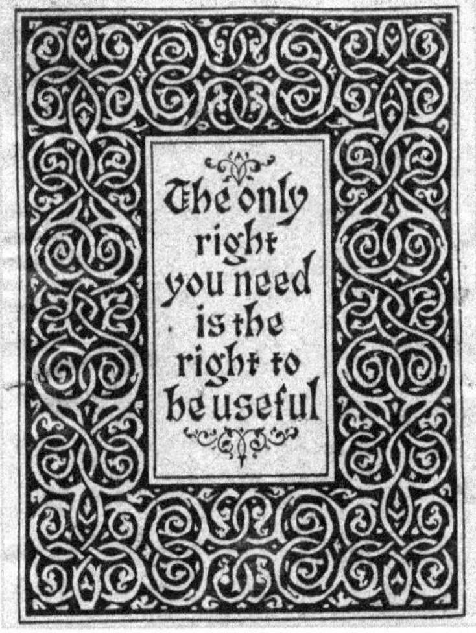

Vol. 14 No. 4, March 1902

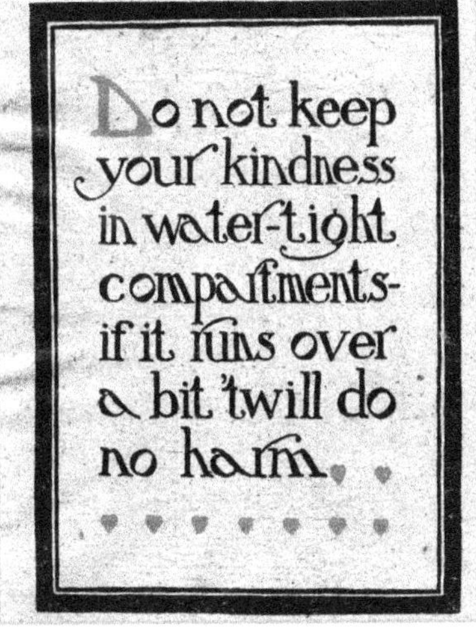

Vol. 20 No. 6, May 1905

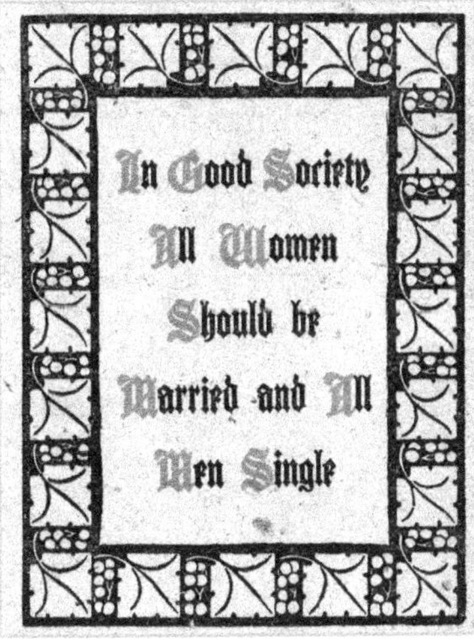

Vol. 31 No. 1, June 1910

Vol. 26 No. 4, March 1908

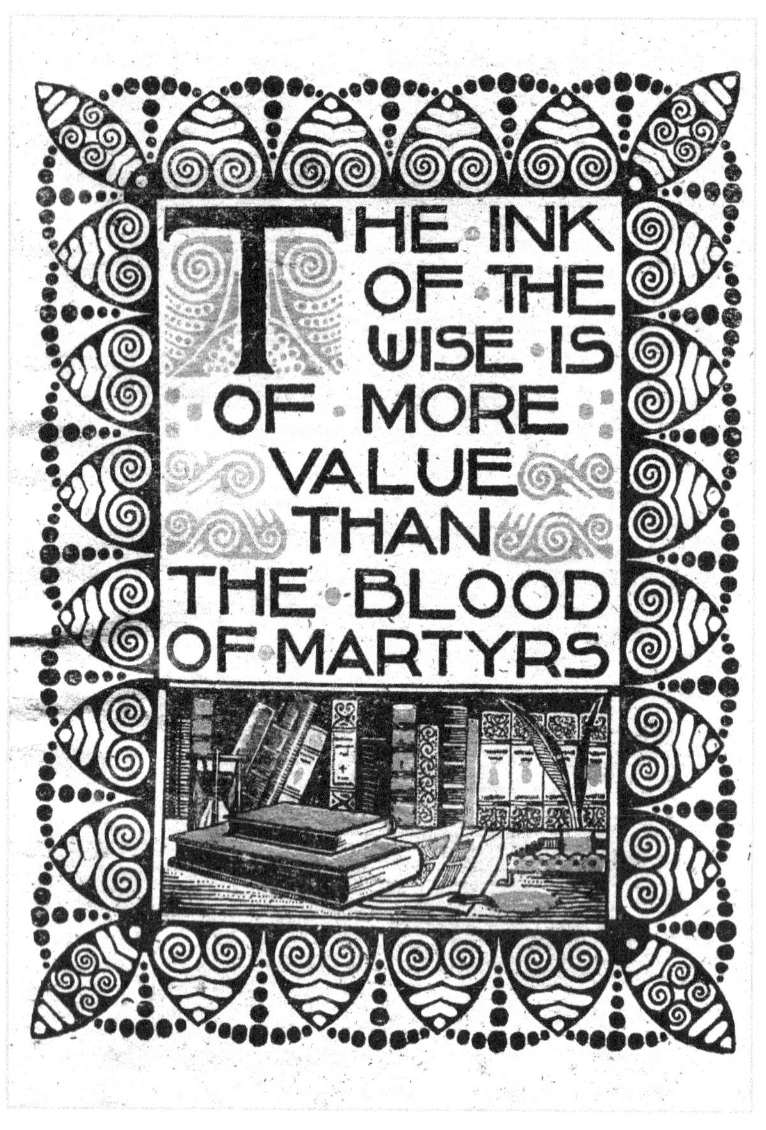

Vol. 22 No. 6, May 1906

Vol. 27 No. 4, September 1908

Vol. 26 No. 2, January 1908

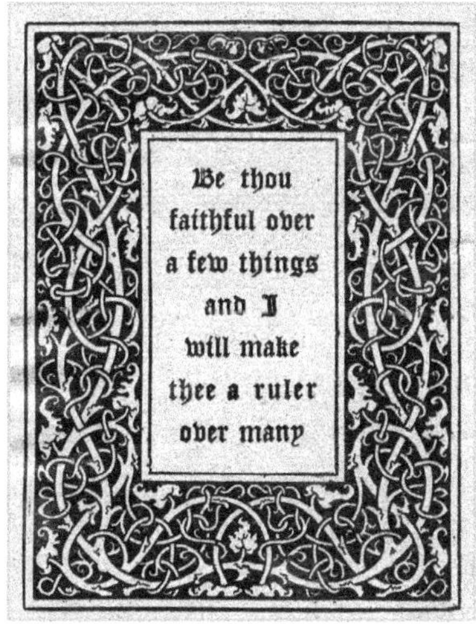

Vol. 15 No. 4, September 1902

Vol. 31 No. 6, November 1910

Appendix E

"Max Stirner" by Benjamin DeCasseres

Ghost-written for Elbert Hubbard's

The Fra, Vol. 6 No. 4, January 1911

IN Ralph Waldo Emerson's revolutionary essay, "Self-Reliance"—a passionate call to arms from a mighty soul on fire with the glorified vision of its own individualized destiny—occur, among other memorable sentences, these words: "Society is everywhere in conspiracy against the manhood of each one of its members. The only right is what is after my constitution; the only wrong what is against it."

Walt Whitman and Henry David Thoreau uttered equally radical words. But neither of these men was an anarchist. They were too sane to take themselves literally. What they believed in was the spiritual evolution of the individual, a self-overcoming, a throttling of the ghosts in one's own soul—the ghosts of fear and ignorance, the ghosts that within ourselves stand at the crossroads of every crisis that invites to action, demanding toll of our self-reliance.

Self-emancipation must precede social emancipation. If you want to abolish a mass you must begin by reconstructing the units of that mass. Of course you can blow the mass up with gunpowder, but you blow up the units with it.

If society everywhere conspires against the individual it is because the individual has not yet freed his mind of the fixed idea that he can do without a State. The fault comes back to each one of us. The State is not a thing; it is an organized instinct; one of the skins of evolution not yet sloughed off; a tool that has not yet completed its work in the hands of the World-Ego.

The weaknesses of "society" are the shadows of our individual weaknesses. Its transgressions are the sum of all individual transgressions. Society is no better than the average between the best and the worst individuals living within its pale. Its crimes against the individual are in exact ratio to the crimes of individuals against one another. Organized society will exist so long as there is an instinct to organize among individuals.

Emerson says, let each one of us fit ourselves to do without society—just as we have outgrown the old monstrous theologies. The State will then be sloughed. "Physician, heal thy self!" Social workers and anarchists today are fighting what they call "general ills." There are no such things.

There are only individual ills. Be yourself, emancipate yourself, abolish the State by learning to do without it—that is the message of Emerson, Whitman, Thoreau, Ibsen.

The latter cried, "Away with the State!" and, clairvoyant thinker that he was, he added as an afterthought—"of course, I mean by spiritual means."

Nietzsche wrenched man out of his social socket and made him a beatified Cain. He was the poet of the Ego. Had he ever heard of Max Stirner, the War-Lord of the Ego?

"The Ego and His Own"

STIRNER'S book, "The Ego and His Own," is the last word in egoism—the last word in revolt. It is not the most dangerous book ever written, because its philosophy is hopelessly impracticable. Ibsen and Emerson and Whitman are more dangerous in their teachings than Stirner. The latter has given us one of the most stimulating books ever written, a book that thrills, invites a man to himself; a book that lays all the sacred spooks and ultimately brings the reader 'round. Egoism makes strange bedfellows!

You shall leave all; the Kingdom of God is within you. Max Stirner makes the Ego of man God, and to serve it you shall leave the State, the home, the family, religion and everything that battens on the aspiring soul of man, though after he has gotten rid of all these "earthly spooks," just what you should aspire toward is not clear, unless it be what Stirner calls man's "Ownness"—a word that Kipling makes comprehensible in his famous injunction,—"What you want go and take."

Stirner's Individualism

THE individualism of Stirner is thus founded on the most rational idea in the world—the idea that only the individual is glorified, that only I matter—with the most irrational implications. Away with State, Church and family!—they prevent my Ego from realizing itself. Crime is my business. Citizenship is slavery. Parents maim their children from the cradle. Society tickets me. Laws prevent me from getting my "own." What I can do, that is right. Evil is failure. Success is the only righteousness. All regulation is emasculation. Only I, myself, am holy. The thing I can use is good; the thing that uses me is bad. Altruism is merely sickness of the will.

All this is not as dangerous as it sounds, for as a matter of fact all strong men-all men who do anything in life at all, all those who differentiate themselves from the mass—act on those principles in one degree or another, generally unconsciously.

Men never like to have their motives to action formulated. They hate even to formulate the matter secretly to themselves.

And Max Stirner's boldness merely consisted in putting what he thought into print. The Albany and Harrisburg legislatures are reeking with men who would no doubt suppress Stirner's book if they ever heard of it—men would long ago have known the book if it had been titled, "Cash; or Grab Your Own." Stirner's anarchy is purely analytic and idealistic. But at Albany and Harrisburg the brand of anarchy is intensely practical.

And to Stirner's individualism there is a rational, majestic, sublime side. His Ego is the hungry animal inside of us all, an animal that has intelligence and imagination, it is true, but an animal nevertheless in that every movement of its psychic, physical and emotional nature is toward its own. Men will only marry and procreate, they will only pay taxes and support churches, as long as they can be made to believe that they are getting something out of these things; they are good so long as the good gives them pleasure —that is, swells their own Ego. They are good and altruistic for the same reasons that they are bad and egoistic: they believe there is a gain somewhere to them. For at bottom when you tear away the rags and tatters of hypocrisy and the moldy crusts of convention that cover the real palpitating core of a man, what will you find? A being that adores itself and loves and worships only where it believes it is loved and benefited by that worship in return. Stirner asks, "What is good?" And he answers, "What I can use."

Conservation of the Ego

MAN is a warrior. No matter how subtle and complex life becomes, as in New York City today, no matter how highly "civilized" we boast of being, it is our own—our "ownness," Stirner calls it—that we are battling for. We each of us, whether in a "state of nature" or a state of society, are fighting for the conservation of the Ego. Some of us believe that the marriage institution, children, the State, help us to conserve that Ego; others believe that these adjuncts suppress it. It depends on the Ego. A business man, generally speaking, finds it aids him to subscribe to the common plan of life. A thinker like Herbert Spencer or Schopenhauer finds it does not. But both classes of men worship at the shrine of the same god-the Ego. Self was the first law; today, as ever, it is the first virtue.

The Ego is a blood-smeared fact. Man once lived in a perpetual state of war; he brutally struck down whatever stood in his way—if he was not struck down first. Today we are still in a state of war, but for the same reason that we found it necessary to kill in the old time we find it necessary now to preserve. The Ego seeks its own through destruction and construction. There was a time when kindness and goodness and charity would have destroyed the race. Use was God; Use is still God. We, the men and women of today, with top-hats and lorgnettes and tin pails and steam-shovels, are not different in our aims from the caveman and shaggy brute that peered out of the forest brambles. Scratch us and the old ghost walks again. We are still the victims of egomania. Our methods are different—that's all.

This warrior instinct can not die. It is our virtue. It is our sap and our virility. We are becoming masters now of the death-dealing forces in us and around us; we have disciplined the things that disciplined us. It is another mask for Ego. It is on these unquestionable truths that Max

Stirner has reared his doctrine of the Ego.

Self-Sacrifice

HENCE it follows that this announcer of Ego does not admit the idea of self-sacrifice into his scheme of life. And here again Stirner thinks boldly and clairvoyantly. For no doctrine has had more adherents and fewer sincere believers than the doctrine of self-sacrifice. Ego will not be sacrificed. It will lend, but will not vanish. Self-sacrifice should be the prerogative of power; as it is, it is most often the excuse that weakness makes for its inability to live for itself alone. Suppose the doctrine of self-sacrifice became universal! We should have the absurd spectacle of each person living for the good of some other person. That, of course, is unthinkable. Self-sacrifice must, in the very nature of things, be subterranean egoism. Stirner speaks of the "egoism of the stars." It is a good example. Each star shines for itself; as an incidence of power it throws its radiance into space, giving light to the darkness, shedding warmth. But its giving is incidental. It exists first of all for itself. The good it causes comes out of its surplus. And self-sacrifice should be self-glorification. All gifts should be gifts of power, not a hand-out from Duty. "Everything is for me!" cries Stirner.

Even what he gives is still his. And there can be nothing to give unless one has cultivated his Ego before conferring the gift. Unless the gardener has given his time to raising the most beautiful plants, how can his gift be worthy? Strangle your instincts, throttle your inner nature, stifle the soul's cry for joy and power and its hunger for its "ownness"—and Nature will brand you a sloven in your very gait and secrete the venom of your secret spite in all your "gifts."

The Socialistic Bugbear

STIRNER'S doctrine of the Ego leaves no room for the Socialistic state. He deals sledge-hammer blows at that fallacy. Socialism is to him, as it appeared to Herbert Spencer and Gustave Le Bon, another form of slavery.

Socialism is only that old enemy, the State, popularized. The mantle has fallen from the shoulders of the old gods onto a newer being—the People. The Socialist believes that the State can do what the individual can not do, forgetting that the State is no other thing than the people.

As Stirner truly says, there is no such thing as a body; there are only bodies—that is, the State, like all abstractions, is a myth; there are only individuals with Ego. The Socialist believes there are individuals and a State. He makes a thing out of a word, galvanizes it into a semblance of life, sticks a crown on its head, puts a gilded wand in its hand, sits it on a throne of theories, and cries, "Behold the Deliverer of Man—the State, the People!"

Always the slave of words—this poor bewildered Man!

Always there is a New Jerusalem—a lazy man's Utopia! Once it was Paradise—now it is Socialism. It is only the latest illusion. There is no short cut to happiness. There is no backstairs to the House of Life. What the individual can not do for himself the State can not do for him. Nothing degrades like dependence; nothing undermines a man like the certain guarantee of a living. The Ego must fight and bleed for its "own"—that makes the Ego godlike.

The Social Slavery

STIRNER foresaw this great Socialistic propaganda that is on us. He foresaw a slavery more terrible than that which ever prevailed in ancient times following the erection of the Socialistic State. By destroying the competitive system, the principle of individuality, the profoundest principle in Nature, would be sapped at the core. Men, always certain of life and the necessities, would lose the one supreme characteristic of their manhood-the ability to struggle and to conquer.

Under Socialism we should be ruled by a gigantic Trust called the State or the People—all names for one thing. The Ego would be regulated as in medieval times, and on the same theory, the theory of all tyrants—"public improvement." Instead of a few politicians we would have a world of 'em. What should a man be helped to do, then? To make a better fight, to give a deadlier blow, to strike surer, to battle for the preservation of Ego. But he should be guaranteed nothing except death if he fails. What is injustice? The equal distribution of goods—guaranteeing to those who can not fight; preserving the weak at the expense of the strong. All men are born unequal. Socialism—the Social State, Stirner calls it—is confiscation of Ego. It is popular with those who have nothing.

Nature's Unit Value

WHATEVER of great things has been done in the world has been done by the individual.

The individual—not the State or the family—is Nature's unit value.

All that makes for material or mental development has sprung from individual initiative, lashed by the thongs of Pride and Necessity—lured by the lust for Power. And wherever the State or the Church has attempted to regulate the individual and the activity of the Ego, decay has followed. The Dark Ages were dark because the Ego was dead. The Ego awakened with Dante, Gutenberg, Michelangelo and Martin Luther.

The old autocracy reigned on the theory that one man should rule all men.

The new autocracy is called Socialism; it merely reverses the scheme. It believes that all men should rule each man. Socialism abolishes the fear of danger in the Ego of the individual. She smashes his mainsprings, fear and courage. No man is born with a right to a living, or to anything else. Man's only right is a competitive right. The State is always evil, asserts Stirner—and Socialism is merely another gag for our tongues and fetters for our feet.

Max Stirner's dream of an emancipated Ego is futile, but his reasons for dreaming it were sublime. The direction his thought takes is right, but he had visions beyond the reaches of our souls. He imposes on our brains a sublime ideal of human development. It is like the North Star, a great light to steer by, but he who tries to reach it is mad, mad, mad, my lords.

Index

www.ingramcontent.com/pod-product-compliance
Lightning Source LLC
Chambersburg PA
CBHW021616270326
41931CB00008B/723

* 9 7 8 1 9 4 3 6 8 7 1 3 8 *